THE POLITICS OF CULTURAL PRACTICE

THE POLITICS OF CULTURAL PRACTICE

THINKING THROUGH THEATRE
IN AN AGE OF GLOBALIZATION

RUSTOM BHARUCHA

WESLEYAN UNIVERSITY PRESS

Published by University Press of New England

Hanover and London

Wesleyan University Press
Published by University Press of New England, Hanover, NH 03755

© 2000 by Rustom Bharucha

Simultaneously published in Great Britain by The Athlone Press

Printed in Great Britain   5 4 3 2 1

Library of Congress Cataloging-in-Publication Data

Bharucha, Rustom, 1953–
    The politics of cultural practice: thinking through theatre in an age of globalization /
Rustom Bharucha.
        p.   cm.
    Includes index.
    ISBN 0–8195–6423–0 (alk. paper)—ISBN 0–8195–6424–9 (pbk.: alk. paper)
    1. Theater. 2. Drama—History and criticism. I. Title.

PN2021 .B53 2000
792′.01—dc21
                                                                        99–85991

To all my friends,
who sustained this book,
and
in memory of Fritz Bennewitz,
an intercultural seeker and one-eyed director,
who saw the world differently

CONTENTS

ACKNOWLEDGEMENTS

The intercultural investigations of this book have been catalysed by numerous interventions in cultural and activist forums in different parts of the world. My first acknowledgement, therefore, would be to my diaspora of friends, whose generosity and hospitality have made the vulnerabilities and risks of border-crossing not merely tolerable, but intellectually exhilarating.

Most of the essays in this book can be regarded as experiments in 'travelling theory'. 'Interculturalism and its Discriminations', for instance, has gone through many incarnations in the following forums: the First Dom Tower lecture organized by Passepartout in Utrecht; the 'Inroads' conference at the Centre for Intercultural Performance in the University of California at Los Angeles; 'Frameworks for Art' at the Mohile Parikh Centre for the Visual Arts in Mumbai; 'Bodies in Question' at the ADSA conference in Hamilton, New Zealand; the Arts Summit II conference on multiculturalism in Jakarta, Indonesia; 'Intersections' organized by the New World Theatre in Amherst, Massachusetts; and the National Congress of Japanese Society for Theatre Research in Tokyo. I am grateful to Emile Schra, Judy Mitoma, Noreen Tomassi, Radhika Subramaniam, Shaila Parikh, Sal Murgiyanto, William Peterson, and Mitsuya Mori for their invitations, and most of all, to Roberta Uno and Jules Holledge for continuing the dialogue on interculturalism with their inspired net-working of marginalized theatre cultures in Asia.

At least three of the essays have been inspired by the specific themes and concepts of different forums. 'Phantoms of the Other' was first presented as a lecture on 'Somebody's Other' at the National Theatre in Britain on the invitation of Rose Fenton and Lucy Neal, the two stalwarts of the London International Festival of Theatre (LIFT). 'When "Eternal India" Meets the YPO' was sparked by the theatrical audacity and play of an itinerant, site-specific conference on tourism and performance organized by the Centre of Performance Research in Aberystwyth, Wales. The first draft of 'Towards a Politics of Sexuality' was provoked by an invitation to participate in a conference on the City of Women in Ljubljana, Slovenia. For reasons that will become apparent in the course of this narrative, I remain grateful to the organizers of this conference and to my friend Aldo Milohnic in particular for making me think about 'interculturalism in the state of malaria'.

'The Shifting Sites of Secularism' was first delivered as a lecture at the Institute of Contemporary Arts in London, for which I must thank Alan Read for his generous invitation. This essay, however, could not have been adequately conceptualized without the political insights that I have received from conferences on secularism, Third World activism, globalization, and transitions in contemporary India, organized by the Indian Institute of Advanced Studies in Shimla, the South Asia Solidarity Group in London, the Indian National Social Action Forum in Mumbai, and the Fundacao Oriente in Lisbon, Portugal, respectively. I am particularly grateful to those interlocutors from other disciplines, notably Romila Thapar, Sumit Sarkar, Achin Vanaik, K.N. Panikkar, Jairus Banaji, Rohini Hensman, Kumkum Sangari, Urvashi Butalia, Rajeev Bhargava, Peter D'Souza, Sudhir Chandra, Satish Kolluri, and Javeed Alam, whose scholarly and activist investments in the secular struggle of contemporary India have been deeply inspiring.

On the editorial front, I would like to thank Tristan Palmer of the Athlone Press for his patience and understanding in negotiating the intercultural agenda of my book, both at theoretical levels and in its distribution through co-publishing collaborations in the United States and India. I am also grateful to Krishna Raj of the *Economic and Political Weekly* and Rasheed Araeen of *Third Text*, who have consistently supported my work over the years. Earlier versions of 'Gundegowda meets Peer Gynt' and my fable on 'Eternal India and the YPO' appeared in the *New Theatre Quarterly* and *Performance Research*. The story of the '*saligrama*' drawn from U.R. Anantha Murthy's powerful novel *Bharathipura*, which ends my essay on 'Phantoms of the Other', was first shared in the IDEA conference on 'Reflections in the River' in Brisbane, Australia, and later published in *The Drama Review*.

For my theatre practice, I remain indebted to the Ninasam Theatre Institute in the village of Heggodu, Karnataka, which has been the testing ground for most of the intracultural experiments in theatre discussed in this book. I would also like to acknowledge the sponsorship of the Rangayana Theatre in Mysore for my production of *Peer Gynt*, who could never have metamorphosed into *Gundegowda* without the inspired translation of S. Raghunandan. Max Mueller Bhavan (New Delhi), Vivadi, and NORAD are also to be thanked for their administrative and financial support of the other productions discussed in the book. While my focus in these productions is on dramaturgy rather than performance, I would acknowledge the deep insights that I have received from all the actors, particularly from those who have alerted me to the hegemonic role of the director. To my old friend Anuradha Kapur, who intervened at a particularly problematic moment in my representation of a feminist text, I remain grateful not only for the grace of her intervention, but for the dialogue that followed on the politics of gender.

On a more formal note, I would like to acknowledge a grant from the Prince Claus Fund for Culture and Development in the Netherlands that has enabled me to collate and rework the different essays of this book written between 1993 and 1999. For their personalized interest in the larger social dimensions of my writing project, I am grateful to three of the foundation's officers – Els van der Plas, Geerte Wachter, and Marlous Willemsen whom I first met by chance at the Arab Arts Project in Amman, Jordan, for which I must thank Kiki Davies and Hassan El-Geretly for their invitation.

It should be clear by now that the multiple locations of my friends and the world of my writing are deeply interrelated. Indeed, I can only reiterate that as an independent writer I could not have sustained my research in other cultures without the hospitality that I have received from Dan and Mary-Frances Dunham, Richard and Nina Toller, Vijaya Nagarajan and Lee Swenson, Mehlli Gobhai, Joost Smiers, Mae Paner, and Richard Emmert, who have welcomed me in their own homes. As for my extended theatre family, it gives me pleasure to acknowledge the warmth I have received from Christine Nygren, Eugene van Erven, Geoff Gillham, PETA in the Philippines, Sardono and Amna Kusumo in Indonesia, and above all, Ong Keng Sen and his associates at TheatreWorks and, the Flying Circus Project in Singapore, whose intercultural explorations have compelled me to write another narrative that crosses the boundaries of this particular book.

Not everything that one experiences in the world of cultural practice can be accounted for in writing; indeed, not every friendship can be acknowledged in words. The memory of Fritz Bennewitz, who sustained twenty-five years of active intercultural theatre research in India, Bangladesh, and the Philippines, has yet to be adequately documented. I do believe, however, that these seeming absences are internalized in an inner map of the world that inspires new imaginaries of cultural exchange. For the moment, as I look back on some of the critical intersections that have contributed to the life of this book, I am tempted to rewrite the closing lines from one of my favourite plays – Brecht's *In the Jungle of Cities*: 'The chaos has been used up. And it was the best time.' The chaos persists – I live in Calcutta, after all – but the writing of this book has been, if not the 'best time', then certainly the most intense and turbulent of times that I would like to share with you now.

Calcutta
October 1999

A Brechtian maxim: don't build on the good old days, but the bad new ones.

Walter Benjamin

INTRODUCTION

This book is concerned with emergent cultural practices in India and other parts of the world that resist the larger forces of globalization and communalism (or religious sectarianism, as it is more widely understood, in the different manifestations of racism, xenophobia, and ethnic cleansing that affect the world today). While India is the 'lens' through which I see the world, it is also the stimulus that brings together any number of sites that are embedded in an intricate network of social, historical, political, and economic contexts at once localized and mediated by global and national agencies. These sites, as will become clear in the course of this book, are not predetermined cultural realities but constructions that are held together not so much by what is 'given' in any culture, but by what is 'invented' through their negotiations of specific interventions, assaults, inputs, and collaborations.

Within the spectrum of national and global forces that determine the politics of cultural practice examined in this book, the word 'cultural' becomes a highly conflictual term linked to the increasingly contested field of 'culturalism'. Theorized by Arjun Appadurai as 'the conscious mobilization of cultural differences in the service of a larger national or transnational politics', culturalism is invariably 'hitched' to certain 'prefixes' (Appadurai 1997: 15). In this study, I will be focusing on *inter*culturalism, *intra*culturalism, *multi*culturalism, and secularism. The last term would seem to be the 'odd man out', but it is vital for my reading of cultural theory and practice in this book, as will become evident in the critical genealogy that follows on the keywords in this narrative.

My purpose is not to historicize the 'intercultural', the 'intracultural', the 'multicultural', and the 'secular' in their larger ideational contexts, but, more simply, to note how they have entered my critical vocabulary at particular junctures in time. If I am wary of beginning any study of culturalism with definitions (see Pavis 1996: 1–10), it is not merely because I find them too prescriptive, but because I prefer to engage with working propositions that actually challenge the articulation of practices as they are in the process of being explored. What concerns me, therefore, is not the essential meaning of cultural terms, but how meanings mutate and metabolize in the course of their transportation, translation, and specific uses in other cultures.

In this context, I was alerted as early as 1977 to the problematic of translation in intercultural theatre practice through Peter Brook's production of *The Ik*, based on Colin Turnbull's anthropological study of an African tribe that has been dehumanized through hunger and displacement. In a memorable interview, Kenneth Tynan had called the reader's attention to an appalling lapse in Brook's representation: '[I]n the programme it just said "as far as anyone knows the Ik still exist." As far as anyone knows? I mean, here we were, invited to feel compassion and horror at their plight, but, nobody in the production had even bothered to find out whether they still existed' (quoted in Bharucha 1978: 59).

The provocation of this statement challenged me as a first-year graduate student at the Yale School of Drama, where 'interculturalism' did not exist either as a subject or as a critical category. At that time I was used to asking questions of productions and performances: 'Does it "work"?, 'Is it "true"?', 'How "real" is it?' Now I found myself asking: Is this *right*? Is it right to do a play about people from another part of the world, with whom you have no real contact, but whose condition provides you with a convenient metaphor for 'inhumanity'? Brook's 'despondent nihilism' has been aptly summarized by Tynan in his pithy description of the maestro's world-view: 'human beings, left to themselves, stripped of social restraints, are animals, and are inherently rotten, and destructive' (Tynan 1977: 23). Indeed, *The Ik* in its chic use of non-verbal babble to suggest the primitivization of African 'natives' will surely go down in intercultural theatre history as a paradigmatic example of primordializing the Other as an anthropological object.

In 1977, my problem was not with Brook as such, but with the troubling questions that were triggered on reading Tynan's interview: Is there an ethics of representation in theatre? What are the alternative modalities of representing the Other with responsibility and engagement? How does one begin to respect – and not just tolerate – cultural differences? Can economic inequalities be included in one's respect for cultural difference? Questions unlimited, but with no answers in sight. There was nothing in the intellectual milieu of Yale, despite its prodigious resources of other cultures in the Sterling Library, that could begin to prepare me for an adequate recognition of the Other. Forget the Ik – they did not exist in my entirely white, liberal, and Eurocentric curriculum at the School of Drama – but what about blacks? In 1977, they were not particularly visible on campus either, and they socialized almost entirely among themselves. Between the African American Department and the Drama School, adjacent to each other in the same complex, there was almost no dialogue. The irony deepens when one confronts the demographic reality of New Haven – the alleged ghetto surrounding Yale – where more than half the population continues to be black.

How can one presume to talk about interculturalism, I would argue, if one hasn't begun to encounter the diverse social and ethnic communities inhabiting one's own public space? Rhapsodizing (or agonizing) about the Other 'out there' in some faraway place, without addressing the others in one's own neighbourhood or work place, is a kind of cosmopolitan affectation that one would have imagined to be entirely anachronistic in our times.

In 1977, it is true that 'multiculturalism' was not a buzz-word; the politics of identity relating to gays, lesbians, and other minorities was in an embryonic stage; debates around 'political correctness' and 'hate-speech' had not yet disturbed the complacencies of implicit racism. It is obvious that times have changed. Or is this a self-deception, a politically correct reflex on our part that is not substantiated by any significant alteration in our respect for others? One could ask: To what extent have times changed? For whom have they changed? In which constituencies? Certainly, there is more talk about 'cultural difference' than ever before, but is it really making a difference to the shaping of a multicultural society? Has the largely academic production of new alterities succeeded in the crossing of borders across class and race, or is it reinforcing new insularities embedded in the rhetoric of cultural difference? Do we cross some borders only to close others?

Increasingly, I have a perverse way of dealing with the seeming vulnerabilities of those privileged groups that attempt to legitimize their absence of interaction with other (generally coloured) minorities. 'We're likely to be misunderstood'; 'It could seem that we're patronizing them'; 'What would I say to them?; 'I don't want to be rejected': these are some of the responses that one is likely to encounter in a litany of excuses. Instead of false reassurance – 'Don't worry, you'll be welcomed by them' – I offer the possible benefits of being excluded. As I shall be elaborating on my experiments in dismantling the hegemony of direction in intracultural contexts of theatre (where I may not know the language of the actors), there are some unprecedented insights that can be gained from being silent, decentred, marginalized to the corners of a room, excluded from the intimacy of certain bondings. There are lessons in humility to be learned from being 'left out', and perhaps they need to be extended beyond the practice of theatre into the actual vulnerabilities of engaging with the Other not as a tokenistic presence or as a nice foreigner, but as a person with whom one can dialogically redefine the world.

It is obvious that we have shifted ground from my preliminary observations on the 'intercultural' (through Brook's representation of the Ik) to a broader perspective on the 'multicultural' (through my critical retrospective on the actual site of my study of dramaturgy at Yale, within the larger constraints of interactions with 'other' cultures in public life). Such jostlings of the 'inter' and the 'multi' will continue to punctuate the narrative of this book. However, for the sake of clarity, it would be useful not to shift gears yet again, by focusing on what I had described earlier as a 'working proposition' on my use of specific cultural terms, beginning with the 'intercultural'.

To get to the point, therefore, I was introduced to the 'intercultural' through some rather random reflections on a particular kind of Euro-American theatrical practice involving interactions and borrowings across cultures. Indeed, I continue to be struck by how the intercultural continues to be invoked more readily by artists than by political thinkers, or by philosophers, or for that matter by politicians (who have become increasingly more eloquent on the virtues of multiculturalism). While I will be suggesting in the conclusion to my book how the intercultural can enter other fields of critical inquiry outside the realm of performance, I would acknowledge that the word remains, at least within the narrative of this book, immersed within the actual practices not merely of understanding other cultures (more specifically, outside one's national boundaries), but of interacting with them through the specific disciplines and languages of theatre.

At one level therefore, I would uphold the perspective on interculturalism offered by Richard Schechner, who has to be credited for his persistence in initiating and pursuing the term through the 1970s, when the word gained a free-wheeling resonance in *avant-garde* performance circles. Not interested in perpetuating what has been described not inaccurately as my penchant for 'daddy-bashing', I will not reiterate here my considerable polemic (Bharucha 1993: 28–40) on Schechner's neo-liberal celebration of interculturalism in terms of its naive, if not ethnocentric, embrace of the cultures of the world, with insufficient regard for their social, economic, and political contexts. What concerns me instead is Schechner's more recent clarification (Pavis 1996: 42) that he began to use the word 'interculturalism' in the 1970s as 'a contrast to "internationalism"', in order to emphasize the 'the real exchange of importance to artists was not that among nations, which really suggests official exchanges and artificial kinds of boundaries, but the exchange among cultures, something which could be done by individuals or by non-official groupings, and it doesn't obey national boundaries' (ibid.).

While this perspective corresponds broadly to how I respond to the 'intercultural', I will try to give it a more rigorous reading within the framework of voluntarism and the circumscribed autonomies of individuals and non-official cultural groups. I stress 'circumscribed' autonomies because, unlike Schechner's rather cavalier distinction between 'nations' (which are 'official') and 'cultures' (which are assumedly 'free'), I have no such illusion that intercultural interactions can be entirely free from the mediations of the nation-state. In particularly authoritarian states like Singapore, for instance, the state *will* inscribe its presence in the intercultural narrative, even if it is not ready to support its activity (see Bharucha 2000 for a contextualization of this political intervention). In short, there should be no false euphoria about the celebration of autonomy in interculturalism. The autonomy exists, but I believe it has to be negotiated, tested, and protected against any number of censoring, administrative, and funding agencies that circumscribe the ostensibly good faith of cultural exchange itself.

At a more complex political level, I would like to highlight the necessity of not entirely abandoning the 'national' in one's redefinition of the 'cultural'. While I am not a nationalist, I am not entirely prepared to let go of the legitimacy and potentially liberating force of the 'national', particularly in relation to those people's movements against globalization in Third World countries, which could be the only hope for challenging and redemocratizing the state. In short, I would like to acknowledge here my political affinities with Samir Amin's important consideration that in an age of 'uneven' globalization' (where, contrary to the liberal rhetoric of global 'flows', there is 'no free movement of workers worldwide'), popular nationalist movements in the periphery are necessary 'to save the state from capitulation to the demands of transnationalization. They alone can renationalize the state and allow it to gain control over accumulation' (Cheah 1998a: 34–35).

It seems to me that this perspective is more valid – and certainly, more realistic – than the post-national pitch offered engagingly by Arjun Appadurai who in his scathing dismissal of the moribund nation-state, is nonetheless blank when it comes to providing a viable alternative. 'I do not know' is his disturbingly candid answer, in response to his own valid questions: '[I]f the nation-state disappears, what mechanism will assure the protection of minorities, the minimal distribution of democratic rights, and the reasonable possibility of the growth of civil society?' (Appadurai 1997: 19). Unfortunately, I *do* know what could replace the nation-state, and it is disingenuous on Appadurai's part not to acknowledge what already exists as a surrogate, if not an accomplice, of the state – the market, as determined by the agencies of the International Monetary Fund and the World Bank, which are unaccountably absent in Appadurai's discussion on the cultural dimensions of globalization.

'Economic determinism' has been the charge raised against those Third World scholars and activists who would seem to reduce globalization to the expansion of capitalism through multinational and transnational corporations across national sovereignties and borders. These scholars have no particular interest in exploring Madonna's cultural assimilation in the fashion industry of the Congo, or the hybridity of pop songs across borders. The discourse on globalization in India, it should be admitted, is positively puritanical in its refusal to engage with the salacious gossip that is such an integral element of metropolitan cultural discourse these days. Instead, there is the unequivocality of activist rage against the encroachments of power plants and industries that have decimated entire environments and deprived entire communities of their livelihood. This rage may be uninflected, but is it unjustified? It would seem to me that the silencing of economic realities in cultural discourse can only obfuscate our search for what Gayatri Spivak has so accurately highlighted as 'ecological sanity', where we must 'learn to learn' the 'knowledge' that is being ruthlessly substituted by the 'telematic postmodern terrain of information command' (Spivak 1998: 343).

Therefore, in addition to the erasure of the 'national' in intercultural discourse, it becomes necessary to be extremely vigilant about how the 'global' is in a position to hijack the assumedly democratic interactions within the 'autonomous' agendas of interculturalism. Needless to say, the 'national' and the 'global' are insufficiently inscribed in Schechner's largely non-theoretical writings on interculturalism. While the 'national' tends to be erased through what I will describe in the next chapter as an 'eternalist fallacy', by which interculturalism is imagined to precede the birth of nations, the 'global' is subsumed within an uncritical acceptance of the modes, mechanisms, and agencies that constitute First World affluence.

Indeed, this totally unproblematized (non-)reading of capital is equally evident in the growing number of writers on performance and queer theory ostensibly on 'the Left', who for all their transgressions continue to live in a cocoon of performativity that is curiously indifferent to those very agencies of capitalism that have rendered so many of their colleagues unemployed and denied their right to livelihood. Indeed, the right to *life* has been called into question by some of the harsher manifestations of global capital in the propagation of the gene, pesticide and pharmaceutical industries. While these seemingly large and remote manipulations of the world's natural resources would seem to be very distant from the immediacies of cultural practice, they are, in actuality, transforming the cultural discourse around rights, ownership, and belonging. Therefore, a critique (or at least, a cognizance) of global capital would seem to be mandatory for the democratization of intercultural practice and discourse.

Allow me to jump-cut the narrative at this point and address the 'intracultural', which first entered my critical vocabulary around 1987, by which time I had returned to India after an approximately ten-year stay in the United States. Why did I return? It's a long story. Suffice it to say that it was a choice, I'm grateful that it existed, I have never regretted acting on it, and, perhaps, I wouldn't be writing this book if I had not reflected on its implications. A more caustic interpretation has been provided by an NRI (Non-Resident Indian) friend who, while thoroughly disapproving of my foolishness in giving up the Green Card, was none the less compelled to acknowledge that my return could be understood in relation to 'the Law of Diminishing Returns'. I shall leave you to ponder this enigma of economics.

At a biographical level, it is very obvious (but only in critical hindsight) that my *inter*culturalism was precipitated on leaving India for the first time, and that my *intra*culturalism was catalysed on my return. In *Theatre and the World* (1990/1993), I have described at length how an intercultural theatre project around Franz Xaver Kroetz's one-woman, wordless monodrama *Request Concert* was my pretext, at a certain level, for returning to India. I will not repeat that story here, except to indicate that this project catalysed my articulation of the 'intracultural' – a term that I was compelled to invent for myself as a critical shorthand to differentiate intercultural relations *across* national boundaries, and the intracultural dynamics between and across specific communities and regions *within* the boundaries of the nation-state. Once again, this is not a definition, but a working proposition that I will elaborate on in my drama-turgical investigations of intracultural theatre in Chapters 3–5.

At this theoretical juncture in the narrative, it would be useful to inscribe the *politics of relocation* within the inevitable narrative of homecoming that I had written into my journey in *Theatre and the World*. 'Relocation' to one's own home challenges the dominant narratives of migrancy that have been valorized in recent postmodern cultural theory. It is assumed in such narratives that the formerly colonized peoples will seek other futures in former colonies where they will be in a position to challenge the civilizational premises of their erstwhile rulers. But that such migrants should even aspire to return-ing to their homelands would seem to be a regressive, if not unproduc-tively nostalgic manoeuvre. Thus, as Pheng Cheah has put it bluntly in his larger contextualization of Homi Bhabha's affirmation of hybridity as cul-tural agency:

Bhabha is not interested in those who cannot migrate and for whom coerced economic migration would be a plus ... Indeed, he cannot even be said to be very interested in those who leave the South temporarily, in order to return, or in the repatriation of funds by migrant workers to feed their kin in the Third World. In Bhabha's world, postcoloniality is the hybridity of metropolitan migrancy. Everything happens as if there are no postcolonials left in decolonized space. (Cheah 1998b: 301)

This is, indeed, an accurate description of the implicit closures in hybridity theory, which seems to have reached an impasse in the refusal on the part of theorists like Bhabha to deconstruct their privileging of migrancy in First World, academic, metropolitan locations. Likewise, in fictional celebrations of hybridity, notably in Salman Rushdie's *The Satanic Verses*, which has been described by the author as a 'love song to our mongrel selves', the 'migrant condition' of metropolitan London becomes 'a metaphor for all humanity' (Rushdie 1990). Not only does this essentialization (and universalization) of 'the migrant condition' deny the different historicities of migrancy for which there may be – at times, for some people – nothing to celebrate, it also fails to account for those individuals and communities that resist migrancy on the basis of other loyalties and bonds to family, tradition, community, language, and religion that are not always translatable within the norms of liberal individualism. To endorse Rushdie's presumptuous claim, therefore, that 'the truest eye may now belong to the migrant's double vision' (Bhabha 1994: 5) is to play into what I would describe as the residual narrative of migrancy that may need to be dislodged by a sharper and more reflexive assessment of the continued inscriptions of 'home' in the mutabilities of the world.

For a start, it may be necessary to dispute the assumptions that invariably underlie the absorption of transnational migrant communities in what Arjun Appadurai has described as 'diasporic public spheres'. We need to question the virtuosity of such constructions through the unsubstantiated evidence of other such claims in populist postmodern theory that 'everybody's on the move these days', or more extravagantly, that 'we are all tourists'. Once again, I turn to Pheng Cheah for some much-needed crude thinking on the relatively uninvestigated perceptual processes of identity in migrant contexts from the perspective of migrants themselves.

Countering the blind faith in global cosmopolitanism, Cheah rightly suggests that '[i]t is unclear how many ... migrants feel that they belong to a world. Nor has it been ascertained whether this purported feeling of belonging to a world is analytically distinguishable from long-distance, absentee national feeling' (Cheah 1998a: 37). He goes on to state the obvious, which is sometimes totally undermined in the theoretical climate of our times, where the dematerialisation of reality is almost mandatory for the positing of a new politics: '[T]he argument that transnational print and media networks extend a world community beyond transnational migrancy to include peoples dwelling in the South has to reckon with the banal fact that many in the South are illiterate [this would include half the adult population of India]' (ibid.). What Cheah refers to as the 'banal fact' of not having access to global communicative mechanisms – and I will be dealing with the lacunae in Benedict Anderson's assumptions relating to 'print capitalism' later in the book – has to be acknowledged as the stark reality for millions of people, who continue to live outside of modernity not necessarily by choice but because of the poverty that continues to be thrust on them by the agencies (and collusions) of the state and the market.

Against this background, the politics of my relocation in India cannot be read outside of the framework of privilege. I have no desire either to camouflage or to disown this privilege; rather I would like to test it within certain trajectories that do not readily fall into the narrative suggested by 'The Return of the Native'. This is not my narrative, I should emphasize, even though this is how my relocation can be read, and, indeed, does get read, as in Patrice Pavis's unaccountable caricature of my return: 'Bharucha ultimately only wants one thing: to return home, to go back to India, to work in small isolated villages with pupils from a rural background, and to confront his own traditional cultures with "the tensions and immediate realities of their history"' (Pavis 1996: 196). To set the record straight, I have never subscribed to a one-point agenda, and my desire to return to India was not motivated (as Pavis seems to imply) by any altruistic need on my part to work with rural actors in 'small isolated villages'.

Heggodu, the village in the Malnad district of Karnataka, has, indeed, been the site of many of my most potent theatrical experiments, some of which I describe in this book. But it would be disingenuous to de-link Heggodu from the Ninasam Theatre Institute, which is consciously committed for all its communitarian ideology to a *modern* Indian theatre practice. At Ninasam, I have found a space in which I have worked long hours with the students on issues and problems that I do believe have extended my research beginning with *The Request Concert Project*. If in its site I have found ground realities that challenge my metropolitan, cosmopolitan, and secular assumptions, I should also add that I in turn have challenged the brahminic and patriarchal structuring of the institution through its tacit evasion of realities dealing with gender and caste. While I no longer work at Ninasam on a regular basis, my dialogue continues with its participants not just, I might add, on 'rural' matters, but on theoretical issues relating to the 'cosmopolitan vernacular', the ongoing debates between secularists and communitarians in India, and the politics of funding. This dialogue, I should add, could be one of the strongest contributing factors to my definition and practice of intraculturality in India today.

At a conceptual level of cultural practice, the 'intra' denotes the possible relationships between different cultures at *regional* levels – for example, between the states of West Bengal and Kerala, Manipur and Maharashtra. Tellingly, in the absence of viable infrastructures for such exchanges on an ongoing basis – a problem that I will elaborate later in the book – the 'intra' in my theatre work refers more pertinently to the differences that exist within the boundaries of a particular region in what is assumed to be a homogenized culture ('Kannada culture', 'Bengali culture', etc.). It is in calling attention to these internal cultural diversities (and differences) within specific regions that the intracultural can be most effectively activized.

While my work in this area is marginal, I would claim that intracultural interventions have the capacity to challenge the generalized tenets of citizenship that ostensibly connect all social actors to the idea of 'the nation', in and through their assumed 'diversities'. The intracultural also facilitates a critical examination of those differences relating to caste and economic inequality that are more often than not evaded in valorizations of 'regional culture'. My purpose is not to deny the intricate network of bonds and affiliations that do exist within the framework of regional cultures, but to question how they are produced within the cultural hegemonies of dominant groups. For all their affirmation of civility and regional brotherhood, these groups may exclude a spectrum of cultural languages marginalized by the strictures of caste, poverty, and other forms of social alienation.

While it could be argued that the 'intracultural' has an extremely limited dissemination as a term, I persist in using it not least to counter the more readily accepted official terms of 'inter-regional' and 'inter-state'. More critically, the 'intracultural' is, perhaps, the sharpest way of puncturing the homogenized categories and pretensions of the multicultural state. Indeed, the 'intra' can be said to camouflage its ideological infiltration, in so far as it would seem to be almost synonymous with the 'multi', and yet its agenda is decidedly different. At a purely demographic level, both the 'intra' and the 'multi' would seem to share a common ground in so far as they assume either the interaction or the coexistence of regional and local cultures within the larger framework of the nation-state. However, while the 'intra' prioritizes the interactivity and trans-lation of diverse cultures, the 'multi' upholds a notion of cohesiveness that is based, as the former Culture Secretary of the Indian state once put it, on '5,000 years of uninterrupted civilization' (Singh 1998).

The 'intra' is useful precisely because it has the potential to debunk such organicist notions of culture by highlighting the deeply fragmented and divided society of India that the multicultural rhetoric of the state refuses to acknowl-edge. If it is a force to reckon with, it is because its agencies are linked to cultures of struggle that are almost inevitably pitted against the culture of the state. While the agencies of the state have the power, and, indeed, the onus to order differences − and minoritarian ones in particular − within the prescribed norms of citizenship, the agencies of intraculturalism are more concerned with mobiliz-ing a consciousness of differences among its participants. Functioning within the framework of popular nationalist movements and coalitions, including non-governmental organizations (NGOs), voluntary associations, social action groups, citizenship and civil society initiatives, these intracultural agencies have the oppositional capacities to work against the globalizing and fascist tendencies of the state. It is in calling attention to their democratization of society at ground levels that I hope to broaden the political base of the intracultural beyond the explorations that I have made so far within the domain of theatre.

In the concluding section of my essay on cultural activism in the 'shifting sites of secularism', I provide some clues as to how the politics of intracultural practice can converge with the larger struggle for 'political society'. Whether or not the 'intracultural' continues to have any semantic significance within this convergence will have to be further investigated, as my research continues beyond the boundaries of this book. But from the unresolved immediacies of my research today, I would say that the linkage of cultures of struggle in India today could be the most potent form of strengthening intraculturality, whereby the dynamics of *living together* can be complemented by the creative strategies of *fighting together*.

On a less militant note, let me insert into the discussion at this point some perspective on 'multiculturalism', which has already interrupted my description of inter/intra-cultural initiatives with the somewhat retarding force of its statist rhetoric and agenda. No culturalism, to my mind, has been more obsessively prefixed by qualifying adjectives like 'liberal', 'authoritarian', 'corporate', 'insurgent', 'boutique', 'critical', 'aggregative', 'universalist', 'essentialist', 'paradigmatic', 'modular': a veritable shopping-list of seemingly differentiated multiculturalisms that ultimately resonate a disturbing sameness. Symptomatic of our times, and more specifically, of social conditions in Europe where borders seem to be disappearing (at least for some privileged communities), multiculturalism is the most over-inscribed catch-word of seeming change in the polities of the developed world. Tellingly, it exemplifies that old truism: *Plus ça change, plus c'est la même chose.*

In order to account for my cultural biases, from which no study of culturalism is entirely free, I should acknowledge that I feel much closer in my cultural and critical affinities to the tensions of the 'inter' – 'the cutting edge of translation and negotiation, the *in-between* space' (Bhabha 1994: 38) – than I do to the comprehensiveness that is suggested by the 'multi'. If in the first modality there is a greater room for difference, play, disagreement, counterpoint, breakdown, there is almost an in-built expectation written into the 'multi' which assumes that 'we *have* to get along and live together'. In short, it would seem to deny the 'right to exit' a particular society or to subvert the premises of 'living together'. These restraints do not condition inter/intracultural endeavours, where there is no onus as such on its agencies to conform to the norms of any prescribed culture. Nor is there any demand in such interactions that they need to outlast their efficacy or capacity to hold together. The 'multi', however, is obliged to last for the 'good' of society at large in all its ostensibly democratic manifestations relating to the management of justice, harmony, and peace.

I acknowledge that this is a somewhat biased reading in which I am unable to remove the spectre of the State from the narrative of multiculturalism. While I resist the tendency to demonize the state – this is counterproductive, as I have argued earlier, in the larger context of resisting the onslaught of globalization – I do not necessarily see the State as an ally or as an uncritical point of reference for the articulation and execution of cultural practice. In other words, I am assuming a privilege here: that it is possible to absent, marginalize, and oppose the control of the State in any form of culturalism – a privilege that comes somewhat unquestioningly from my location as a freethinking citizen in the fractious and increasingly threatened democracy of India. In contrast, I would acknowledge that there are other political contexts where the State cannot be so readily absented, such as the State in Singapore, for instance, whose synony-mous policies of multiculturalism and multiracialism prescribe very specific limits as to what is 'political' (the domain of the state) and what can be accepted as 'cultural' (the inherited legacies of specific 'races' through language and religion). Needless to say, this is not my context in India where the sheer turbulence of the political situation enables me to question the limits of the State in determining the culture of its citizens.

In this book, I will extend this questioning to confront the seemingly beneficent policies of multiculturalism as legislated in western democratic societies. I will argue that, for all their good intentions, these policies have tended to mark, segregate, and ultimately divide entire communities through tokenistic and pseudo-communitarian strategies that have resulted in what Slavoj Žižek has described somewhat too dangerously as a 'disavowed, inverted, self-referential form of racism' (Žižek 1997: 44). Balancing the extremity of this position with the more measured communitarian stance of Charles Taylor (1994) and the 'polycentric' multiculturalism of Ella Shohat and Robert Stam (1994), I also make a case for retrieving and supporting the democratic possibilities of multicultralism, not least to counter the vicious denigration of minority rights and cultures that is so rampant in different parts of the world today.

Here there is a lacuna in the book, or so it could be perceived, in so far as I deal with the communalized representation of 'minorities' only in a few fragments of performance. I do not, however, provide a comprehensive reading of 'minority rights', as outlined in the increasingly dense multicultural debates on the subject. Not only am I incompetent to engage in the philosophical and legal intricacies of these debates (Rawls 1993, Kymlicka 1995, Walzer 1994, Habermas 1994), I am concerned primarily in this book with the actual strategies and making of cultural practice at a time when communities are increasingly marked and divided. I would also acknowledge that the schisms between the languages of political philosophy and cultural practice continue to be so staggering that they are not easily inscribed even within the gaps and fissures of this book.

Within the Indian context, the narrative of multiculturalism is not merely vexed at the level of cultural practice; it is also perhaps an inadequate philosophy to deal with the growing threat of communalism and subsequent erosion of democratic norms. At least this is the view offered by a sympathetic critic of multiculturalism, the marxist political theorist Achin Vanaik, who is compelled to emphasize that multicultural politics in India cannot have 'the same weight, thrust, tactical or strategic significance as in the West' (Vanaik 1998: 642).

At one level, it could be argued that multiculturalism in India has to be strengthened beyond the 'unity in diversity' model of the state, not least to counter the increasingly strident monoculturalism of Hindutva, the political ideology of the Hindu Right. This ideology advocates 'one nation, one language, one religion', even as it flaunts the intrinsic 'plurality' of Hinduism. Such is the strategic doublespeak at work here that the anti-secularism of Hindutva can masquerade as an authentic 'Indian' secularism based on the innate principles of tolerance embedded in the Hindu pantheon of beliefs. Significantly, the same Hindutva can provide the legitimacy for marking religious minorities as 'foreigners' and 'traitors', thereby indicating the tense borderlines that exist between what is assumed to be 'pluralist', and what is, in actuality, through political manipulation, a profoundly sectarian, if not racist, ideology.

Unlike in western societies where the anti-multiculturalist forces of the Right have attempted to control and censor, for example, the progressive changes in the curriculum of the core courses in universities, or the education policy for minorities, or the now defunct agencies for affirmative action in the United States, the monocultural thrust in the policies of the Hindu Right has extended, as Achin Vanaik correctly emphasizes, 'to the whole fabric of Indian society including its liberal democratic and secular state' (Vanaik 1998: 642). To counter the scale of its operation, one needs not merely a resurgence of multiculturalism in contemporary India, but a 'holistic project of opposition' in which the task of 'preserving and deepening cultural diversities' can be extended beyond the privileging of 'culture' to the enhancement of its social, economic, and political implications in society (ibid.).

Without undermining the political validity of this position, I would claim that Vanaik's insistence on heuristic distinctions between 'culture' and 'society' rests too heavily on Raymond Williams's reading of culture as a 'realized signifying system'. The problem today, not just in India, but in almost any part of the world, is that the rationales underlying such 'realized' systems have collapsed, while other cultures of struggle are in the making at very fragmentary, inchoate, and, perhaps, unrecognized levels. The task is to identify, link, and mobilize these cultures of struggle out of which new signifying systems may be realized. While this is obviously a task that encompasses more than the consolidation of a spectrum of cultural practices – and I do not share Vanaik's valorization of culture as a 'field of values' rather than as a 'field of practices' (I would argue that values are embedded in – and indeed, inseparable from – practices) – I would emphasize that the 'holistic project of opposition' envisioned by Vanaik is not possible today without a critical embrace of more than one 'signifying system' of culture. The Anglo-Saxon cultural grounding and presuppositions of Raymond Williams's justifiably respected socialism no longer provide adequate 'resources of hope' for the multicultural realities of our increasingly contested and differentiated modes of resistance in an age of globalization.

While there can be contrary arguments offered at this point, which I will briefly indicate in the next chapter in the socialist critique of multiculturalism, I am more interested in exploring the relatively uninvestigated relationship between 'multiculturalism' and 'secularism'. While it can be argued that almost any philosophy of multiculturalism is broadly secular in its acceptance or at least grudging tolerance of a diversity of positions, the opposite does not necessarily hold true. In other words, a secular state does not necessarily endorse multi-culturalism, and may even be actively opposed to it. The shifting dynamics of this interpretation, however, will depend to a large extent on what is meant by the 'secular' in the first place.

This brings me to the last of my key-words in the introduction to this book. Perhaps, there is no word that illuminates the incredible distance that exists between the cultural contexts analysed in this narrative than the word 'secular'. This most contested of concepts in the political culture of contemporary India is almost a forgotten word in the West today. Certainly, it is the least theorized of categories in the overdetermined and jargon-ridden discourse of cultural studies. It is almost as if the secular has been so thoroughly assimilated in western consciousness that it is not worth thinking about any longer. This, I believe, is a profound illusion that may need to be unlearned.

In one of the few attempts to recontextualize the secular within Anglo-American academia, Bruce Robbins (1994) has drawn on Edward Said's (1983) reflections on 'secular criticism' to dislodge the received meanings of the secular. By positing it not against 'religious concerns or beliefs per se but to the national and nationalism as belief systems' (Mufti 1998: 96), Robbins tacitly endorses Said's own resistance to any serious consideration of religion as a component of cultural consciousness, even within those contexts and constituencies of the non-western world where God is neither officially nor philosophically dead. In Said's categorical view, 'the amount of heat as opposed to light generated by religious practices' has done more harm than good, and he is 'not interested in the elucidation of ideas of the Divine or of the sacred, except as they are secular facts and historical experiences' (Williams and Said 1989: 182). The problem is that there is little or no evidence in the corpus of Said's influential writings that religion is anything more than 'a token of submerged feelings of identity, of tribal solidarity' (quoted in Wicke and Sprinker 1992: 232). And therefore, his reading of the secular proceeds as if religion is a non-issue, or, at best, a crude nationalist reflex.

Significantly, the attempt to dislodge the received meanings of the secular in the Indian context has been strategized on different grounds. In my own interventions in this volatile field, I began by speculating on the possibilities of retrieving the pluralist bases of religion for secular consideration, in my tract on *The Question of Faith* (1993). This was followed by my book *In the Name of the Secular* (1998), which attempted to map secular histories and strategies of opposition to fundamentalist forces within the emergent field of cultural activism in contemporary India. In Chapter 6, I will elaborate on why it was necessary to shift gears in my reading of the secular, from a focus on 'faith' (which is not the prerogative of fundamentalists) to a more reflexive cultural practice of the secular. In this book, I will continue to deepen the reflection on cultural practice with the qualification that while I share Said's affirmation of worldliness in his reading of secular criticism, I have arrived at it through a very different route. While religion is not specifically addressed in my essay on secularism in this book, it is refracted and fragmented in unprecedented ways and disguises – for instance, through the interruption of a religious festival in the north-eastern state of Manipur with a performance of 'Michael Jackson', or, more directly, through the inscription of four boy-priests in the form of a widely disseminated secular image. While my evidence for 'secular culture' drawn from grass-root cultural practices may seem eccentric to the political philosophers of secularism, the point is that they substantiate the *instability* that I read in the secular, as opposed to the *weight* that Said endows in the term. Secularism, I believe, is still in the making.

Calling attention to the mode of 'catachresis' – Gayatri Spivak's reading device that deploys a 'meaningful and productive misuse' of a particular term – Aamir Mufti provides a succinct encapsulation of Said's redefinition of the secular:

> Secular implies for Said a critique of nationalism as an ideology of hearth and home, of collective *Gemütlichkeit*; a critique of the assurance, 'confidence', and 'majority sense' that claims on behalf of national culture always imply, a critique of the entire matrix of meanings we associate with 'home', belonging and community ... It contains the charge that organi-cism of national belonging, its mobilization of the filiative metaphors of kinship and regeneration, obscures its exclusionary nature ... Secular criticism seeks continually to make it perceptible that the experience of being at home can only be produced by rendering some other homeless.
> (Mufti 1998: 10)

This strikes me as being an over-dichotomized reading of the secular that actually obscures some of its complexities, at least as they register in the contemporary Indian context.

First of all, there seems to be a confusion of categories in the description of nationalism as an 'ideology of hearth and home ... belonging and community', which is perhaps better read as communitarianism, that component in the anti-secularist discourse of India that privileges itself precisely on the grounds that its fragmented and marginalized subaltern discourses cannot – or will not – enter the 'imagined community' of the nation-state. In India, the struggle today is not just between secularists and fundamentalists, but between secularists and communitarians, such as Ashis Nandy and Partha Chatterjee, whose anti-nationalist stances have been juxtaposed – and contrasted – by Aamir Mufti with the Saidian reading of secularism. The point is that there is also a secularist ground in India that may endorse nationalism ironically on the very lines of Said's cosmopolitan discourse, which would reject the anti-modernist 'hearth and home' philosophy of Indian communitarians. Said's secularism would seem to be not just anti-nationalist, but anti-communitarian.

In my reading of the secular, I will try to explicate why one needs to be vigilant about the insufficient critique of patriarchy and gender in the 'narrative of community', as valorized by communitarian thinkers like Partha Chatterjee. Simultaneously, one is obliged to contend with the anti-democratic tendencies of globalization as endorsed by the nation-state in its increasing capitulation to the 'narrative of capital'. The simultaneity of these dual sources of contention is totally missing in Said's reading of secularism, not least because it is not specifically concerned with the critique of capital or the reinforcement of 'social justice', which is one of the central tropes for the propagation of secularism in India today. Instead, Said upholds an almost militant, if not fierce, cosmopolitanism, with a scarcely disguised embrace of western liberal culture from a minoritarian perspective. 'Displacing its assignation as the site of the local', as Mufti correctly points out, Said 'rescues' the perspective of the minority as 'one from which to rethink and remake universalist (ethical, political, cultural) claims' (Mufti 1998: 112).

While I would accept Mufti's somewhat hyperbolic claim that Said's intervention has been made 'in the interest ... of all those who would be minoritized in the name of a uniform "national" culture', I find it harder to go along with his emphasis that this intervention has been made *from the perspective* of the homeless. This lies at the root of the criticism that has justifiably, to my mind, been raised against Said's 'elitist', though by no means 'empty', cosmopolitanism. For all his qualifications, his reading of 'minority', at least within the framework of secular criticism, is almost entirely mediated by the elegiac figure of Erich Auerbach, whose exile in Istanbul during the Second World War has been unduly fetishized by Said and his disciples. I fail to see how the undeniably poignant predicament of a minority writer in exile, reflecting on the corpus of western literature, can be metaphorized for the dehumanized condition of minorities at large. For all the critical sensitivity of this reading that justifiably honours the courage of Auerbach's enterprise, it provides too precise a lens for the epic canvas of the millions of homeless and displaced who are, for theoretical purposes, categorized as 'minority'.

A somewhat less essentialized reading of this historically determined and mutable term is needed, which could keep in mind the prescient statement made by Dr Babasaheb Ambedkar, the seminal philosopher of the rights of the *dalits*, or the downtrodden communities in India: 'It is wrong for the majority to deny the existence of the minorities. It is equally wrong for the minorities to perpetuate themselves.' While I will be contextualizing this statement within the cultural representation of minorities, as described in Chapter 5, I would also suggest that in order to enhance the 'contrapuntal' possibilities of Saidian secularism in other cultural contexts, it should be juxtaposed with differentiated minority experiences and histories that can challenge the ostensibly enlightened genealogy and legacy of the secular in which Said's reading of minorities is irrevocably placed.

This is what I try to do in my chapter on the 'shifting sites of secularism', where in a consciously disjunctive narrative mode, I enter the varied sites of a communalized cinema hall and the anti-communal *mohalla* (neighbourhood) committees in the slums of Mumbai. While I would not claim that this reading has emerged 'from the perspective of minorities', I try to engage with the specific practices of their largely unacknowledged 'secular culture' that challenge not only the cosmopolitan affinities of Saidian secularism, but the residual signs of my own cosmopolitanism as well (as echoed in the nostalgic evocations of the 1950s in the fiction of writers like Salman Rushdie and Vikram Seth). My cosmopolitanism, I would say, is in the process of becoming 'cosmopolitical', to use the felicitous term invented by Pheng Cheah and Bruce Robbins (1998) in their contestation of the assumptions of privilege in earlier modes of cosmopolitanism. Unfortunately, since books have life-spans, and consequent limits to what gets included in the telling of any narrative, I will have to leave out a reading of the cosmopolitical in this particular book, though I trust it will further catalyse my understanding of the secular.

From the 'inter' to the 'intra' to the 'multi' to the 'secular', I have roughly sketched the key-words of this book, though I will leave you to read how they intersect in each chapter. Clearly, this is not a linear narrative that engages with the histories of these individual terms in heuristic contexts. On the contrary, the reader has to be prepared for criss-crossing trajectories of different modes of culturalism, which exist in differing relationships to the specific sites of inquiry in each chapter. Following this somewhat volatile methodology, I have consciously attempted to highlight the shifts in this narrative, rather than to blur their differences.

Thus, to provide a short tour-guide of the 'shifts' in sight, 'Interculturalism and its Discriminations' offers a theoretical overview on the imbrications of intercultural practice within the global economy and nationalist politics, along with its conceptual differences from the statist and assimilationist tendencies in multicultural political philosophy. 'When "Eternal India" Meets the YPO' provides some much-needed comic relief on the consequences of packaging the intracultural diversities of 'Indian culture' for the consumption of the corporate world. 'Gundegowda meets Peer Gynt', 'Towards a Politics of Sexuality', and 'Phantoms of the Other' focus primarily on the politics of identity within the larger frameworks of translation and the naming of minorities, including Muslims, *dalits* (low-caste communities), gays, lesbians, and survivors of communal riots. With 'Phantoms of the Other', the search for a secular imaginary, which has already been inscribed in the earlier chapters, leads directly to a more activist confrontation of different modes of secular cultural practice in 'The Shifting Sites of Secularism'. Following this attempt to theorize the essential instability of secular identities within emergent modes of cultural activism, the book ends somewhat elliptically on 'Afterwords', which speculates on the future of the intercultural in the form of a personal story rather than an ideological blueprint. Suffice it to say that I am happy to be alive to be sharing this story with you, which I trust you will be patient in learning about in the due course of reading this book, instead of sneaking to the end.

Undeniably, the shifting sites of this book have been tricky to negotiate not merely at conceptual and theoretical levels, but, more concretely, at the level of writing. The challenge has been not merely to order the shifts through a strategic erasure of their tensions, but rather to hold on to the narrative even while allowing it to be steered in some rather unpredictable directions. If there is a holding principle in this narrative, I would say that it comes from my discipline in theatre, which I continue to regard as a laboratory of the world. While at one level it could be argued that there is far less documentation of actual performances and productions in this book than its title would suggest, I would also emphasize that I could not have addressed the overlapping narratives of globalization, communalism, and culturalism without the concrete insights that I have gained about these phenomena through the immediacies of theatre. The preposition 'through' indicates my dramaturgical relationship to theatre in this book. Here I am not specifically concerned with theatre as a 'place for seeing' (as its etymological origin in the Greek word *theatron* suggests). Rather, what concerns me is how I am able to see the global and communal realities of our times *through* the transient illuminations of theatre.

But perhaps it is not just what one sees, but what one does not see in theatre that incites the deepest questions. In writing the most difficult section in this book on communal violence, for instance, which would seem to defy any adequate representation in theatre, I have come to realize that the act of seeing may be unduly fetishized in the writing of performance. Indeed, my critical methodology has been most challenged in my attempt to address those '*sights*' that I have not seen with my own eyes – for example, the grief bordering on madness of those survivors of communal riots, who 're-enact' the atrocities that have been inflicted on them by their assailants. What one is capable of 'seeing' here cannot be separated from the fragments in which the survivors have been documented, and in which they momentarily come alive, crying out to be cited.

It could be argued that realities like communal violence are far too culture-specific to be translated meaningfully into other social and political contexts. The spectre of caste as well may not resonate in western contexts in the intricate and deeply internalized ways by which it continues to dominate social and cultural relationships in India. And yet, is it possible to deny differing histories of racism, sectarianism, bigotry, and intolerance by which underprivileged and downtrodden communities in almost any society continue to be dehumanized with varying degrees and modes of violence, at explicit, implicit, and perhaps even invisible levels? The point here, I would suggest, is not to seek equivalencies in different states of degradation, nor to set up false hierarchies of the 'better-off' and the 'worse-off' victims, still less to periodize histories of pain in neat chronologies and sequences. We need to develop more complex ways of translating not just the texts but also the contexts of differing histories of violence in individual cultures. Then only can we proceed towards an intercontextual reading of violence, as indeed of other social and cultural phenomena.

To highlight the intercontextual demands of cultural translation, I would like to dwell briefly on a specific example that could help in formulating the critical task that lies ahead in reading this book. Consider, for instance, the extremely marginalized working-class community of the *burakumin* in Japan, whose condition should not be arbitrarily equated with the *harijans* of India. And yet, both communities have been described as 'untouchables' in terms of their social ostracism from the more 'civilized' sections of their respective societies; both are marked by their names and segregated sites of residence; both are denied rights of intermarriage with upper 'castes'; and indeed, both continue to be identified with menial jobs and occupations involving animal-slaughter and leather-related activities. The difference between these communities could be that while the oppression of the 'untouchables' in India continues, it has been politicized at mass levels not least through the political affirmation of *dalit* identities, movements, and parties; in contrast, the *burakumin*, who have also fought bravely for self-respect and recognition at civic levels, continue to remain in the shadows of one of the most highly developed, industrialized, capitalist-intensive societies in the world.

The argument here is not that their condition is better (or worse) than that of the *dalits* in India today, or even (though this would be more plausible) that the *burakumin* and the *harijans* have a common struggle. All I would say is that their comparable conditions of dehumanization and social humiliation exist in very different locations in the map of the world – indeed, in very different proximities to (and distances from) the power structures, institutions, and technologies of globalization. We would be better off as citizens of the world if we were prepared to exchange not just the imagined achievements or lost heritages of our respective cultures, but the very real differences of caste and social injustice (as indicated in the present condition of *dalit* and *burakumin* communities) that continue to remain unresolved, even as they are in the process of being contested. To argue against the exchange of these differences on the ground that the silences of cultures need to be respected is worth considering, so long as it does not legitimize a total evasion of the difference in question.

On the complex issue of 'context', therefore, what I seek most specifically from the western reader of this book is not a mere endorsement of the Indian social and political realities that have informed my analysis of cultural practice in an age of globalization. Nor would I particularly welcome the blithe denial 'Your context is not ours', which at one level is an intellectually lazy (and perhaps, unconsciously ethnocentric) truism. What interests me more are the possibilities of my context being translated in other locations, where the languages of communalism and secularism (as they have been outlined in this book) may not be immediately familiar to readers outside India. Likewise, my seemingly unequivocal critique of globalization may come across as too harsh, even anachronistic, to those readers for whom the benefits of global capitalism far outweigh its negative impact in those parts of the world where the basic necessities of life – water, food, health care, education – have yet to be equitably distributed. The point is not to valorize or to demonize globalization but to be critically alert to its vastly differentiated contexts. In this book, I offer one context that I trust will be addressed in good faith, even though it may seem jarringly unfamiliar to some readers, and oppressively familiar to others.

To seek the familiar in the unfamiliar, the unfamiliar in the familiar, is one of the critical tasks that Bertolt Brecht had confronted in his search for a new dialectics in theatre. We can continue to probe the challenge of this task in its new permutations as they have evolved in the burgeoning fields of cultural and performance studies. As Arjun Appadurai has acknowledged, 'A strong theory of globalization from a sociocultural point of view is likely to require something we certainly do not now have: a theory of intercontextual relations that incorporates our existing sense of intertexts' (Appadurai 1997: 187). It is my hope that the intercultural impetus of this text will contribute in its own way to the larger search for intercontextual relations without which any study of cultural practice across borders would be somewhat redundant.

1

INTERCULTURALISM AND ITS
DISCRIMINATIONS

SHIFTING THE AGENDAS
OF THE NATIONAL,
THE MULTICULTURAL,
AND THE GLOBAL

BEGINNINGS

To begin with an image that anticipated my articulation of interculturalism – indeed, I was not yet aware that such an 'ism' already existed – I would like to retrieve a critical moment in my viewing of a Chhau performance that I remember seeing in Calcutta in 1977, shortly before I had left home for the first time. Not only was this my first exposure to the 'folk' dance-theatre tradition of Chhau from the eastern states of India, it was also my introduction to interculturalists from different parts of the world. Indeed, as I retrieve the image that is at once catalysed by and buried in my memory of the Chhau performance, what concerns me here is not the evocation of nostalgia but an exposition of unresolved contradictions.

As I see it today, the Chhau performance was not so much the site of my image, but the backdrop against which I remember seeing another 'performance' that was going on simultaneously in front of the stage. This real-life improvisation was being enacted rather unconsciously by a group of interculturalists from the First World, who were totally absorbed in clicking their cameras throughout the Chhau dance. I remember seeing the backs of these interculturalists, and a very glittering array of cameras, zoom lenses, videos, and projectors, which at that point in time signified for me, at a very visceral level, an image of western technology and power: the power of capital. Today, when I look back on this image, I realize that it was refracted in so far as I was seeing at least two things at the same time: the Chhau dance on a makeshift stage, cut by the bodies and technology of the interculturalists.

This image, which has now become a visual trope in my intercultural imaginary, raises some troubling questions. At an existential level, I remember asking myself: Who are these people? What are they seeing? And why are they so oblivious to the hundreds and thousands of people sitting behind them? Today these questions suggest a context of exclusion on my part, implying a relatively uninterrogated sense of cultural belongingness and territoriality that is being assumed, even as it is in the process of being disturbed.

In a more reflexive mode, therefore, I would turn the critical gaze on to myself: Was I overreacting to what I saw? Were we being made into voyeurs of our own culture as we saw Chhau through the screen of alien bodies? To what extent can Chhau be regarded exclusively as 'our' culture? What goes into the construction of this possessive adjective 'our' – our culture, our language, our nation? As I shall be demonstrating in the course of this book, the regional hegemonies of 'Indian culture' attempt to subsume indigenous, folk, and tribal cultures within their ostensibly homogenized linguistic and cultural frames. Tellingly, the practitioners of these cultures from the most downtrodden sections of society can be marginalized and demeaned by upper-caste patriarchies in everyday life – the very patriarchies that would claim minority cultures as part of a larger regional cultural heritage. I will be theorizing this problem later in the book specifically within the politics of intraculturality.

In this chapter, however, I am specifically concerned with the different yet overlapping narratives of the intercultural, the multicultural, and the global, which should not be arbitrarily conflated. I am concerned with both the political dynamics of these phenomena and their implications in the actual making of specific cultural practices. With this agenda in mind, let us return to the Chhau performance in order to interrogate a seemingly innocuous set of details: the photographs, images, and recordings that were taken during the performance.

Today I am compelled to ask: Where has the documentation of this performance been circulated over the years, among so many other unacknow-ledged recordings of rituals, ceremonies, and non-commercial performance traditions from Third World countries? To whom have the images of such performances been distributed? And with whose permission? Does access to technology ensure the rights of ownership, representation, and distribution? It is with these questions that I would like to open some contentious issues relating to 'intellectual property rights', which have yet to be adequately addressed within the emergent debates on the globalization of cultures in our times.

THE RIGHTS OF CULTURE

Along with the policing of human rights by which First World nations legitimize their control of Third World economies on humanitarian grounds, there is now, increasingly, a bombardment of threats around the alleged violation of intellectual property rights. Third World countries like India, for instance, are often accused of abusing these rights by multinational corporations and pharmaceutical companies, the consciences of the First World. But is it possible to reverse the charges, as indeed environmentalists (Shiva and Holla-Bhar 1996) have succeeded in doing, by exposing the hypocrisies of those industries that have presumed to patent indigenous plants like *neem*, which is used by millions of Indians for dental and medicinal purposes? How do we counter similar instances of 'cultural piracy' that have yet to be acknowledged?

It is heartening in this regard to acknowledge the growing sensitivity among many western artists, theorists, lawyers, environmentalists, and anthropologists to the global transactions and appropriations of non-western cultural resources and practices. Increasingly, there is a critical consensus that intellectual property laws are 'selectively blind to the scientific and artistic contributions of many of the world's cultures'; ironically, when these cultures are recognized, they are denied the rights of authorship (quoted in Boyle 1996: 193). There is also an increasing cognizance of the imbalance between the 'traditional knowledge, folklore, genetic material and native medical knowledge' that are flowing *out* of Third World countries 'unprotected by intellectual property', in contrast to the surfeit of works from developed countries that are flowing *in*, 'well protected by international intellectual property agreements, backed by the threat of trade sanctions' (ibid.).

It could be argued that this increased vigilance around intellectual property violations is an exaggerated form of political correctness that plays more on the fears of cultural piracy than on empirical evidence. Critics of intellectual property could also be accused of speaking falsely on behalf of oppressed communities, who may not be aware of their exploitation and who could even be philosophically opposed to the idea of patenting their traditional wisdoms. These arguments, I would emphasize, are made in bad faith; they underestimate both the casual complicities of a wide range of professionals in acts of cultural piracy, and also the increased alertness on the part of indigenous communities to the economic value of their traditional skills and resources.

Besides, in an age of globalization, when the future in a sense is already in the process of being patented, a pre-emptive attitude to the exploitative potential of intellectual property cannot be sufficiently emphasized. Within the very real risks posed by the tradable intellectual properties (TRIPs) that have now been sanctioned within the General Agreement on Tariffs and Trade (GATT), it is possible to speculate with some conviction that

> transnational cultural corporations may obtain all rights to exploit for profit any piece of music, any image, any text they believe to have commercial potential. The consequence will be that these corporations may become the exclusive owners of substantial pieces of artistic cultures wherever in the world and thereby influence, perhaps even determine, the direction in which these cultures may develop.   (Smiers 1997: 3)

While it could be argued that these fears apply more readily to highly marketable cultural products, artefacts, and skills relating to the mass media, graphics design, and the fine arts, it would be disingenuous to exempt less commercially viable activities such as the performing arts from the control of the global market. Even if non-western theatrical productions and performances as such are not likely to interest the transnational corporate sector, the raw materials, techniques, and resources from non-western countries can easily be transported, channelized, and converted into 'original' products (performance pieces, video demonstrations, research programmes), which can then become eminently marketable through the funding available to festivals, universities, and a select body of avant-garde world.

The question that needs to be addressed is unavoidably polemical: What do the home countries and communities, from where these resources emanated, receive for their contribution to the creative process? Are they even acknowledged? The difficulties posed by these questions are invariably elided within the hype of global cultural enterprise, which for all its transcendence of specific national and cultural boundaries, remains doggedly loyal to the most conservative assumptions of what constitutes a work of art in the first place. If this 'art' belongs to anyone, it is indisputably the 'property' of an inspired 'author'. ('Genius' is the word that is still used to describe the most celebrated of global cultural impresarios.)

In this regard, the cult of the author has rightly been exposed by critics of intellectual property rights like James Boyle (1996), who traces the tenacious hold of an eighteenth-century romantic notion of authorship on the most blatant distortions of environmental loot. 'The romantic author', as Boyle points out, 'was defined not by the mastery of a prior set of rules, but instead by the transformation of genre, the revision of form' (1996: 54). Ultimately, it is this stamp of originality and invention that is upheld in claims around intellectual property rights, at the expense of taking into account collaborative and communitarian modes of production, inherited legacies of oral and folk wisdom. In this context, the cultural resources of indigenous peoples and tribal communities are particularly vulnerable to misuse because they are not *owned* by any defined party; they *belong* to the entire community. Unfortunately, 'individual' ownership is more accountable at legal levels than 'community' belonging and sharing, just as 'innovation' is more assessable than 'tradition', 'transformation' more precise in the specificity of its altered form than the vagaries of 'evolution' (Frow 1996: 98).

Within the framework of these biases, the double standards of the upholders of intellectual property rights become only too evident, as the border lines between 'ideas' and 'expressions', 'inventions' and 'discoveries' are proving to be more blurred than globalists are prepared to acknowledge (Frow 1996: 93). Admittedly, these blurrings are harder to specify within cultural practices than in the more scientific terrain of gene technology, for instance, where 'seed as "seed" and seed as "grain"' are discriminated for commercial purposes, the 'use-value' of the seed being supplanted by the 'exchange-value' of the grain (Kloppenburg 1988: 3). In contrast, artistic endeavours are not so easily discriminated; if a contemporary visual artist, for instance, incorporates the skills of an indigenous craftsman into his/her art work, there is no obligation as such to acknowledge this contribution.[1] The skill of the indigenous craftsman is, at best, a facilitating agency for which payment is due. Recognition, however, goes to the artist who has the 'idea' in the first place to use the skill of the craftsman in order to realize a particular 'expression'. Likewise, there are any number of complexities in determining the authorship of collaborative and interdisciplinary works of art like installations, which can be further complicated through new techniques of quotation, *bricolage*, and re-mixing.[2]

One could argue that these new modes of authorship have evolved in response to the availability of new technologies in the metropolis, but they should not be valorized at the expense of acknowledging communitarian systems of knowledge in which authorship is often anonymous. The ultimate perversity in exploiting this anonymity lies in the ruthless appropriation of the principle of 'universality', whereby the 'common heritage of mankind' that is embodied and celebrated in so many holistic disciplines, rituals, and ceremonies, can, with a few strategic adjustments, become the 'property' of particular individuals and agencies. How, in such demeaning and exploitative circumstances, can the 'cultural commons' of indigenous cultures be democratically recognized and shared in the 'public domain' without being ripped off by the speculators of the culture industry?

There is a loaded political context in such questions relating to different cultural practices and art forms, which has yet to be extrapolated adequately from the more rigorous readings of bio-imperialism and biodiversity in environmental agendas. In contrast, the concern for the ecology of cultures would seem to be, at this point in time, more rhetorical than real. Even in the most scrupulously liberal of cultural exchanges, ostensibly tuned to the demands of political correctness, there can be any number of blind spots and slippages in the ethics of cross-cultural representation and borrowing. When does the 'fair use' of resources from other cultures, even in the least commercial of endeavours like academic research in the non-western performing arts, for instance, become an alibi for the production of a new expertise at the expense of acknowledging local knowledge? What are the perks of this expertise that remain unaccounted for through the promotion of individual careers and the empowerment of new categories of cultural representation? If we have not begun to answer these questions, it is because they are in the process of being articulated from the oblivion of their assumed privilege: the privilege of silence that academics invariably secrete within the apolitical aura of their seemingly unadulterated search for knowledge.

THE INTERCULTURAL AND THE GLOBAL

Shifting the discussion away from the globalization of intellectual property rights, one needs to discriminate between those intercultural endeavours that, if not already globalized, are in the process of being globalized, and those that work against the grain of dominant global narratives. This is not an easy discrimination to sustain, but let me attempt some clarifications on the subject. Not every cultural exchange, I would acknowledge, needs to subscribe to the global agenda determined by the market economy, the satellite media culture, the McDonaldization of commodities, among other phenomena of global capitalism. There are artists in the world who seek each other out at personal and creative levels, through the harshest of economic circumstances, with no particular hope of recognition even within the framework of their respective national cultures. The work of these relatively unknown artists is not likely to be commodified by the agencies of corporate culture. On the other hand, there can be established artists whose narratives can work against the demands of the market that they are in a position to negotiate. Still others can opt out of the market altogether, pursuing a different set of cultural interventions that bring together a wide spectrum of activists, drop-outs and dissidents, representing the non-conformist, if not subversive, elements of any society.

Interculturalism, I would affirm, embraces all these possibilities of dissent, and therefore it is ironic that its most ardent advocates should so naively equate the 'intercultural' and the 'global' – terms which are often used synonymously, and even harmoniously, particularly in First World cultural contexts, where globalization is not just taken for granted but actively promoted. In India, however, there is a tremendous resistance at ground level to the homogenizing, commoditizing, and anti-democratic tendencies of globalization, as exemplified in people's movements directed against mega-enterprises like the Sardar Sarovar Dam project in Narmada. The resistance to globalization has also extended more arbitrarily to its cultural ancillaries, which would include corporate media spectacles like the Miss World Beauty Pageant in Bangalore (November 1996), which was attacked by sections of feminists, who specifically linked the commodification of beauty to the consumerist propaganda of the global market.

In this opposition, they received support from the farmers' lobby as well, which had earlier opposed the introduction of Kentucky Fried Chicken (KFC) into the Indian market. It is worth keeping in mind that while KFC is a thoroughly domesticated global icon in developed societies, so much so that it would be regarded as 'indigenous', if not disparagingly associated with the kind of junk food that the poorer sections of society eat, this very KFC becomes a status symbol in countries like India. In other words, the cultural signs of this commodity are totally different in Third World economies, thereby challenging one of the most illusory norms of globalization that it is capable of levelling differences across borders.

Without exposing the economic hegemony of globalization, it becomes disingenuous to accept its 'emancipatory results' in the cultural sphere. As posited tentatively by Geeta Kapur (1997), these 'results' can be related to the 'freedom' from 'the national/collective/communitarian straitjacket', along with the 'paternalistic patronage system of the state' and the rigidities of 'anti-imperialism' (Kapur 1997: 30). There is no reason to my mind why artists should be inhibited from exploring 'other discourses of opposition' relating to gender and minority issues, which Kapur associates with yet another liberatory aspect of global culture. I would contend that the right to criticize the official agendas of the State is eminently possible within the seeming constraints of a national imaginary, along with new articulations of cultural representation relating to women, *dalits*, tribal communities, and other minorities. The 'emancipatory results' by which Kapur attempts to inflect her critique of globalization are illusions of freedom; they are the phantoms of the market, which reduce possibilities of dissent to a pastiche of their co-optation.

I am more in agreement with Kapur when she claims the privilege as a resident in the Third World to resist globalization within the framework of a contested national culture – a privilege that may not be available, as she correctly points out, to our colleagues from more globalized economies. This privilege, I believe, needs to be extended to the practice of interculturalism, in order to subvert its affiliations to global capitalism from within its ranks. In other words, an opposition to globalization cannot be restricted to the national boundaries of Third World contexts, even if such an opposition would appear to make more sense in such contexts than in First World locations, where globalization has been normalized both in the financial and in the cultural sectors. To oppose globalization in one political context, and to conform to its agenda in another, is the surest way of subscribing to cultural schizophrenia.

The interculturalist, I would like to believe, is not a schizoid opportunist who shifts his/her position out of convenience. Nor is the interculturalist a free-floating signifier oscillating in a seemingly permanent state of liminality and in-betweenness. The interculturalist is more of an infiltrator in specific domains of cultural capital which could exist in First and Third World contexts as well. The ubiquity of global capitalism compels the interculturalist to negotiate different systems of power in order to sustain the exchange of cultures at democratic and equitable levels.

THE INTERCULTURAL AND THE NATIONAL

To shift the time-frame of this chapter back to 1977, when I first saw the Chhau performance that provoked me into thinking about interculturalism, I should acknowledge that I was not thinking about globalization at that time. The new economic policies of the Indian government had not yet been articulated. Nor could one have predicted the imminence of the satellite media invasion, for the simple reason that television had yet to enter our homes. In 1977, I found myself implicated within an increasingly uncomfortable awareness of what Frantz Fanon has described so memorably as 'the pitfalls of national consciousness'. Within the transposition of these 'pitfalls' in the Indian context, where the process of decolonization continues to elude us at so many levels, one was a witness to the post-Emergency euphoria of a nation attempting to re-establish its authenticity, through a retrieval of a pre-Nehruvian past.[3]

At an idealized political level (which, unfortunately, failed to materialize in a sustained secular political alternative to the Congress Party), there was an advocacy of decentralization through an upsurge of alternative activist initiatives. In the more institutionalized sectors of cultural practice as well, there was a vacuous retrieval of the past through an 'invention of tradition', whereby a 'back to the roots' anti-modern/anti-realist/anti-western policy was crudely, yet tenaciously, propagated by the State and its accomplices (Bharucha 1993: 205–208). These proponents of an authentic 'Indianness' were for the most part neither nativist visionaries nor ideologues, but cultural bureaucrats who exemplified the 'intellectual laziness' that marks the defunct state of the national bourgeoisie: 'Not engaged in production, nor building, nor labour ... the innermost vocation of [the national bourgeoisie] seems to be to keep in the running and to be part of the racket' (Fanon 1967: 120). It is in this nationalist framework of 'being part of the racket' that my first exposure to interculturalism needs to be contextualized.

I remember thinking to myself at that time: If the interculturalists at the Chhau performance were there, it's because they had been invited to be there. They were not intruders, but the honoured guests of the local impresarios of the organization and state cultural officials, who sought some kind of foreign endorsement for their display of indigenous culture at home. Such endorsements in the intercultural scenario are invariably made possible through a series of complicities not just at economic, political, and professional levels, but, more acutely, through the ideological bases and biases of different cultural institutions and modes of expertise across systems of power that would like to believe in the *autonomy* of their interactions. This autonomy is, perhaps, most emphatically asserted in the seeming transcendence of intercultural practice over all national boundaries and considerations. Indeed, if there is one premise that would bring together the widest spectrum of Euro-American interculturalists, it would be a rejection, if not a denial, of their own national identities and affiliations.

In the world of intercultural theatre, for instance, there is much evidence to support the resistance to nationalism in the 'transcultural' search for a universal theatre language across cultures in the work of Peter Brook and his 'ultracultural' quest for the origins of theatre in the spectacle of *Orghast*.[4] Different variations of this anti-national resistance can also be traced in the exploration of the 'essential human being' in the paratheatrical experiments of Jerzy Grotowski and his Theatre of the Sources. In the theatre anthropology of Eugenio Barba as well, one finds an almost virulent obsession with the 'pre-expressivity' of cultures that underlies their acculturation in specific contexts. These seeming discriminations between the 'transcultural', the 'ultracultural', and the 'pre-cultural' (Pavis 1996: 6–7) share a common ground in their distance from, if not resistance to, the realities of history, political struggle, and, above all, nationalism. There is no point in reiterating here my intense discomfort with the apolitical/asocial and subtly orientalist premises underlying these established examples of Euro-American intercultural theatre practice (see Bharucha 1993: 13–87 for an extended analysis on the subject). Rather, what concerns me is where I stand in relation to the 'national', a category that was not theorized sufficiently in my earlier critiques of interculturalism.

As suggested somewhat euphorically in liberal manifestos of interculturalism (Schechner 1982a), 'The world ... is in the process of moving from its nationalistic phase to its cultural phase, and it is preferable to distinguish cultural areas rather than nations' (quoted in Pavis 1996: 5). Not only is this statement one of profound wish-fulfilment that is not actually substantiated by the events in the *realpolitik*, where we have witnessed since 1989 an upsurge of nationalism, secessionism, insurgency, and fascism in almost all parts of the world, but also it is debatable whether 'nationalistic' and 'cultural' phases can be separated quite so easily in any discussion of culture, particularly in postcolonial contexts. One obvious paradox that liberal supporters of interculturalism fail to confront is that in the countering of one nationalism, other nationalisms are invariably in the making. But perhaps a more politically engaged reading of culture would indicate, as Frantz Fanon has emphasized, that 'national consciousness' could be 'the most elaborate form of culture' itself (Fanon 1967: 199).

There is an obvious provocation in this statement that challenges not just the anathema to nationalism assumed by a wide range of interculturalists. This prejudice is reinforced by those postcolonial theorists who have opposed nationalist discourses of resistance, which have been marked as 'coercive, totalizing, elitist, authoritarian, essentialist and reactionary' (Lazarus 1993: 70–71). The nationalist underpinnings of my own critique of interculturalism have not spared me from being described as 'demagogic' and even 'ridiculous' (Pavis 1992: 179). Turning to Fanon for ideological support, therefore, one is aware of the specific struggle for independence in Algeria to which his writings were committed. Though that historical moment cannot be replicated, its contradictions in other contexts of struggle and underdevelopment, as in India, and the foresight with which Fanon was able to anticipate the degeneration of nationalism in post-independence societies, are among the most chastening reminders in my cultural context of how history can repeat itself in disturbingly familiar ways. I turn, therefore, to Fanon not for answers, nor to be mystified by his 'occult instability' (needlessly valorized by Homi Bhabha in his own search for 'cultural undecidability'), but to find a ground in which the 'national' can be repositioned against nativist celebrations of community and the glib advocacy of post-nationalism. This repositioning of the 'national' cannot be separated in the Indian context from the emergent cultures of struggle in search of a more participatory people's democracy.

Fanon's provocation lies precisely in not clarifying the enigmas that he sets forth in his militant, yet contradictory – I will not say equivocal – statements. For example:

> National consciousness, which is not nationalism, is the only thing that will give us an international dimension ... It is at the heart of national consciousness that international consciousness lives and grows. And this two-fold emerging is ultimately the source of all culture.
>
> (Fanon 1967: 199)

Neil Lazarus probably comes as close as we are likely to get in identifying 'national consciousness' as 'a liberationist, anti-imperialist, nationalist internationalism' (Lazarus 1993: 72), which has been named 'nationalitarian' by Anwar Abdel-Malek in order to discriminate its agenda from the more negative associations of 'nationalism'. Fanon himself emphasizes more than once that nationalism – the 'magnificent song' that fuels the struggle for independence – has a great capacity to degenerate into 'ultra-nationalism', 'chauvinism', and eventually 'racism' (1967: 125).

This degeneration is part of a narrative that most postcolonial/intercultural thinkers would endorse because it plays into the demonization of what is assumed to be an intrinsically tainted phenomenon. Thus, we find in Fanon's critique of nationalism, the familiar charges of the tyranny associated with blaming other communities for the predicament of the post-independence nation. This process of othering minorities invariably thrives on the resuscitation of 'old tribal attitudes', 'spiritual rivalries', 'drivelling paternalism', and 'region-alism': 'African unity takes off the mask, and crumbles into regionalism inside the hollow shell of nationality itself' (1967: 128). Fuelling this degeneration of nationalism into a 'racism of contempt' is the steady decline of 'the party' (ostensibly the party that provided the leadership in the independence struggle; for example, the Congress Party in India). The bankruptcy of such parties is not spared by Fanon in the choicest of epithets: 'trade union of individual interests', 'skeleton of its former self', 'a means of private advancement', 'accomplice of the merchant bourgeoisie', 'a screen between the masses and the leaders' (ibid.: 136–137).

Clearly, there is no 'undecidability' in this critique of the party, which represents the most hollow manifestation of nationalism itself. *But* – Fanon does not stop here. In countering a degenerate nationalism, he does not posit any utopian postnationalism, nor does he lapse into pre-modern commu-nitarianism, or into a nativist valorization of the authentic past. 'A national culture', as he emphasizes, 'is not a folklore, nor an abstract populism that believes it can discover the people's true nature' (1967: 188). On the contrary, Fanon returns to an intensification of struggle at ground level with somewhat different priorities: 'If you really wish your country to avoid regression, or at best halts and uncertainties, a rapid step must be taken from national consciousness to political and social consciousness ... [I]f nationalism is not enriched and deepened by a very rapid transformation into a consciousness of social and political needs, in other words into humanism, it leads up a blind alley' (ibid.: 163–165). While Fanon does not substantiate these discriminations between the 'national', the 'political', the 'social', the 'human', their resonances in the contemporary political context of India are almost uncanny, particularly in relation to people's movements, whose social dimensions relating to caste and gender are assuming new political identities and formations.

To bring the discussion back to the intercultural abhorrence of nationalism, it becomes obvious that one needs to 'break down the equivalences between "national" and "nationalism"', as Stuart Hall has suggested in his own inflected reading of Fanon (Hall 1996: 42). One also needs to work against moribund notions of an 'empty international humanism' (ibid.) and seek out a new critical internationalism that would include a profound respect for intercultural exchange through the mediation of different histories and postcolonial struggles. There is a lot of work that lies ahead in actualizing these discriminations within cultural practices, but perhaps one can begin by addressing the nullity of those prejudices that equate the 'national' with the regimentation of nation-states, the policing of borders, and the construction of 'good citizens'. This demonization of the 'national' can only homogenize nationalisms, apart from undermining the very real struggles and sacrifices that have gone into the activization of social and political movements in different parts of the world.

On a more personal note, I would suggest to the neo-liberal, anti-nationalist seekers of interculturalism from First World cultural contexts that they should first begin to account for their own implicit nationalisms, and their very real privileges that are so often taken for granted in their ownership of passports from First World nations – the ultimate sign of global privilege – which enables them to travel to almost any part of the world without difficulty. This is not a privilege that many of us from Third World countries can assume. As I have often emphasized in my critical interventions, our interculturalism begins with the trauma of having to obtain a visa on our much maligned, if not degraded, passports, in order to travel not merely to 'the West', but to almost any country in Asia, Africa, or the Middle East. I confront the injustices of competing and disparate nationalisms every time I am invited to an intercultural forum. For all my seeming 'privilege' as a seasoned traveller, I am marked along with my fellow citizens as a potential illegal immigrant, if not a terrorist, so much so that my negotiation to cross the border in face-to-face encounters with visa officers has now become a performative act in its own right. It is not surprising, therefore, that my closest compatriots in intercultural performance should be border artists, who, unlike their liberal counterparts who assume the crossing of borders as their birthright, never fail to take the border for granted.

BORDERS AND CHOICES: INTERCULTURALITY IS (NOT) ORDINARY

Intercultural decision-makers would like to believe that they function with a certain map of the world that counters the official maps and borders. But one finds that even on these seemingly altruistic, humanitarian, border-free/border-less maps, the routes of cultural exchange have already been charted, the zones of interaction have already been fixed. And some zones may not exist at all, which means that one could be reduced to an absence. If one wanted to shift these zones (break the dichotomies of the North and South, East and West) or if one desired to re-route the map (bring the cultures of the South closer together), the possibilities of doing so are extremely remote in the absence of alternative routes, structures of representation, and infrastructures of support. Indeed, the 'crossroads' of cultural exchange are often substituted by the 'inroads' of institutionalized interculturalism, whereby the South–South cultural exchange is unavoidably mediated by the North.[5] While it could be argued that these mediations are not necessarily undemocratic, I would acknowledge that they are extremely constraining because they work against the basic premises of voluntarism on which interculturalism is based as a theory and practice.

Voluntarism as a critical principle is unavoidably linked to the larger philosophical framework of liberalism that assumes a freedom of choice, which may not, in reality, exist for all its assumed beneficiaries. At an ideational level, however, it is a useful term in so far as it enables us to discriminate interculturalism from the larger, more emphatic, if not overdetermined, narratives of multiculturalism, which does not function on a voluntarist basis. For all its constraints, interculturalism is not thrust on us: it is a process of exchange that artists, for example, seek out for any number of reasons – curiosity about other cultures and a desire to interact and collaborate with them; a need for spiritual rejuvenation or exotic diversion; or perhaps, to travel (at someone else's expense) and, thereby, to deflect (or reinforce) the agendas of cultural tourism.

While there are any number of reasons that can contribute to the voluntarist dynamics of intercultural encounters, interculturalism itself as a cultural phenomenon should not be reduced to a pre-existing beneficent state of being. This needs to be stressed because there is often a tendency among the advocates of interculturalism to essentialize its ubiquity by assuming its seeming timelessness. In some readings, interculturalism is almost evoked as a primordial state that has been arbitrarily disrupted by the ruptures of the nation-state:

> Clearly nationalism, and its rivalries, armaments, boundaries – culminating in the nuclear catastrophe of mass extinction – is something we humans are going to have to learn to get rid of. Learn to be intercultural? More like unlearn what is blocking us from returning to the intercultural. For as far back as we can look in human history, people have been deeply, continuously, unashamedly intercultural.   (Schechner 1982b: 71)

While nationalism is clearly the villain of this breezy utopian universalism, there are other contexts in which interculturalism has been nurtured through the fall-out of global trade, war, and colonial history. Tellingly, these realities can be elided, if not silenced under the sign of 'ordinariness'. Thus, in Kobena Mercer's witty observation that 'interculturality is ordinary', we learn that

> All the symbols of the nation's cultural identity have come from somewhere else. What could be more English than a cup of tea? Brewed with leaves from India and sweetened with sugar from the West Indies. She's as fair as an English rose? Excuse me, roses do not spontaneously grow in Watford or Wiltshire, they were imported from fourteenth-century China. One could go on to find yet many other examples of interculturation in popular culture – in the realms of food, sports,

clothing, and music – yet all of this is erased and denied in narratives that
reproduce a monolithic concept of belonging whose values of purity,
authenticity and homogeneity are all based on a negation of the dynamic
exchanges that bring all cultures into being.   (Mercer 1997: 42)

There are far too many elisions in this undeniably ironic celebration of
ordinariness, not least the contexts of historicity that determine the 'exchanges'
of cultures in specific ways. Not every exchange is necessarily 'dynamic'; it can
also be coercive or assimilationist, if not blatantly colonial. Likewise, not every
importation can qualify as intercultural; if roses are a sign of unacknowledged
interculturality in England, as Mercer suggests, surely the eucalyptus tree that
proliferates all over India, killing the natural soil, is not 'intercultural', even
though it was imported from Australia. What is needed in any study of
interculturality in everyday life, which is an infinitely wider and more elusive
field of research than intercultural performance, is some critical perspective on
the temporality and contextualization of borrowings.

A cup of tea, for instance, has obviously been indigenized at some point in
time, not just in England but in India as well (and more specifically in North
India – a cup of coffee would be more welcome in the southern states of India).
The point is that once importations and borrowings become indigenized, they
cease to be 'intercultural' after some time. Indeed, they begin to represent new
norms, the very ordinariness that has been hegemonized by 'monolithic
concepts of belonging' upheld by the ruling elite. In this context, the task that
lies ahead in popularizing 'a new consensus about intercultural histories'
(Mercer 1997: 41), necessitates not merely a defence of what was (always)
intercultural, but a de-hegemonization of what is assumed to be 'ordinary'.
There needs to be a constant update on the process of intercultural borrowings,
so that if a cup of tea has become 'English' at least within my reading of
intercultural signs, perhaps the increasing popularity of *chai* in Britain can be
regarded as a more recent intercultural phenomenon. It is not just the tea, but
the way in which it is prepared and served, in particular contexts of domesticity
and socialization, that shifts its normative cultural significance.

For all the sophistication of Mercer's pitch for the ordinariness of
interculturality, which cannot fail to echo and, at some level, to distend
Raymond Williams's affirmation that 'culture is ordinary', there is an implicit
valorization in his reading of the innate state of flow in intercultural exchanges.
Not only does this flow idealize the actual processes of exchange, which can be
fraught with the deepest tensions, blockages, ruptures, and breakdowns, it
also suggests that the intercultural is somehow independent of larger political
processes. Thus, we are reminded that 'Politics and ideology draw on the
energies of interculturation, but always seek to fix and freeze the underlying
fluidity into rigid codes that reproduce the balance of power' (Mercer 1997: 42).
Perhaps, the intercultural process is less fluid than Mercer assumes, in so far as it
is imbricated within the 'politics' and 'ideology' of specific contexts. The
challenge for any intercultural worker is to disimbricate his/her intervention

from existing hegemonies by working consciously, if not subversively, against the grain of assumed norms. Perhaps, in its most radical manifestations, interculturalism is not ordinary, but an extra-ordinary act.

THE INTERCULTURAL AND THE MULTICULTURAL

To introduce the most obligatory of words in cultural discourse today – the 'multicultural' – which more often than not passes as 'intercultural', I would reiterate that the principle of voluntarism enables us to differentiate between these terms at rudimentary levels. While interculturalism is, within the framework of this argument, a voluntarist intervention circumscribed by the agencies of the State and the market, multiculturalism is increasingly identified with the official cultural policies of western democracies like Australia, Canada, and Britain. While the governments of these countries can formulate multicultural policies, none of them can presume to have an intercultural policy: the 'inter' will invariably lie outside of the direct control of the state. Unlike the 'multi', which is concerned with the cohabitation of different cultural and ethnic groups negotiating an ostensibly common framework of citizenship, intercultural practitioners have a greater flexibility in exploring – and subverting – different modes of citizenship across different national contexts, through subjectivities that are less mediated by the agencies of the state.

Unlike interculturalism, which has yet to be cogently theorized – it is at once too processual and scattered in its multiple locations and modes of expression to be subsumed under any one theoretical framework – multiculturalism has been over-theorized in a plethora of conflicting narratives that suffer from an overkill of ideology. Hegemonized as a state policy in countries like Britain, for instance, the narrative of multiculturalism is inextricably linked to the influx of labour from the ex-colonial countries in the late 1950s; its process of making immigrants into compliant citizens has been engineered by the most established agencies of the State and civil society monitoring the systems of law, education, employment, language, and social welfare. Significantly, it was the propagation of a liberal 'integrationist' mode of multiculturalism in Britain from the mid-1970s onwards (in opposition to the 'nationalist' assimilationist policies of immigration upheld earlier) that precipitated a crisis that still continues.

Many activist writers on the Left in Britain have reflected forcefully on how the State propagation of multiculturalism has resulted in a breakdown of a consensus built around a 'black' political identity and class solidarity that had unified a wide spectrum of Asian and Afro-Caribbean workers against the discriminatory practices of the state. Within the rhetoric of respecting cultural differences, the liberalization of multicultural policies has merely succeeded in 'depoliticizing race and substituting (a narrowly defined) "culture" for anti-racist consciousness' (Mohanty 1998: 17). Furthermore, at a grass-roots level of community organization, 'the government funding of self-help groups undermined the self-reliance, the self-created social and economic base of these groups; they were no longer responsive to or responsible for the people they served – and service itself became a profitable concern' (Sivanandan 1985: 6). In the name of freeing communities from the 'objectivist delusion' and 'essentialist nostalgia' of race, to use Satya Mohanty's ironic categories, multiculturalism divided communities – against each other, within themselves. It became another mode of promoting sectarianism, thereby perpetuating the policy of 'divide and rule' in former colonies, but camouflaged within the multicultural aura of respecting a plurality of cultural identities and ethnicities.

Satya Mohanty has argued that this reading of multiculturalism has echoes in other political contexts as well – for instance, in the United States, where, as Michael Omi and Howard Winant (1986) have pointed out, 'an objective analysis of racist domination was obscured by an intellectual [post-modern/post-colonial] agenda that emphasized the cultural multiciplicity of "ethnic" identities' (quoted in Mohanty 1998: 18). Whether or not one subscribes to the socialist register and reassertion of 'race' as a political category in these readings of multiculturalism, one cannot deny that the multicultural narrative is beginning to implode from within the unresolved tensions of its inner contradictions, even within neo-liberal endorsements of its framework.

Having acknowledged this predicament, one is also obliged, as I have indicated in the introduction, to defend more historically inflected readings of multiculturalism against the recent backlash of conservative opinion that would like to reduce its agenda to a caricature of affirmative action for essentially undeserving minorities. It is out of this compulsion that I would like to focus now on a spectrum of radical, liberal, and communitarian perspectives on Euro-American multiculturalism. This is not intended to be a comprehensive or even a selective overview, but rather a series of schematic positions (and provocations) on multiculturalism that I would like to interrogate – and interrupt – with some emergent lessons drawn from intercultural practices. At a methodological level, I will be intersecting different languages relating to the practice and philosophy of multiculturalism – languages that are rarely brought into collision because they incorporate radically different grammars, vocabularies, and epistemologies of thought. In this collision of languages, there is the risk of a certain theoretical awkwardness, but perhaps this is unavoidable in any attempt to heighten the intercontextuality of a layered and polyphonic phenomenon like multiculturalism.

1   The Problem of Universality

I begin with Slavoj Žižek's incomparably subversive reading of multiculturalism as much for its capacity to exhume the spectres of earlier liberationist modes of thinking, as for its lethal demolition of contemporary myths of coexistence:

[M]ulticulturalism is a disavowed, inverted, self-referential form of racism, a 'racism with a distance' – it respects the Other's identity, conceiving the Other as a self-enclosed 'authentic' community towards which he, the multiculturalist, maintains a distance rendered possible by his privileged

universal position ... [T]he multiculturalist respect for the Other's
specificity is the very form of asserting one's own superiority.

(Žižek 1997: 44)

In this exposure of multiculturalism, there are some immediate provocations of
the universalist assumptions underlying intercultural practices, which tend to be
critiqued (if at all) within the context of ethnocentricity rather than racism.
Unlike the multiculturalist who, in Žižek's formulation, 'distances' himself from
the Other through a privileged universality, the interculturalist, at least in
his/her most idealized manifestations, erases all distinctions through an assumption of a shared universality. In the empty space of the intercultural meeting
ground, which assumes the 'point zero' of an authentic 'first contact' between
'essential human beings', there is a total erasure of the participants' ethnicities in
favour of their universal human identities, creativities, and potentialities. The
interculturalist is above ethnicity; he/she is always already human. And
therefore, he/she can afford to propose a universality for all, cast in an invariably
white, patriarchal, heterosexist image.

This naive acceptance of an innately human 'universality' is quite different in
its implications from the kind of 'moral' and 'radical' universalism that is
affirmed by cultural thinkers like Satya Mohanty, whose reading is opposed in
its own right to Žižek's more shifty and strategic use of the 'universal'.
In Mohanty's anti-foundationalist, 'realist' defence of multiculturalism, a
'minimal rationality' is posited as the base for any inter/multi-cultural communication: 'No matter how different cultural Others are, they are never so
different that they are ... incapable of acting purposefully, or evaluating their
actions in the light of their ideas and previous experiences, and of being
"rational" in this minimal way' (Mohanty 1998: 198). It is this inherent capacity
for critical and collective reflexivity that defines 'human agency', thereby
providing the 'universal' foundation for all kinds of progressive movements in
the cultural and political sectors. While Mohanty's 'objectivist' rebuttal of the
'relativist' readings of cultural pluralism works refreshingly against the grain of
postmodern theoretical fashion, it also risks seeming reductive, if not formulaic,
in its axiomatic endorsement of an unproblematized 'rationality'.

In contrast, Žižek's endorsement of 'the true Universality to come' is almost
over-problematized in its opposition to the 'neutral universality' of existing
systems and the 'anti-universality' of rightist groups steeped in their own
particularistic agendas (Žižek 1997: 50). The Left, as Žižek presents the problem
of universality, has no other option but to confront the 'paradox' of its
allegiance to an ideal of 'universal emancipation', along with its acceptance of
'the antagonistic character of society' (ibid.). In other words, it is only by
accepting 'the radically antagonistic – that is, *political* – character of social life'
that one can be 'effectively *universal*' (ibid.; emphases in original). This is
quite different in effect from assuming, as Mohanty does, that the 'universal'
(of 'minimal rationality') already exists, thereby precipitating the possibilities of
radical action.

Working on the premise that *'antagonism is inherent to universality itself'*, Žižek splits the unitary concept of universality into 'the "false" concrete universality' of existing systems of knowledge, and 'the impossible/real demand of "abstract" universality' (1997: 50; emphases in original). It would seem that the 'true Universality to come' cannot be posited within what already exists in the name of the universal, by which systems like multiculturalism legitimize their racist practice. However – and this is the point of a closer rapprochement between Žižek's and Mohanty's seemingly incommensurable positions – the 'assertion of the universality of antagonism' (which coexists with the 'antagonism inherent to universality itself') does not foreclose the possibilities of a dialogue with the Other. Without spelling out how this is actually implemented, Žižek believes that culture can continue to serve as an 'efficient answer to the gun', and that its struggle is embodied in and through *'reflective knowledge'* (ibid.: 51; emphases in original).

At this very fundamental level of the human capacity to discriminate and make choices, it would seem that there is a meeting, though not necessarily a fusion, between two different readings of 'universality' as offered by Mohanty and Žižek. But – the routes by which these cultural strangers on the Left arrive at the critical inflection of 'reflective knowledge' in 'our' world, are fundamentally different. While Mohanty would seem to retrieve a notion of the 'universal' from earlier political struggles, which he then attempts to catalyse in the creation of 'the shared epistemic and social space' of multicultural discourse and practice, Žižek introjects the 'universality to come' into his subversion of the existing multicultural frames that have been hegemonized by the State and the global order, in order to reinflect new strategies of coping with the closure of political spaces in our times. While multiculturalism for Mohanty continues to offer the possibilities of a 'democratic project' within a moral and realist framework of values, Žižek is more sceptical of 'morality' in his 'ethical suspension of the Law', by which he consciously thrusts the narrative of multiculturalism into 'the cultural logic of multinational capitalism', which is coterminous with the upsurge of ethnic cleansings and other forms of fascism in our world. If Mohanty is still capable of seeing 'the world' as the common site of inter/multi-cultural endeavours, Žižek's vision is far less unmediated, as he chooses to see the world not through a glass darkly, but through a consciously distorted lens, not unlike the upturned eyelids of a contemporary Butoh dancer surveying the relics of a post-Hiroshima present.

Through the interplay of these collisive readings on universality, it becomes more viable to accept that while the human desire for creative interaction can serve as the minimal 'universal' base for interculteral encounters, this desire is fraught with tensions, compulsions, hidden agendas, and funding realities, as I have indicated earlier in the context of the existing inequities of intercultural exchange. *There is no 'pure' universal base for intercultural practice in the theatre, or for that matter, in any other art form.* The 'universal minimum' that can be said to initiate any intercultural exchange is extremely fragile, based more on intuition and good faith than on any real cognizance of the Other. It is only through the process of exchanging differences, not only through specific cultural languages but the contexts supporting them, that another, more reflexive realization of 'universality' can be produced and shared through creative consensus and dialogue. There is no reason to believe, however, that this evolved 'universality' will remain intact; indeed, in the field of theatre, for instance, the phenomenology of performance (and its inherent condition of 'dying' within the concretization of its practice) would resist the illusion of any permanent state of universality. Ironically, the artists who flaunt their 'universal' credentials are invariably the most insular practitioners of their art.

Through Žižek, it also becomes possible to unread the somewhat naive assumption that the interculturalist's universality is a kind of mask that disguises his/her 'real' ethnocentricity. Perhaps, it is this ethnocentricity that is the 'phantasmatic screen' in Žižek's words, which 'conceals the fact that the subject is already thoroughly "rootless", that his true position is the void of universality' (Žižek 1997: 44). In addition, there is a less startling reversal as well that may need to be addressed here, in so far as the 'void of universality' can be *filled* with a thoroughly 'rooted' Eurocentricity that does not attempt to screen its arrogance. Racism does not always work with screens; it can be most respectably enunciated through the most cultivated opinions.

2 Eurocentricity, Racism, Multiculturalism

At this point, it would be expedient to inflect the relationships between Eurocentricity, racism and multiculturalism. While Žižek has no difficulty in describing multiculturalism as racism, the film theorists Ella Shohat and Robert Stam would not merely oppose such an equation, they would even insist that Eurocentrism and racism are in no way 'equatable', even though they may be 'historically intertwined' (Shohat and Stam 1994: 4). Regarding Eurocentrism as an 'implicit positioning rather than a conscious political stance' (ibid.), Shohat and Stam would stress that it is possible to be anti-racist and Eurocentric at the same time. While this is undeniably true, the possibility that racism can be nurtured in and through Eurocentrist values should not be summarily denied. Unfortunately, this is precisely the elision that underlies Stam and Shohat's otherwise persuasive reading of 'critical and polycentric multiculturalism' that is related at 'reciprocal' and 'dialogic' levels to a critique of Eurocentricity. This critique results in what I would describe as a wish-list of multicultural virtues – 'no pseudo-equality of viewpoints', 'no established hierarchy of cultures', 'no essentialist concept of identities', even an acknowledgement of the 'pain, anger, resentment' that inevitably surface in the meeting of historically differentiated and colliding cultures (ibid.: 48, 958).

Despite their disclaimers that a radical multiculturalism cannot be 'nice' or 'politically correct', Shohat and Stam's prescriptions of multiculturalism succumb to these very traps in their overly modulated master text that ultimately rises above all controversies, even as it claims the right to represent them. In a consciously non-subalternist mode of representation – 'Can the non-subaltern speak?' is their plaintive reversal of Gayatri Spivak's radical question – Shohat and Stam's discourse on 'unthinking Eurocentrism' is, perhaps, unthinkingly exclusionary in its refusal to submit the liberal premises of their text to sub-alternist scrutiny. An emphatic tolerance pervades their reading of intolerance, so much so that while racism is acknowledged at implicit and xenophobic levels in other writers, it has no place within their ontologies of either Eurocentrism or multiculturalism.

This erasure of racism in multicultural agendas is particularly problematic in those contexts where ambivalent responses to racism need to be highlighted. Consider, for example, the following notorious statement allegedly made by the American novelist Saul Bellow: 'When the Zulus produce a Tolstoy, we will read him' (read, that is, the Zulu Tolstoy). The explicit cultural superiority of this statement, which can be read as racist (not least by the Zulus themselves), needs no elaboration. As Charles Taylor, one of the more reflective interlocutors in the debate around multiculturalism has pointed out, it obviously assumes:

1 The Zulus have to produce a *Tolstoy* in order to prove themselves (Taylor 1994: 71). Nothing within their own cultural heritage can serve as an appropriate point of reference. The standards of excellence have already been determined in Europe, and the Zulus have to live up to them.

2 The Zulus *have yet* to produce a Tolstoy ('*When* the Zulus ...'). This indicates some kind of feigned familiarity with the existing *oeuvre* of Zulu literature, with which Mr Bellow might be quite unfamiliar. In this regard, he would not be essentially different from our very own Salman Rushdie (and here I am consciously shifting the context in order to emphasize that cultural superiority is not the prerogative of European authors alone). In response to 'fifty years of [Indian] independence', Rushdie has had the audacity to affirm a pantheon of Indian literature in a volume of select writings (Rushdie and West 1997) that has the dubious distinction of excluding all contemporary Indian writers writing in Indian languages, apart from English – languages that Rushdie might not have read, even in translation. This 'privileged voice of the diaspora', to appropriate a phrase used by Geeta Kapur in another context, is legitimized not through the invocation of a legacy (as in Bellow's invocation of Tolstoy), but through the sanction of the market and the liberal endorsement of the *New Yorker*.

3 Going back to the Zulus and Tolstoy, I would add a third reservation: perhaps the Zulus are not interested in producing a Tolstoy. He would, in all probability, bore them to death. Not reading Tolstoy could be a 'cultural choice' that should not be denied to them. Rejecting Tolstoy, however, without having read him, could pose a liberal dilemma.

4 Taylor, however, adds a more provocative complication to the argument: 'The possibility that the Zulus, while having the same potential for culture formation as anyone else, might nevertheless have come up with a culture that is less valuable than others is ruled out from the start. Even to

entertain this possibility is to deny human equality' (Taylor 1994: 42). In the articulation of this 'possibility', a critical dialogue on the contesting criteria of assessing and evaluating other cultures becomes imperative.

3   Contesting Criteria

Let us focus now on Taylor's demand for an adequate set of criteria in order to evaluate the relative worth of other cultures. To assume the equality of cultures without knowing anything about them, amounts, in his view, to another kind of patronization. While this reasoning is eminently sound, it barely conceals a vehement rejection of those 'subjectivist, half-baked, neo-Nietzschean' positions (1994: 70), which assume that all judgements of worth are based on standards that are intrinsically hegemonistic and power-ridden.

At one level, it could be argued in Taylor's favour that while multicultural artists, for instance, have every right to question the standards of the decision-makers, who determine what is 'good' and 'bad' in multicultural practice (and, consequently, what should be funded and what shouldn't), these artists cannot fetishize their condition to such an extent so as to believe: 'Because we are so marginal, and no one understands us anyway, we alone have the right to determine our own standards and critical criteria.' This attitude can easily lead to another kind of intolerance, if not self-mystification, that Taylor castigates for its undermining of the human capacity to discriminate and to make choices.

On the other hand, to argue against Taylor's position, one could say that it is so entrenched within the rigour of a continental philosophical system (Rousseau, Herder, Hegel) that it theorizes multiculturalism from above without taking into account the humiliation and rejection of a wide spectrum of people, notably artists from non-western cultures, who may have no other option but to create their own 'neo-Nietzschean' criteria for their own self-respect, if not survival. At no point in Taylor's scrupulously argued theory is there an awareness of how the spectre of 'worth' can hegemonize the norms of 'quality' in essentially monocultural practices. Not only is this elusive 'quality' denied *ipso facto* to multicultural artists without, of course, being defined in any coherent way, it is also protected within elitist frameworks that legitimize the non-trespassing zones of established theatres, art galleries, and other cultural centres to which immigrant and foreign artists are denied access. The outsiders who dare to infiltrate these zones and cross the threshold of 'quality', could be rejected for being

1   *too different* ('Your work is interesting but we don't know where you're coming from. Of course, we wouldn't want to misrepresent you, therefore ...')
2   *not different enough* ('Your work is not sufficiently authentic. We're looking for something typically Indian.')
3   *just like us* ('Why is your work so modern?')

These axioms are almost platitudinous to the growing number of the multi-cultural unemployed.

While artists from marginalized backgrounds are getting sharper at recognising difference and sameness as two sides of the same coin, the painful reality, as Kobena Mercer puts it pithily, is that 'Black artists are never allowed to be ordinary but have to visibly embody a prescribed difference' (Mercer 1997: 37). This difference is compelled to validate what Paul Gilroy has termed 'ethnic insiderism', a stricture from which no community is entirely free, in so far as it is not just blacks and Asians who are expected to work on things black and Asian; whites as well are not expected to cross the threshold of their privileged whiteness (which, of course, doesn't mean that they don't).

It is disingenuous in this regard for critics like Richard Schechner to raise the charge of 'reverse patriarchalism', whereby 'the native can "step up", but the Western "developed" person ought not to "step down"' (Schechner 1996: 45). Not only is the epistemology of this perspective problematic in its own right, it becomes even more unconvincing in Schechner's use of Zubin Mehta as an example of an Indian conductor who is highly successful in the western classical music world, as opposed to 'a western master of the sitar', whose very existence is a source of scepticism (ibid.). For a start, Zubin Mehta exemplifies what needs to be avoided in any intercultural search for equity, namely, the cult of the maestro, reinforced by exotic meritocracy. More critically, Schechner relativizes (and in the process, conflates) two different musical systems – and classical ones at that too – which have very different modes of internal assessment, evaluation, and public accountability.

In the world of intercultural theatre, one would be compelled to ask whether non-western directors share the same intercultural opportunities that have been made available to western directors like Schechner himself, who has recently worked on a Chinese opera adaptation of the *Oresteia* in Taiwan. Without denying the creative legitimacy of such an enterprise, one is questioning here the politics of expertise that enables an American director to direct a Greek classic in an unknown language and mode of representation, when a reciprocal opportunity for an English-speaking, non-western director to direct a western classic in English at a nationally recognized theatre company in Britain or the USA would be far less forthcoming. This is somewhat different in effect from a German director wanting to direct an 'Indian' classic like Tagore's *Raktakarabi* ('Red Oleander') in Bengali without knowing the language. While the creative possibilities of such intercultural processes should not be summarily rejected, I would simply ask: Would the decision-makers ever consider the possibility of an Indian director doing Goethe or Brecht in German without knowing German? Indeed, even if we did know German, we would be expected to direct 'something Indian' – maybe a folk-tale, or *Shakuntala* (regardless of whether or not we know a word of Sanskrit). So much for 'reverse patriarchalism'.

I would contend that it is harder for artists and cultural workers from the Third World to work against the strictures of 'ethnic insiderism' for the simple reason that there are fewer opportunities for employment outside ethnic stereotypes (and the politically correct 'alternative' forums that have emerged to counter them). Therefore, the temptation to 'fill the slots' in whatever ethnic manifestation is unavoidably strong. 'Be othered or perish' would seem to be the *sine qua non* of multicultural survival, though there are any number of subversions – like Trinh Minh-ha's advocacy of the 'Inappropriate Other' (Trinh 1991), for instance[6] – which admittedly do not always make sense to those artists who are doubly alienated, not only from themselves but also from the high theory of postcolonial discourse that is supposed to represent their predicament.

Returning to Charles Taylor's insistence on the need for an adequate criterion in order to evaluate, recognize, and understand other cultures on a relative basis, it needs to be acknowledged that while critical criteria are necessary for the exchange of cultures on an inter/multi-cultural basis, they may be fuzzy in their contours and orientations. Indeed, as Susan Wolf has argued perceptively in the context of pluralism in ethics, *indeterminacy* could be one of the primary constituents of a pluralist sensibility that works against the premises of absolutism, relativism, and subjectivism (Wolf 1992: 786–790). While an absolutist position assumes that there is only one right answer overruling the relativist claim that 'what is right for you is different from what is right for me' (ibid.: 789), a subjectivist position, on the other hand, would claim that 'anything goes' (ibid.: 790), countering the more reflexive pluralist position which acknowledges that 'if there is no right answer ... this does not imply that there are no wrong answers' (ibid.). The seeming equivocality of the pluralist position does not mean that it is without commitment; nor does it fear the finality of answers. However, it is aware that, in certain contexts, the 'question of what is right ... lacks a unique and determinate answer'; 'rightness' in such cases is, as Susan Wolf puts it succinctly, 'neither relative to anything', nor 'a matter of perspective'; it is simply 'indeterminate' (ibid.: 789).

PHILOSOPHY AND PRACTICE

There is much for intercultural workers – and decision-makers, in particular – to learn from these philosophical investigations, particularly when the task of negotiating different cultural frames (as opposed to a singular one) poses additional challenges of perceiving how, and indeed of preparing the ground, to interact with other cultures. We may need to develop in this regard a *respect for imperfection* in our shaping and viewing of inter/multi-cultural collaborations, which should not be equated with the valorization of half-knowledge that so often passes as 'expertise' among the *aficionados* of 'other' cultures.[7] Without engaging sufficiently with the difficulties involved in perceiving inter/multi-cultural practices – From whose eyes, and from which perspective do we observe the 'inter'? On what frames of reference can we draw to encompass the 'multi'? Through which and whose criteria? – it becomes somewhat premature to settle for a 'fusion of horizons' (Hans-Georg Gadamer), as Taylor does in a seemingly regressive, if not utopic, postponement of any real interaction with ongoing cultural differences. Besides, do we need a 'fusion' in order to meet through differences? Surely an intersection or a collision or an ellipsis of horizons is more likely to resist the risks of cultural homogenization.

At this juncture, one is compelled to acknowledge the crisis of practice in much philosophical and social scientist thinking on multiculturalism, and, more specifically, the insufficient engagement of philosophers with emergent cultural practices. On the one hand, earlier methodologies and disciplines of con-ceptualizing 'culture' (including its practices) are incorporated within larger social and political theories of multiculturalism, but they are proving to be inadequate to deal with the influx of new forces and circumstances constituting unprecedented mobilizations of energy in the public sphere. While it may not be the responsibility of political philosophers to figure out *how* new cultural languages can be created – and perhaps there is a certain theoretical rigour in *not* intersecting political philosophy and cultural practice as I am attempting to do in this chapter – the point is that without a cognizance of these new cultural languages there can be no real breakthroughs in conceptualizing the matrices and paradigms of multicultural theory.[8]

Thus, we find Charles Taylor acknowledging the necessity of being 'open to comparative cultural study of the kind that must displace our [*sic*] horizons in the resulting fusions' (Taylor 1994: 73). As he puts it, 'To approach a raga with the presumptions of value implicit in the well-tempered clavier would be forever to miss the point' (ibid.: 67). But perhaps it is Taylor who is missing the point in restricting multiculturalism to an evaluation of what already exists (and tellingly, in the uncontested realm of 'high culture'), instead of figuring out the 'multicultures' in the making through popular and mass mediations (to which immigrant communities have greater access).

In this context, while one can agree in principle with Taylor that human identities are created dialogically through an encounter with 'significant others' (George Herbert Mead), one is nonetheless compelled to recognize the existing cultures of '*insignificant* others'. Why does the narrative of multiculturalism need to perpetuate a post-enlightenment notion of 'enrichment' through the 'significance' derived from the 'rich human languages' of other cultures? Surely multiculturalism is enriched not through accretion and absorption alone, but through a dismantling of predetermined legacies and genealogies. In order to gain something, we may have to give something up. Taylor does not begin to grasp the pertinence of this axiom, which assumes, in my view, the multicultural necessity of *betraying* one's culture of origins. This betrayal is not merely the burden of the immigrant who is displaced from his/her homeland: those who assume a citizenship that is being granted to others need to re-think their own norms. The challenge is not merely, as Taylor puts it, 'to deal with *their* sense of marginalization without compromising *our* basic political principles' (1994: 63). Taylor, I would suggest, needs to accept the dialogic possibility of *his* marginalization as well. Why should minorities always be 'othered' for the enrichment of their assumed benefactors?

Finally, one may assume, as Taylor does, a fundamental continuum between assessing the worth of cultures and developing a politics of recognition and respect that is due to them. But when, at some hypothetical point in time, one is in a position to say that this culture is 'superior-in-a-certain-respect' to another, hopefully it will not follow that one also says that its community needs to be more respected than other communities. Surely the preoccupation with 'worth' sidelines the larger issue of 'justice', as Susan Wolf (1994) has correctly pointed out, thereby playing into the prejudices of the 'Saul Bellows' of this world, who would prefer to retain their liberal aura of omniscient tolerance in the absence of a 'fusion of horizons'.

RETHINKING POLITICS IN CULTURAL PRACTICE

If Taylor suffers from an excess of caution that almost legitimizes the absence of an active, exploratory (and, necessarily, messy) relationship with other cultures, most inter/multi-cultural artists whom I have encountered, would seem to function with an excess of desire for the Other. Clearly, their preoccupation is not with the worth of other cultures, but with the mystique of their difference ('I'd love to work with the Zulus' would be their enthusiastic response). It would be necessary to question whether 'the Zulus' share this enthusiasm to the same degree. While much theoretical work has been done on 'desiring the Other', relatively little attention has been paid to the somewhat bleaker prospects of being *rejected* by the Other. Indeed, the desire for the Other in actual practice need not always be reciprocated by the Other for very strong social, historical, and political reasons. This resistance to an assumed reciprocity in cultural exchanges needs to be inscribed in our search for collaborations.

Keeping this in mind, I would emphasize the euphoria underlying the neo-liberal pursuit of 'cultures of choice' (Schechner 1996: 49) from within the comforts of a metropolis, where cultures can be readily consumed along with their cuisines. It would be necessary to question whether these cultures want to be consumed in the first place. Secondly, one needs to resist the fatuous belief that ethnicities are so fluid that they can be 'bartered' and 'swapped'; they can 'hybridize' and enter into all kinds of 'promiscuous' relationships (ibid.). The individuals who can afford to barter and swap their ethnicities have obviously no difficulty in affirming their multiple selves. But if one considers the pre-dicament of underprivileged communities, such as the *dalits* (low castes) in India, for instance, whose ethnicities have been stamped on, demeaned, and inferiorized for centuries, surely the task of upholding a *dalit* identity is part of a long and hard-earned struggle, which has involved a disidentification from earlier, hallowed, patronizing descriptions of untouchables as *harijans* ('children of God'). In this struggle, where identity is politicized in a consciously affirma-tive mode, a *dalit* cultural worker or activist is not likely to let go of his/her ethnicity, which could be the only lever for self-respect through social and political mobilization.

At this point, the counter-argument could be that interculturalism is not dealing with the *dalits* of this world, the wretched of the earth. Who then are the appropriate candidates for intercultural exchange? Are we – and I include myself here – part of an exclusive club of frequent flyers, the privileged diaspora, the global intelligentsia, the enlightened exiles? If that, indeed, is the case, could we then account for our exclusions? Or can we perhaps extend the privilege of interculturalism not merely to 'one of us', but to non-metropolitan community workers and activists as well, who have as much right as we do to cross borders? This extension of privilege, however, is possible only through an implosion of its values by its most self-confident beneficiaries. A crisis of faith is needed – yet another betrayal, if not an infiltration of global capitalism from within its cultural enclaves – before the resources that make interculturalism possible can be redistributed at more subversive, yet democratic, levels.[9]

While multiculturalism works within the 'cultural logic of multinational capitalism' (Žižek 1997), I would like to believe – and perhaps this is the utopic thrust in my own discourse – that interculturalism has the potential to work against this logic. But for this to happen, its practitioners will have to dispense with many proliferating myths of globalization – namely its invincibility, and the accompanying hoax of a liberalized world economy that has emerged through the apparent dissolution of national sovereignties and borders. Along with 'the myth of the powerless State' (Weiss 1997), we need to undermine the bogey of the essentially demonic anachronistic state that has been reinforced by recent theories of postnationalism, which have attempted to displace conventional (yet tenacious) notions of place, community, and belonging, in favour of emergent identities in 'diasporic public spheres' (Appadurai 1997).

Emergent cultural identities, as I will argue later in the chapter on secularism, are not the prerogatives of the diaspora alone. Indeed, they are very much in the making along with new subject-formations within the fractious and contradictory processes of people's movements in India, wherein the 'national' is in the process of being re-articulated against the hegemony of the nation-state and its global affiliations. Within this democratization of 'political society', as Partha Chatterjee (1997) has conceptualized the process, it becomes imperative for artists and cultural workers to realign their own increasingly atomized constituencies to cultures of struggle, wherever they may exist in the world. It is within these contexts of struggle that the most critical debates on intellectual property rights and the destruction of the ecological bases of world cultures can be most meaningfully contextualized and shared across different locations. It is also around these struggles that intercultural dialogue can deepen beyond an exchange of existing cultural practices to a translation of the political and economic differences constituting their emergent forms. Without a confrontation of these differences, the existing South–South inequities can only continue to be subsumed within North–South agendas, thereby postponing the possibilities of a more reflexive and sustainable intercultural praxis.

2

WHEN 'ETERNAL INDIA' MEETS THE YPO

CULTURE AND GLOBALIZATION

PROLOGUE

This is a story about fifty years of dependence. Located within the immediate context of a unique performance event, it can be read either as a 'thick description' of this event, or as a post-independence allegory of how India is positioned today *vis-à-vis* globalization and its effects on cultural capital. All the characters and events in this story, I should emphasize, are real, even though they may seem to be fictional, if not totally bizarre. Indeed, I have been struck by the surreality of the 'real' in documenting the collision of contexts that has made this narrative possible. I trust that my interruptions in contextualizing the ruptures in the narrative will not prevent me from telling you a story.

But before we get to the story, a little history would be in order. Not the countdown to independence, but rather our continuing tryst with fifty years of dependence, which has resulted in the total squandering of the possibilities of *swaraj* ('self-rule') at political, economic, social, and personal levels. Nothing less than our self-respect is in question as we celebrate the dubious development of the nation. It does not help to be reminded that development itself is in a state of crisis, not merely within our borders, where millions of people continue to be denied the basic necessities of water, food, accommodation, fuel, education, but in the world at large.

The dominant platitude in disillusioned development circles would seem to suggest that there is now a First World in the Third World, and a Third World in the First World. This illusory collapse of binaries can be attributed to the jolts and shifts in the manoeuvres of global capitalism, which have created unprecedented pockets of poverty in advanced developed societies, and some equally unprecedented ghettos of affluence in the poorer nations. This emergence of the 'new poor' and the 'neo-liberal elite', however, should not make us believe that 'we are all in the same boat (so we can afford to sink together)'. Or, in a more euphoric register, that 'we're all part of one world where national and economic boundaries no longer matter'.

Even a cursory acknowledgement of the imbalances, inequities, injustices, and disparities between rich and poor nations, would reveal that the gap has widened. From the 1996 Human Development Report, we learn that the distance between industrial and developing countries with regard to per capita income has tripled since 1960 (Sachs 1996: 3). Despite home-truths in recent First World studies of sustainable economic welfare that 'growth in GNP does not relate any longer to a growth in quality of life' (Cobb and Cobb 1994), the reality is that there seems to be no retreat from the excessive consumption of natural and environmental resources in the North to 'sustain' this 'quality of life', at the expense of reducing the South to some kind of dumping ground for developmental waste.

Even with a radical change of heart which could result in the North repaying its 'ecological debt', there can be no real evidence of 'good global neighbourhood', constituting a 'new kind of rationality', to use Wolfgang Sachs's positive recommendations, without a cutback of between 70 and 90 per cent in the consumption of energy and materials over the next forty to fifty years (Schmid-Bleek 1994). This is a tall order even by utopian standards, though one welcomes the shift in moving the burden of responsibility from the South to the North. As the white man's burden deepens with the detritus of development, the wretched of the earth refuse to die in order to accommodate the blueprints of structural adjustment envisioned by the messiahs of the World Bank and the IMF.

So be it. The task for us in the Third World is not to berate ourselves unduly for the over-development of the First World that has resulted in the increased pauperization of indigenous peoples and the systematic destruction of nature, nor to seek solace in overnight miracles resulting from a renewed ethics in environmental management. Our problems are not going to disappear overnight. Working against the grain of the compliance that is expected of us by our financial beneficiaries, we need to persist in disrupting the illusions of global capitalism by reinflecting our seemingly anachronistic, yet tenacious, problems.

In this regard, what is imagined to be the *residual* reality of poverty in the Third World is in actuality the *dominant* reality faced by millions of people, whose lives are more scrupulously erased than ever before from the agendas of liberalization, as well as from the postcolonial discourse manufactured in the more privileged diasporic sectors in First World academia. The postcolonial preoccupation with 'cultural difference' at the expense of 'political and economic inequalities' has resulted, in Masao Myoshi's pithy analysis, in 'a form of liberal self-deception', whereby postcoloniality has begun to 'look suspiciously like another alibi to conceal the actuality of global politics', thereby deepening the 'complicity' of intellectuals in 'the TNC version of neocolonialism' (1993: 728, 751).

The residual, the dominant, the emergent: these are the underlying motifs of almost any history, which assume shifting significances in different contexts. I have been struck, for instance, by the predominance, if not surfeit, of theoretical production relating to the phenomena of orientalism and Eurocentricity, which has almost overburdened the market with critiques that feed on each other with an incestuous, parasitic intensity. And yet, with all the developing political correctness and sensitivity to marginalized non-western cultures, the spectre of the Orient continues to haunt even those sensibilities seemingly resistant to ethnocentricity, racism, and intolerance. How does the Orient continue to be perpetuated, how does it continue to reinvent itself? Why does the Orient refuse to die?

Earlier I had stated that poverty refuses to disappear as a problem, thereby countering the wish-fulfilment of global moguls. Conversely, capitalism as a narrative and practice continues to thrive, assuming increasingly invisible and chimerical manifestations, which would seem to reduce the earlier modes of capitalism to a state of spectrality. These refusals to die – of poverty, capitalism, and the Orient – are what concern me in this story, which has yet to begin. I am not seeking a cosy synthesis, a 'happy end' of their implicated, yet colliding narratives. Rather, I invite you to enter their contradictions through a description of a seemingly irrelevant spectacle, which exposes our fifty years of dependence more sharply than any other narrative that I have witnessed in the seemingly unreal world of performance. My story begins not 'once upon a time', but just a few years ago, on the eve of a fiction called independence.

THE BACKGROUND

It all started with gossip of an exclusive, 'invitees-only' workshop in Mumbai that would culminate in a cultural spectacle tentatively entitled *The Woman in Us*. Under the tantalizing sign of this archetypal 'Woman' – would she be the same in men as she would be in women? – a cultural organization called Sarthi, which claims to be committed to 'artists in need', primarily from the rural, folk, and tribal sectors of Indian performance, wanted to explore the 'feminine principle' in the arts by bringing together a wide spectrum of performers from the length and breadth of India, covering both the *margi* (classical) and *desi* (indigenous) traditions of our performance culture. The invitees' list was like a 'Who's Who' of celebrities, including the most renowned gurus like Kudanaloor Karunakaran Nair (Kathakali), Ammannur Madhava Chakyar (Kutiyattam), and Kelucharan Mahapatra (Odissi), as well as the first Pandwani woman story-teller Teejanbai, epic balladeers like the Manganiyars from Rajasthan and the Bauls from Bengal along with many other ritual and tribal artists, percussionists, acrobats, street performers ... in short, a panorama of India's cultural diversity.

Sarthi (which literally means 'charioteer') is synonymous with a cultural operator *par excellence* called Rajeev Sethi, who came into prominence as a designer and creator of spectacles during the Festivals of India, which I have critiqued earlier in the context of the 'invention of tradition' (Bharucha 1990/1993). It would seem that we have yet to distance ourselves from the fall-out of this phenomenon, initiated by Indira Gandhi and later institutionalized by her son, in which performers from different parts of India were transported arbitrarily by government agencies to Delhi, where their histrionic skills were decontextualized, reassembled, and synthesized to form packages, which were then exported to foreign capitals where 'India' was displayed and consumed, with very little thought given to what would happen to the performers on their return home. I believe that while the hype around festival culture seems to have ebbed in the absence of any lucrative returns, this 'culture' continues to get recycled under different schemes with cosmetic changes in its rhetoric and style of functioning. These schemes can range from the variety entertainment programmes of zonal cultural festivals to the more high-tech '*kuchra*' (garbage) passed off as Indian 'culture' in the 1996 Miss World Beauty Pageant in Bangalore, which was beamed on satellite television to the rest of the world.

Tellingly, as the State gets maligned even by those artists who would like to retain their earlier status as the *ad hoc* representatives of an 'inner circle', the privatization of cultural spectacle gets increasingly legitimized through the lure of global patronage and recognition. This globalization of culture in turn gets rhetoricized within intercultural frames of collaboration. Sarthi, for instance, had organized one of its first pan-Indian spectacles in Paris, on the invitation of the director Ariane Mnouchkine at the Théâtre du Soleil. Here are some excerpts from Hélène Cixous's rhapsodic account of the meeting, which can be read as a story in its own right.

To begin:

The Gods have fled Europe. We know it from the time of Holderlin. Leaving fleeting traces in our memory.   (n.d.: 2)

But all is not lost.

Visitors have come to this place ... [C]olourful travellers playing a music that has come through millennia – bursts of rose, saffron, and gold ... Where are they from?   (ibid.)

India, of course, in all its intracultural splendour.

There are the Rajasthanis rising from the arms of the Indian body, the Oriyas jumping from her hips, the Andhras and the Marathis stepping out of her limbs, yet others beat at the heart of Madhya Pradesh.   (ibid.)

Though these emissaries are 'innocent' ('they hold the Gods by the hems of their brightly coloured garments'), they represent a cruel paradox.

In India – this paradox is the tragedy of our young centuries – never had they met nor heard each other. Because 'in reality' everything separates them or places them in confrontation: starting with religion – in which they are confined, Hindus and Muslims alike.   (ibid.)

We are back to the primary assumptions of 'enumerated' communities, as opposed to 'fuzzy' communities, to use the categories of Sudipta Kaviraj (1987), through which the colonial rulers practised their familiar policy of 'divide and rule'. Eschewing the colonial legacy of communalism, by which communities were marked by religion, designated in census reports, and set against each others, Cixous invokes the 'evil spirit of Ayodhya' in atavistic terms of 'hate, hostility, alienation, bloodshed'.

In this hell-hole of contemporary India, however, there is a way out for the emissaries of God:

> It was vital for them to come here [i.e. France], these human fragments of the large Continent, to 'recognise' each other for the first time.
>
> (n.d.: 3)

The sheer effrontery of this Eurocentric protectionism gets lost in ecstasy:

> We cross all borders, astride music, and the borders dissipate with pleasure. A fairy-like bewitchment reigns. The men reel in as women, the women brandish an ornamental masculinity. And the Hindus greet the Muslims respectfully.   (ibid.)

How does that follow? From 'crossing borders' to 'fairy-like bewitchment' to the communal accord between 'Hindus' and 'Muslims'?

Enough, dear reader, I have long given up on how such an anachronistic perpetuation of orientalist rapture continues to be stimulated by the spectre of 'India', and by theorists who are scarcely unaware of the traps of 'cultural essentialism'. In her attempts to break patriarchal binaries by de-essentializing the fixed identities of male/female, father/mother, cultural/nature, logos/pathos, Cixous has not been free of re-essentializing 'femininity' in her concepts relating to *écriture feminine*, the 'other bisexuality', and the 'gift' – a paradox that has both tantalized and provoked a wide range of feminists (Moi 1985: 102–126). This submission to the very 'metaphysics of presence' that she has attempted to dismantle in patriarchal categories is almost flaunted in her feminization of India, whose history she has narrativized beguilingly in her five-act poetic evocation of the freedom struggle in India between 1937 and 1948: *L'Indiade*.

In this celebration of our independence, the *raison d'être* of the dramaturgy is built on the polarization of 'Hindus' and 'Muslims' as two essentialized, religious communities, who are incommensurable, irreconcilable, despite inner contradictions, moderate voices, and cross-overs of identity. These communities are cast within an absolutist enunciation of India as 'the Land of Love', and of Pakistan as 'the Land of the Pure', categories that get further complicated through the almost manichean representation of a relentless, authoritarian, masculinist Jinnah in combat with a loving Gandhi, who radiates the aura of a bisexual 'good mother'. (At one point, he is shown embracing a 'she-bear' Muna Bhalu, who is an expressionist rendering of Third World innocence, instinct, and fun, which gets bestialized through the demons of communalism.) 'This is a play about the human being,' as Cixous reminds us, 'about heroes and dust, about the combat between angel and beast in each of us' (quoted in Carlson 1996: 89). It is also a play about imagining a nation-in-the-making, which, for all the universalist claims of the director Ariane Mnouchkine ('the history of the world is my history'), can be more meaningfully read within the dictates of a political imaginary that is more biased and exclusivist than its expanse of vision would suggest.

Tellingly, in the vast panorama of characters presented in the epic, including full-blown portraits of Nehru, Gandhi, Jinnah, Azad, Sarojini Naidu, Abdul Ghaffar Khan, and Sardar Patel, there are the significant exclusions of potentially disruptive figures like Dr Babasaheb Ambedkar and Netaji Subhas Chandra Bose – exclusions that unwittingly place Cixous in the company of Richard Attenborough. 'The India of their Dreams', as she subtitles her play, is very much the India of *her* dreams, which for all its subjectivity and passion is cast within a Nehruvian legitimization of Indian independence. We are back with a vengeance to the mystique of our 'tryst with destiny', with no real questioning as to what this independence could mean to the marginalized sectors of society. One is not invoking here the eternally oppressed 'common man', but those emergent political constituencies that are compelling nationalists to rearticulate the premises of Indian secularity. To narrativize the India of *our* dreams, fifty years after independence, we may have no other option but to introject the immediacies of political struggle in the present into the betrayals and silenced agendas of the past.

This is not the place to elaborate on Cixous's unconscious endorsement of these betrayals and silences in the context of her very real affinities to a metaphoric 'India' that counters the godless, mechanistic, masculinist site of Europe with the possibilities of redemption, desire, and love. What concerns me here is how these tropes of an unacknowledged neo-orientalism, drawing on the archetypes of 'eternal India', get transported back to contemporary India, thereby endorsing 'secularist' brands of cultural nationalism through valorizations of 'our' inner vitality and spiritual being.

In this context, it became vital for me to check out *The Woman in Us* not for its ontological enigmas, but, more concretely, for its reinvention of an indigenized 'India', first validated in France, and then revalidated within the global mechanisms of the domestic market. In more theoretical terms, one could say that the issue in question concerns the *intercultural* patronage, across nations, of the *intracultural* exchange within the boundaries of India, which feeds the *globalization* of cultural capital through agencies inimical to the ethos of self-sufficiency. To infiltrate the global enclaves of power, mediated by Indian cultural contactors like Sarthi, becomes necessary, if only to counter the unquestioned lure of celebrity events, which tend to be sold out even before they take place. It is one such infiltration, facilitated through the guise of my 'expertise' as a theatre scholar, that enables me to share this story with you. But now let us get on with the narrative by introducing its most powerful (and invisible) player and patron: the YPO.

ENTER THE YPO

It sounds like some exta-terrestrial force – a description that is not entirely off the mark when one considers the omnipresent global status of the Young Presidents Organisation. Consisting of some young and not-so-young presidents of corporations and business houses, it could be described as an exclusive men's club with branches in all parts of the world. Indeed, the Young Presidents (YPs) could be regarded as super-executive tourists, who meet four times a year in different locations in the world, to conduct – not a conference or a seminar or a convention – but a 'university'. The University of Presidents is not only mobile, it is also extremely 'packaged' (from registration to graduation, it lasts for a week), and unlike ordinary universities facing the budget crunch and the very real threat of closures, this university has no financial problems, located as it is within the confines of a five-star hotel. So, to spell out the agenda, *The Woman in Us* is going to be staged as the formal inauguration of the University of Presidents in Mumbai, the first of its kind in India.

Super-executive tourists need something more than sightseeing and local colour. They want not just any spectacle, but the greatest show on earth. So what would be the obvious locations for cultural spectacle in India? The banks of the Ganga in Benares (where Peter Brook had hoped to stage his *Mahabharata*), or the Taj Mahal (where the international musical phenomenon Yanni has been featured to the chagrin of local farmers, whose crops were destroyed in the lavish architectural and security arrangements for the spectacle)? The Taj and the Ganga are the clichéd choices of India's fabled past. Instead, the YPO is more interested in India's potentially lucrative present, its global prospects and free-for-all trade. Within these priorities, the location of Mumbai as the centre of India's industrial capital, is right-on.

The YPs are, of course, almost ignorant of the context by which Bombay has been renamed Mumbai, one of the milder changes of the ruling Hindu communalist party of the Shiv Sena in Maharashtra. Like Michael Jackson, whose first show in India received the blessings of the Sena, they are in all probability unaware of what its leader Bal Thackeray represents in the Indian political context as an 'extra-constitutional authority' and 'remote-control Chief Minister'. They may have read the interview in *Time* magazine (January 1993) where he made some fairly explicit comparisons between the Muslims of India and the Jews in Hitler's Europe, in order to justify his pogroms against 'minorities'. But forget about these communal matters: the YPs are not concerned about the collusions between big business and fascism in India, so long as their business is good.

Mumbai, in short, makes sense for the YPO event – this is where the pulse of India's as-yet dithering response to globalization and liberalization can be most keenly felt. But *where* in Mumbai will *The Woman in Us* regale the YPs? This is where we have to credit Sethiji with a certain flair that marketing people have no hesitation in describing as 'genius'. Like an inspired soul, he doesn't go to the obvious spots of Bollywood; rather, he looks elsewhere in the direction of the Mumbai docks and selects Mukesh Mills as the site for his spectacle.

In its totally derelict and abandoned vista of ruins and warehouses, spanning a panoramic view of the Arabian Sea, Mukesh Mills is a winner. There's a smell of raw capital in its decaying frame, waiting to be sensed by the speculators of global finance. The site is exciting precisely because it is 'way-out'. It's not on any tourist route, and that's what appeals to the super-executive – a premonition of the unknown, a pornography of the 'real', which can always be risked so long as there is five-star luxury to fall back on (a hot shower, a therapeutic massage, etc.).

By the time we enter Mukesh Mills, the performance arena has already been structured around an elaborate labyrinth of platforms and a grid of hundreds of spotlights. The deity *Ardhanarishwara* has already been transported from the workshop site and ritually installed with appropriate pomp and religiosity, conch shells and all. *Ardhanarishwara*: Lord Shiva in his half-male, half-female form, an appropriately androgynous deity for the seeming ambivalences of *The Woman in Us*. On a jocular note, we are informed in the brochure:

> A brash journalist asked a brash socialite: Is God a man? And she answered, No, she isn't. A half-truth answered by a half-truth, the one half replacing the other; man by woman.   (Sarthi 1996)

On a more serious note, however, Sarthi's subtly disguised anti-feminism becomes more explicit, as we learn of the futile attempt by feminists to redefine gender relations within male paradigms and the paternalistic discourse of 'rights'. 'Perpetual grievance articulation' and affinities to 'special interest groups' like gays and religious or ethnic minorities, are also seen as feminist limitations. In this crisis:

> [M]ight it not be possible to formulate an alternative strategy to arrive at gender equality[?] Why not make men conscious of the fact that in every man there is femininity – a femininity that he may not even realise exists? A femininity that, if he will only bother to recognise, harness and release it, would transform him as well as the world for the better.   (Sarthi 1996)

If this was the message that the University of Presidents was meant to imbibe, then either it was a radical gesture on Sarthi's part to counter the masculinity and implicit homophobia of the corporate world, or else it indicates how hopelessly Sarthi is out of touch with reality, including its own unspecified sexual politics. Can one really expect the super-executive YPs to respond to 'femininity' as a self-enhancing principle in the larger context of global capitalism? It would not appear so.

Abruptly – this is going to come as a rude shock to the sexually attentive reader – even before we reach Mukesh Mills, the 'Woman in Us' has been censored as the title of the event. It appears – and this is an interruption that Salman Rushdie would be capable of inventing – that one of the Indian YPs is a devout follower of a *mataji*, a holy woman, who is not just any *mataji*, but an international jet-setting one, whose corpulent face can often be seen on posters in unlikely corners of European cities and California, where she specializes in healing lost souls. This *mataji* is obviously a worldly creature, and so the rumour circulates among some of the participants: Has she detected something like a homosexual subtext in the title? Or is her YPO disciple transferring his own *desi* (indigenous) sexual anxieties onto the 'woman in him'?

(This is not the first time that such a censorship of androgyny has manifested itself in Indian official circles. During the exhibition 'Stree: Women in India' in Moscow [Bharucha 1995], the Indian consul got rid of the film *Sahaja*, on female impersonation in traditional Indian dance, which had attempted to link the concept of *ardhanarishwara* to the primacy of the female principle in the arts. The consul's objection? *Hum to pure mard hai* ['We are entirely men'], not half-and-half like Lord Shiva in his androgynous form. It is another matter that this film was replaced by a documentary on Indira Gandhi, arguably the only 'man' in the parliament of her times.)

Facing the rejection of *The Woman in Us* with equanimity, the ambivalent Sethi has at least two other choices for his precious vision: *The Peacock's Egg*, based on some nebulous mythological reference, which could be more meaning-fully interpreted as a yearning for male pregnancy; and *The Hidden River*, which is of course so hidden that it can mean whatever you want it to mean. We settle for *The Hidden River*.

CULTURAL TOURISM

Now let's get down to business because we have just two run-throughs before the grand spectacle. In any cultural show for tourists, except in the more avant-garde and esoteric explorations in the field – I am thinking of the long trails in the outback of Australia in which particularly intrepid tourists explore days and nights of solitude – a very basic criterion of cultural tourism concerns the management of time. Super-executive tourists are even more time-conscious, tuned as they are to the digitilization of commerce and the stock market. Every second counts, and it follows, therefore, that the YPO inauguration ceremony has to last for exactly one and a half hours. Period. No more, no less. That's the command.

Needless to say, this poses enormous problems in the Indian context, where, at the best of times, we live in several times, which get even more accentuated within the specific time-structures of particular performance traditions. Kutiyattam, for instance, is known for its elaborate dilations of time: it takes six to eight hours for the entrance of a character to be fully established, or for the embellishment of a single episode, and, sometimes, even a verse. In these circumstances, how do you tell the Kutiyattam guru: Please sir, can you make it in eight minutes? Forget whether this reduction has anything to do with the grammar or subtleties of Kutiyattam. What matters is the spectacle, and, more important, the authentication of experience: 'You are watching the greatest guru in the world.' The poor octogenarian is a mere blob of blurred movements on the vast stage, where one cannot decipher a single expression: it is a humiliation of his great art and person.

Apart from the management of time, another *sine qua non* of cultural tourism concerns finding the balance between the sacred and the profane, the exotic and the familiar, the sense of 'This is way-out' and 'I feel at home here'. At a quantitative level, *The Hidden River* has no difficulty in asserting the sacred through yet another recycling of 'eternal India', with all the divine paraphernalia associated with *mantras* and *slokas*, incense and ritual, watering the *tulsi* plant and making *kolams* on the floor. We have hundreds of ways in which the sacred/ the divine/the eternal can be demonstrated *ad infinitum*.

But there's a condition: once you display the sacred, you cannot readily despoil it. So when you are dealing with a cultural show, where audience participation becomes necessary, and this audience includes what would accurately (in proper brahminical terminology) be described as *mlecchas* ('barbarians'), you have to deal with the risks of pollution. In more theoretical language, you have to negotiate the blurred areas where the profane is not merely an element legitimized within the worldliness of the ritual, but a possible source of contamination from outside.

Let me elaborate further. In any touristic scenario of entertainment, there is generally a section towards the end of the show, when one of the tourists (generally an ostentatious representative of his species) enters the performance frame, either dancing with the girls, or mimicking some 'native' trait, or indulging in some kind of improvised cross-dressing. And this is the moment – the play-within-the-play – that is most appreciated by the rest of the party, who click their cameras through this 'spontaneous' act that they have so keenly anticipated in order to confirm their kinship with the 'other' culture. This celebration of 'being there' can leave some of the most poignant memories 'back home'.

In *The Hidden River*, the audience participation has already been choreographed and built into the action. During the finale, when the entire cast would be on-stage in a whirlwind of festive movement, the idea was for the head representatives of the YPO, sitting in their designer outfits in the front row, to bound onto the stage, grab one of the folk performers, hold hands, and then move round and round in the traditional Indian children's game, which has many variations in the world. The head YP is game for this display of frolic and innocence, but as he puts it candidly: 'Do I have to take off my shoes?' The eternal problem of 'eternal India': all those beautiful temples, but those dirty floors.

Tradition prevails over global conveniences: 'I'm afraid, sir, that if you don't take off your Gucci shoes you may be cursed for stamping on sacred ground. And that wouldn't be auspicious, would it?' And what would happen to *The Hidden River*? After all the trouble taken to authenticate the sacred, the *raison d'être* of Sri Sethi's spiritual spectacle would have collapsed in one fell swoop, as this foot fetish – a legacy of many abrasive encounters between booted British officers and barefoot maharajas – would be allowed to assert its dominance.

So, in true postcolonial fashion, negotiations have to be made with the 'minions' in the cast to take care of the shoes, while the consuls of the YPO dance in abandon.

DEHUMANIZATION

In all these complications, a process of dehumanization has entered the proceedings. The performers, so energized in the workshop, with bravura displays of their unparalleled talent, are now passive, apathetic, mechanized, and, above all, nervous. They are made to sit in one area like obedient children. They want to please the *sahibs* but they don't really know what's going on. Therein lies the power of the masterminds controlling cultural tourism. The script is never shared. It is assumed. And the performers have to fill in the appropriate slots and clear off.

A glimpse of dehumanization: it is past midnight as we struggle through the first run-through, which is also the dress rehearsal. The actors are wary of missing their entrances, since all the transitions between the items are voiced in English – a quotation from A. K. Ramanujan, an explanation of a ritual in the mode of a television chat show. Needless to say, this makes no sense to the predominantly non-English-speaking rural performers, who have to be herded on-stage and literally moved around like mobile dummies. 'This is the only way to do it', as the ubiquitous director shrugs his shoulders. He's been through this before.

In one corner of the stage, I see a 'real' Rajasthani family – father, mother, child. The father plays the fiddle, the mother sings, the child dances. They are supposed to be playing 'mendicants', who come early in the morning begging through the streets of 'eternal India'. There is a blank moment in the rehearsal. I am watching the child, who is standing very still, barely 3 feet high, with his brightly coloured *ghagra* (skirt) trailing on the floor. He looks very tired, his shoulders droop, his nose runs, and he has a racking cough. Suddenly, there is a peremptory shout from the other end of the stage, where another Rajasthani family is making its entrance for a symmetrical effect. Like a terrified automaton, the child jerks his body into a dance, which is almost instantaneously captivating. He flashes on a charismatic smile, wiggles his hips, and exudes a charm that can only be described as *chamatkar*. This dance continues for less than a minute, and then is abruptly stopped. The child is reprimanded for his late cue, and he leaves the stage, a very disconsolate figure.

That moment when his fatigue was triggered by a remote-control command into a seemingly effortless dance, remains one of the most violent images that I have ever encountered in my experience of theatre. It was like watching – and I choose my words carefully – a human variation of a monkey dance. In this utterly dehumanized context, one is compelled to ask: What is going on here? What is being justified? And for whom? I am made uncomfortably aware that I could have been witnessing an unconscious and histrionically disguised form of child labour, that very reality which Sarthi claims to be fighting against, in its crusade against the Beggary Act and its sponsorship of health schemes, retirement plans, and accommodation for underprivileged performers. Some of these schemes have been sponsored by the Théâtre du Soleil under the nurturing categories of *Ankur* ('Seed') and *Bargad* ('Banyan').

And yet, with all these good intentions, when one actually begins to test these humanitarian schemes through the dynamics of human interaction in the actual process of rehearsing a performance, one realizes the hollowness of Sarthi's rhetoric in relation to its arbitrary and non-negotiable conditions of work. Once again, actors are being reduced to skills, to the fodder of 'human resource development' as the government puts it, with its inimitable insensitivity to both language and people.

There is also a more theoretical dimension to this questionable ethics of representation, when one considers the implications of decontextualizing the 'extra-daily' energy of 'non-western fictional bodies', which I have critiqued in the writings of Eugenio Barba and other performance theorists (Bharucha 1990/1993). In the movements of the young Rajasthani performer, one can read (if one chooses to) a 'fictional body' – it is captivating, it has energy, freshness, vitality, etc. But what are the implications of abstracting this body from the daily circumstances of the performer's life? Are these realities of no consequence? What does 'extra-daily' energy mean to the performer himself, and how does it get consumed, and by whom? Under which circumstances? What is the relationship of 'energy' not just to the gods or to the body, but to labour and poverty, the daily grind of everyday life which is the condition of most Third World performers?

OPENING NIGHT

These questions remain unanswered as Mukesh Mills goes through even more scenic metamorphoses in preparation for Opening Night. The Oberoi kitchen and dining staff has arrived in full force with burners and tandoors, cutlery and crockery worthy of a five-star banquet. Red carpets are rolled onto the cement quay of the mill. Deserted and grimy corridors and alleys in the periphery of the performance area are spruced up, rather than camouflaged. In earlier days of 'festival culture', the standard technique was to screen what needed to be invisible – for example, slums in the major thoroughfares of New Delhi, which were decoratively erased with Rajasthani tapestries and prints. In Mukesh Mills, the technique is more postmodern, in so far as the ruins are not disguised but highlighted with low-angle, high-density halogens, to illuminate gilt-framed touristy paintings celebrating kitsch.

Abracadabra: there is yet another transformation. Unbelievably, in a corner of the quay, a Taj Mahal of a toilet has magically descended from the heavens. It is an absolute model of a toilet with elegant urinals, shining faucets, gleaming tiles, and even an attendant who is trained to say, 'Good evening, sir' and offer you a serviette, with which you wipe your hands and which you then toss into an immaculate bin. This most expedient of five-star facilities has obviously been designed to reassure the nightmare of most foreign tourists to India: sanitation.

Show time. The YPs and their wives arrive on barges across the Arabian Sea with the sun setting in the background. They are greeted with folk abandon and ritualistic grace, which they take in their stride and with good humour. They are such beautiful people – poised, travelled, and super-executive. We are not dealing with tourists here in the plebeian sense of the word, the bums and perverts hanging around the beaches of Goa and Kovalam. We are dealing with elegance, high culture, and a lot of money.

After an atmospheric hush of great expectations, the show starts . . . It doesn't move. It's stuck. It begins to thud along. It's a crashing bore. It's meant to be a spectacle, but it falls somewhere in between ethnic razzmatazz and an education of the senses (the YPs are attending a 'university' after all). Like a primordial tortoise inching its way through a maze of confusions and dead-ends, the production covers barely one-third of the tortuous script, when the finale should have erupted in a *tillana* of joy.

An Indian YP panics and begins to follow the ubiquitous Sethi around the performance arena. At one point, he corners the maestro and engages him in what appears to be a life-and-death situation, while Guru Kelucharan, oblivious of time, is interacting with the *gotipuas* (young female impersonators). Sethi flies into action. He is all over the place like a frenzied fly. There seems to be a whisper campaign among the artists, who are visible in the pit around the stage. And then, with an inexplicably deafening crescendo of sound, a sudden rise in decibels, the show jump-cuts into the finale. The audience wakes up from its seeming somnolence. The head YPs, looking very ethnic in a matching silk fabric, jump on-stage and do their number. There is absolute mayhem, nothing is co-ordinated, every instrument is out of sync, the *talas* are going berserk, the *srutis* are shrieking, and the show comes to a thunderously embarrassing and abrupt end.

After a smattering of applause – no standing ovation as the YPO organizers might have envisioned – it is time for speeches, which is what any inauguration is ultimately about. Just as the head Indian YP opens his mouth, there is the unkindest of cuts: a fuse blows. As the mikes blank out, Sethi flounces onto the stage in a state of dishevelled array, not trying to disguise the fact that the gods have been cruel. He points an accusing finger at the audience and in a very hoarse voice says: 'It's all your fault. There are too many mobile phones in the audience.' After all, what is a YP without a mobile phone, that postmodern accoutrement of the ear, which is said to cause brain damage? What is less known to the technologically uninitiated is that these instruments emit energies. Whatever the reason, it appears that so many invisible energies were being released in *The Hidden River* that the power supply of Mukesh Mills just couldn't cope with the extra load. Hence, the fuse.

This does not stop our Indian YPO representative from orating at the top of his voice, reminding his foreign colleagues of India's march toward the twenty-first century. He ends his speech by quoting Gandhi's most misappropriated lines about not wanting either that the windows of his house be stuffed or that he be blown off his feet. There is not a hint of irony, just a brazen flaunting of Gandhi within the blatantly anti-*swaraj* context of globalization and liberalization. Not to be outdone, Mrs Indian YP clutches the dead microphone and proceeds to elocute a well rehearsed speech on Indian hospitality, with the kind of plasticity that one has come to associate with the rhetoric of beauty competitions.

The delegates of the YPO receive the speeches in a state of polite stupor. Then there's a burst of music from the banqueting area, fireworks, and it's time to eat. The tables are groaning under the weight of five multicultural cuisines – you can eat anything from lobster to biryani, soufflé to *kheer*. But let us leave these trivialities for the moment: a 'real' interruption has infiltrated the surreal narrative of *The Hidden River*, illuminating the larger political and economic contradictions of contemporary India.

THE REAL STORY

Mukesh Mills (as the reality begins to unfold) didn't just burn down accidentally. It didn't just become a 'sick' unit overnight. On the contrary, it was deliberately neglected and allegedly sabotaged by its owners, thereby displacing hundreds of workers, who continue to live in the squalid quarters around the mill, still seeking adequate compensation for their arbitrary retrenchment. The site, in all its atmospheric decay, has become a convenient (and lucrative) backdrop for the shooting of Hindi films.

In its brochure, Sarthi provides a fairly succinct historical perspective on the decay of the textile industry in India, which at one level destroyed the earlier tradition of handloom weaving, and later capitulated to the connivance of mill owners, who circumvented labour laws by financing independent powerlooms and seeking illegal deals in real estate. The brochure, however, has no difficulty in surrendering its 'political correctness' to the advertising of a gala event:

> Today for the first time and perhaps for the last, this site is being brought back to life with a dialogue on balances. A dialogue between the harbringers [*sic*] of plenty and the pilgrims of joy, the captains of industry and the artists of good fortune.   (Sarthi 1996)

What makes this rhetoric so insidious is its assumption that Mukesh Mills could well return to its state of decay, after this one, masque-like spectacular rescue mission, enacted by 'the artists of good fortune' for the pleasure of the 'captains of industry', had run its course. There is not a word about the workers and their predicament.

This omission is, at one level, typical of the larger enterprise of cultural tourism, where 'tourist sites' can frequently emerge out of the ashes of dead industries. Shut down the slate mines of Wales (as Thatcher did), liquidate the families of miners and their culture, and then create an interactive, performative, living museum *in* the mines for the benefit of tourists. Fortunately in India, we do not (as yet) have sites of the immediate past reconstructed with such virtuosity, for the simple reason that the past is still very much with us. We cannot readily use postmodern touristic categories like 'ex-primitive' and 'ex-peasant', to use Dean MacCannell's terms (1992), because the 'primitive', the 'peasant', as indeed the 'folk' and the 'tribal', continue to relate to living communities, positioned in different proximities to the uneven and disparate process of modernization in India.

Instead of historicizing the differentiated contexts of 'traditional skills' in India, Sarthi has chosen to essentialize their authenticities within the larger context of 'continuity in change'. At the same time, it is sufficiently canny to emphasize 'the imparting of self-managerial negotiative and commercial skills' to non-metropolitan Indian artists, so that they can circumvent 'middlemen' (excluding Sarthi, of course, which would prefer to designate itself as a 'friend'). To what extent Sarthi is a 'friend' of 'artists in need', we shall discover shortly, as this story picks up from where I had interrupted it. But one thing is certain: Sarthi is no friend of 'workers in need'. Or else, it would not have used Mukesh Mills so callously as a site for entertainment, with no real concern for its social ecology.

ENTER THE WORKERS

All is not lost, however, as the workers of Mukesh Mills enter the narrative from which they have been excluded. While the YPs are dining, they seize an ideal opportunity in which to assert their rights as the uninvited guests to the party. In a master stroke of collective action, they barricade the front gates to the mill, so that no one can leave the premises. We are all under siege.

The YPs finish banqueting, then proceed to make polite sounds about returning to the Oberoi. After all, they do have a busy day ahead of them. The term starts, maybe with some meditative yoga or a work-out in the health club. Time stands still, however, as the YPs are compelled to wait, while the police intervene in the negotiations outside the mill between the workers and the management. As the hours pass, and the seconds tick, *amchi* Mumbai, our very own Big Apple, begins to emit its familiar odours in all their fishy, acrid density. There's no possibility of taking the barges back to the hotel. The tide's come in. And there are no helicopters for an escape exit.

The story could end here, but there is another group of people, who are more silently distressed and hurt: the actors. It isn't easy for any actor to spend three to four hours preparing for a show, and then not be allowed to perform. The gurus in particular did not short-change any of their elaborate rituals and make-up in preparation for their abbreviated performances. Such is the sense of betrayal following the production, that it is only appropriate that effusive apologies should be made by Rajeev-*bhaiya* in a *panchayat*-like forum, to which the actors respond with a show of solidarity. Tomorrow, after all, is another performance ('just for us'). Despite the Charioteer's reassurances and display of Indian 'unity' (it's all 'their' fault), something rankles in the hearts of the actors. As the hours pass, and the children in the company get restless and hungry, there is no food offered to them.

No food? But there's a banquet around the corner. Sorry, actors don't dine with the YPO. A few of the more adventurous performers have entered the no-trespassing zone and knocked back a few drinks. But the majority wait in dignified, proud silence for the food that they have been told in advance has been ordered specially for them: good Indian food, the kind that comes from the caterer in white cardboard boxes with rubber bands. The actors' food hasn't arrived because all transportation has been stopped by the workers from entering Mukesh Mills. So it's no one's fault.

Or is it no one's fault? Surely in any emergency, in any human crisis, there needs to be a change in attitude by those who appear to be controlling the *modus operandi* that has broken down. Sarthi's younger volunteers, flapping around like jittery chickens, attempt to reassure the actors about the situation, but they do not communicate. One could suggest: Why not simply invite the actors to eat the food that is lying in massive quantities on the banquet tables? Would this be a further insult, an invitation to eat the left-overs? Perhaps not, if the attitude brought to the invitation could combine grace with humour. One could make a party out of the predicament. Indeed, theatre people are known to transform limitations into possibilities, and they can always be relied on to laugh, if only to subvert the patronage of the ruling class, on which they have depended for centuries.

There is yet another, wilder possibility: would it be too much to ask for an insurrection among the performers, an infiltration from within their ranks, that could challenge Sarthi's cultural politics? Sadly, to forge a dialogue between the striking workers and the actors (who are silently sympathetic to the workers' cause), one would need an activism for which there is very little preparation as yet in Indian performance circles. Our protest continues to be numbed by the respectable clichés of Third Theatre and didactic street plays. It doesn't ignite in response to immediate political situations, for which a 'guerrilla theatre' would need to be improvised on the spot without the mediation of prepared texts. All these possibilities of intervention, however, remain at the level of fantasy. Unable to take a collective stand, the actors continue to wait for their food.

EPILOGUE

On this note of humiliation, and the larger absence of self-respect and civility surrounding it, I will end the story for the moment with hungry actors, red-faced Indian organizers trying to cover up their shame, yet still not prepared to give up on globalization, whose lapses in the Indian context continue to be attributed to a few 'infrastuctural' problems. In the meanwhile, the foreign YPs grind their teeth in frustration: When will India ever get its act together? India, I would counter, does not have to get its act together for them, but for its own people. We have to begin at home, with our ground realities of poverty and hunger, child labour and illiteracy, which have been systematically neglected through fifty years of an incomplete and essentially illusory independence.

As our cultural resources continue to facilitate cosmetic constructions of 'eternal India', which nonetheless break down within the exploitative modes of production in an increasingly globalized India, we face a seeming impasse. And yet, if there is any reason to hope at this critical juncture in time, it would lie in the realization of new political identities and formations that can no longer be taken for granted, neither by brahminical power structures nor by the yuppie imitators of the YPO. In the assertion of the Mukesh Mill workers, we are compelled to acknowledge that, contrary to rumours in postcolonial academia, the working class is not yet dead, even through it may seem to be dispersed through new configurations. It is in the interregnum of workers waiting outside the factory gates from which they have been displaced, and the imminence of their breaking through these gates, that we can evoke one of the most resolute challenges to globalization.

At a cynical level, it could be argued that this insurrection of workers is part of a residual narrative, which in actuality celebrates a politics of nostalgia that is counter-productive within the dominant threats of our times. A more realist perspective would regard the residual as part of an emergent narrative, in a very altered context of labour and industry. The critical task is not to collapse the residual into the emergent, but to examine the tensions that lie in between, which can yet enable us to ignite moments of crisis in our volatile history, by interrupting and infiltrating, if not disrupting, those narratives that have legitimized the exclusions of the oppressed from the agendas of change. It is in de-legitimizing these exclusions that we can combine critique with celebration at this point in time, by igniting our fifty years of dependence into a real affirmation of struggle for a renewed independence.

3

GUNDEGOWDA MEETS
PEER GYNT
INTRACULTURAL
NEGOTIATIONS IN THEATRE

In this chapter, I will elaborate on the social and political dynamics that constitute the making of the intracultural in theatre. While Ibsen's *Peer Gynt* is the testing ground of this elaboration, it is also the catalyst for articulating a spectrum of problems – the politics of language and translation; the colliding contexts of cultural diversity and difference; and the appropriation of folk and epic resources for the shaping of a 'cosmopolitan vernacular' dramaturgy. With such an agenda it should be obvious that my task here is not to foreground the dilemmas of the self, following the example of Ibsen's protagonist who, in his most paradigmatic gesture, peels an onion on-stage only to realize that he has no centre. While such illuminations of the self can be linked to the crisis of secular identity in India today, I am more concerned here with the actual practice of having to negotiate more than one self, more than one history, and more than one language in the shaping of an intracultural narrative.

Before getting to Peer Gynt (or Gundegowda as he was transformed in his Kannada incarnation at the Rangayana theatre in Mysore, Karnataka),[1] it would be useful to begin with some received notions of the intracultural. Patrice Pavis once described the term as referring to 'the traditions of a single nation which have been almost forgotten or deformed and which need to be reconstructed' (Pavis 1992: 20). While it is convenient to focus on the site of a 'single nation' to explore the intracultural dynamics of the cultures existing within its boundaries, the singularity of the nation cannot be so readily assumed. In the political culture of contemporary India, for instance, there are conflicting nationalities that resist the very idea of a 'single nation' in the first place. Secessionist and insurgent groups demand separate nations, while entire communities of tribal and indigenous peoples lie outside of the framework of the nation altogether. Countering Pavis's designation of the 'single nation', therefore, I would suggest that a more cogent framework for determining intracultural practice could be shaped by 'regional' rather than 'national' considerations. In the context of this particular chapter, I will be focusing primarily on the southern state of Karnataka in India, which provides a specific framework of regional culture within which the intracultural negotiations will be contextualized.

Another problematic aspect of Pavis's definition is his equation of intraculturalism with traditions that are 'almost forgotten' or 'deformed'. These words imply the attenuation, if not oblivion, of a cluster of minor traditions, which are implicitly compared with a mainstream, healthy, national tradition that remains unnamed. While Pavis emphasizes the need to reconstruct these marginalized traditions – indeed, this would seem to be the primary function of his intracultural endeavour – one is left speculating on the beneficiaries of this reconstruction. Besides, who or what would be the agents of reconstruction? Which resources would be activized in the process, and at whose expense?

Pavis's definition of intraculturalism, I would submit, has no particular resonance in the context of cultural practice in the Indian subcontinent; indeed, it is restrictive, if not misleading. The task of any intracultural initiative in India is not to reconstruct 'dying' traditions, but to create new possibilities of interaction and exchange within and across a wealth of 'living' traditions from vastly different time frames and cultural contexts. In contrast to the implicit homogenization that underlies Pavis's Eurocentric reading of the intracultural – a reading that is unconsciously determined by the industrialization and capitalist economy assumed by the European theatre cultures that are the focus of his study – we have in India a more differentiated gradation of cultures in tribal, rural, folk, ritual, *mofussil* (district town), urban, and metropolitan contexts. These cultures are not 'deformed' or 'forgotten' in Pavis's terms; rather, they are alive in different states of vibrancy, and in different proximities to the process of modernization, industrialization, and secularization in India that is far from complete.

BETWEEN DIVERSITY AND DIFFERENCE

Within the epic scale and variables of India's diversities, how does one negotiate the intracultural? This question counters the multicultural bombast of the Indian state, which all too often seeks a false reassurance in the sheer number of India's diversities without engaging with the possible implications of their mixing, interaction, and hybridity. Only in recent years has the rhetoric of cultural diversity been subjected to a secular critique. Brainwashed as we have been from our school days by India's 'unity in diversity' – the *mantra* of the nation-state – it is still difficult not to regard diversity as an *a priori* condition of Indian democracy.

However, as the hallowed premises of this democracy have been challenged in recent years by the political establishment of the Hindu Right, the early euphoria around 'diversity' is no longer intact, and there are the beginnings of a new scepticism: is a 'diverse' society necessarily 'pluralist'? Today, as I have already outlined in the introduction, there is a growing critical need to debunk the 'natural' propensities of diversities, which have facilitated the allegedly organic outgrowth of '5,000 years of uninterrupted civilization'.[2] This pseudo-Himalayan perspective of 'Indian' culture, which legitimizes the centralization of cultural activities by the Indian state, has provoked new critiques of the concept of 'diversity' itself, which now tends to be read as a political construction around which an official multiculturalism has been hegemonized.

One of the most trenchant critiques of the 'politics of diversity' has been articulated by Kumkum Sangari (1995) in her larger analysis of the debate surrounding the formation of a uniform civil code in India. Sangari contextualizes the ideology of cultural diversity within 'pre-formed, sealed religious communities' that are 'deprived' of 'internal diversity, looseness, and open boundaries' (Sangari 1995: 3300). Marked by a strongly defined religious identity that is not subject to 'regional or class variations', these diversities are assumed to embody the cultural rights of entire communities. So entrenched is the conflation of religion and culture in such assumptions that the obvious intolerance of religious patriarchies in granting fundamental rights to women and minorities is not exposed. Instead, the defence of community-based 'personal laws' is equated with the assertion of 'plurality' itself.

At one level, Sangari's critique of the politics of diversity is located specifically within the fractious debates around secularism in the Indian context, but it also draws on a larger critique of cultural differentialism, whereby cultures are segregated by impermeable boundaries so that their individual purity can be maintained. In such models of an essentially factitious plurality, there is a 'geographical contiguity' of cultures that coexist 'in mere spatiality, without interpenetrating'; cultures are reduced to particularisms, with 'non-transmissible life styles' (Al-Azmeh 1993; quoted by Sangari 1995: 3309). It is, indeed, telling to note how closely such orientalist perspectives of non-western cultures are echoed and endorsed in official models of multiculturalism in Asia, where communities continue to be marked, categorized, and separated, while contributing to the official rhetoric of solidarity and national integration.

While Sangari resists the strictures of cultural differentialism, she does not go to the other extreme of subscribing to postmodern multiculturalism in which cultural boundaries are imagined to be so porous that they facilitate a total rejection of 'unified, fixed, essentialist identities of communities' (1995: 3310). Rejecting the 'celebratory, transgressive, border-crossing, hybrid, syncretic' strategies of such multiculturalism, which have now been fetishized in much postmodern theory, Sangari emphasizes that the 'hypermobility' and 'flux' of the 'intra-communal alliances' emerging from such theory do not provide a sufficiently strong front to resist the economic pressures of global capitalism. In other words, while she rejects the existing politics of cultural diversity as upheld by the Indian state, she does not celebrate cultural difference as it has been valorized in the postmodern theoretical canon.

This is in sharp contrast to the negotiation of cultural diversity and difference as articulated by the doyen of postcolonial studies Homi Bhabha, in his once sacrosanct, but now increasingly contested, reflections on the subject. Tellingly, there are some apparent overlaps in the readings of cultural diversity by Sangari and Bhabha, though their political investments in the term are radically different. While Bhabha remains almost virulently culturalist in his refusal to link cultural diversity to social disparity, Sangari would claim that '[w]hile we cannot afford to politically confuse cultural diversity with social disparity, we have to simultaneously recognize that in our history disparities have indeed produced specific forms of diversity' (1995: 303).

Though this materialist inscription of disparity is missing in Bhabha's reading of cultural diversity, one notes that his equation of diversity with 'the recognition of pre-given cultural contents and customs' (Bhabha 1994: 34) is not essentially different from Sangari's assumption that cultural diversities are embedded in 'pre-formed' and 'sealed' communities. In addition, Sangari's argument around cultural differentialism is also echoed by Bhabha as he posits cultural diversity as a rhetoric in which the 'separation' of cultures is ensured, 'unsullied by the intertextuality of their historical locations, safe in the Utopianism of a mythic memory of a unique collective identity' (ibid.). Clearly, there is a construction of primordiality in this reading of diversity that is compatible with Sangari's treatment of the subject.

Where Bhabha's postmodernism clearly parts ways from Sangari's highly problematized modernity (and the specific politics of feminist intervention linked to it) is to be found in the play of his rhetoric. Cultural diversity is invariably counterpointed (and neutralized) in his reading by the indeterminacies of cultural difference. If the former ('diversity') is an 'epistemological object', the latter ('difference') is 'a process of signification by which statements of culture or on culture' actually shape the production of 'fields of force' (Bhabha 1994: 34). For Bhabha, the ethnic or cultural traits embedded in particular traditions are less important than their possibilities of hybrid interaction on the 'significatory boundaries of culture, where meanings and values are (mis)read or signs are misappropriated' (ibid.). The problem with such an emphatic valorization of hybridity could lie in the virtuosity by which Bhabha pushes the boundaries of cultural undecidability to such an extent that he totally fails to sustain any dialectical tension between 'cultural diversity' and 'cultural difference'. The rhetorical excess of difference jettisons all considerations of diversity at social, political, and economic levels. In the final analysis, all that one is left with, as has been pointed out by Bhabha's numerous critics, is the bravura of postmodern rhetoric with no significant political content or accountability.

If Sangari stops short of engaging with the possibilities of cultural difference, Bhabha avoids any serious confrontation of the residual, communitarian ingredients of cultural diversity. For my own part, as will become evident in the analysis of intracultural practice in this chapter, it is neither possible to suspend an engagement with the diversities of specific communities, embodied in the cultural legacies that have been passed down through generations in the form of languages, songs, customs, preformance traditions, local knowledge, nor to avoid the creative risks and play involved in incorporating and inscribing differences that emerge across regional and linguistic borders. Significantly, I would uphold the interstitially of my enterprise, but on different grounds from Bhabha's enunciation of the 'Third Space', which somewhat too categorically disrupts 'the historical identity of culture as a homogenizing, unifying force' on the reductive grounds that such an identity has been authenticated by 'the originary Past, kept alive in the national tradition of the People' (Bhabha 1994: 37).

Countering such formulations, one is compelled to question Bhabha's fossilization of historical identity, which is more conflictual and processual than he cares to admit. Let us accept that any construction of the 'originary Past' can legitimize the oppression of minorities through the construction of fundamentalist utopias (the repositories of the Past itself). But are there no other pasts in an historical imaginary that can be negotiated by citizens at creative and democratic levels? Do all pasts necessarily have to affirm fixed origins? And do all communities have to be incarcerated within the monolithic confines of 'the People'? Surely there are fissures and inner dissensions within peoples and their pasts that could reveal the 'internal diversity' of communities, as Kumkum Sangari has suggested, though she too closes the possibilities of any such exposure through her refusal to accept the syncretic possibilities of religion in determining cultural identity. If syncretism and all other in-between modes of mixing beliefs and faiths are ultimately the repressive signs of a disguised patriarchy, are there any spaces left within community that are open to non-sectarian interaction and dialogue?

While Sangari rightly emphasizes the 'organic boundedness' of communities, one cannot essentialize this limitation so as to foreclose all possibilities of intracultural transmission and communication. Likewise, while Bhabha is also accurate in emphasizing that 'the meaning and symbols of culture have no primordial unity or fixity' and are always in the process of being 'appropriated, translated, rehistoricized, and read anew' (ibid: 37), there is no reason to summarily reject the vibrancy of cultural continuities, particularly within specific contexts of non-metropolitan, indigenous cultures.

Perhaps one needs a more historically differentiated reading of cultures in which one could acknowledge different contexts of cultural continuity (and discontinuity) as determined by the trajectories and speeds with which cultures travel, and, at times, seem not to travel at all. Within discontinuities, there can be continuities. A break with the past at certain levels can lead to its reaffirmation at other levels. Indeed, the dialectics of cultures are at once variable and fluid, positioned between the seeming fixities and stabilities of cultural diversity and the indeterminacies of cultural difference. It is precisely this space between diversities and differences wherein the intracultural is most sharply, and productively, negotiated.

THE POLITICS OF LANGUAGE

Having outlined a theoretical framework on the conceptual terrain of intracultural practice, we can now focus on the sharpest indicator of 'cultural diversity' in India: language. The multilingualism of the subcontinent is at once prodigious and intractable, sustained by eighteen constitutionally recognized languages (with many more clamouring to be recognized by the state), and at least eight major script systems besides Perso-Arabic and Roman: 'Nagari, Bengali-Assamese-Manipuri, Oriya, Telugu, Kannada, Tamil, Malalyalam, and Gurumukhi' (Pattanayak 1981: 41–42). I mention these facts to highlight the obvious intensity and range of the linguistic diversities in India, which are far more pronounced than, say, those between continental Indo-European languages such as French, German, Italian, Spanish, which at least share the same script. These diversities become all the more extreme (and segregated) in the absence of any national infrastructure for the translation or systematized learning of Indian languages across regional borders.

This is not the place to elaborate at length on the political complexities of India's multilingualism, but it is necessary to point out that linguistic diversities also conceal social, economic, and political differences. Today the valorization of multilingualism as a fact of Indian life is increasingly punctured by an acknowledgement of its divisiveness. Apart from the continuing hold of English in representing 'state power, corporate power, the social elite and India's interface with the global system', there are new hierarchies among Indian languages through the incursions of the global media and the market (Mohan 1995: 888). While some languages, notably Hindi, Bengali, and Tamil are beginning to be widely disseminated through the media, other regional languages are acquiring a 'junior partner status' (ibid.).

The hierarchization of language continues as the official regional languages of different states dominate the languages of dispossessed and downtrodden communities living within the state boundaries. These languages are either reduced to 'dialects' or obliterated altogether. In this violent scenario, where the 'people who have land, water, money' are 'trying to wipe out the language of bonded labourers',[3] it becomes somewhat insidious to celebrate India's multi-lingualism in terms of 'the maintenance of group identity' and a 'shared common core', among other liberal pieties of harmony and inclusion (Pattanayak 1981: 57). Instead it becomes more pertinent to accept that 'the mind-boggling richness of our linguistic diversity' is, in actuality, 'a manifestation of inequality and underdevelopment' (Mohan 1995: 890).

Within this context of the politics of language in the subcontinent, the most immediate task of intracultural practice could be to reverse the hierarchization of languages, and, in the process, to discover new trajectories of linguistic and cultural exchange not determined by the dictates of the state or the demands of the market. The difficulties of such a venture, however, cannot be under-estimated in the absence of viable infrastructures. Moreover, in the indifference to any sustained experimentation in bilingualism or multilingualism in cultural practice, countering the recent trends in other multicultural societies like Singapore, Australia, and Canada, one is compelled to analyse intracultural practice within the imagined homogeneities of regional culture, and not across the borders of regional states. At least this will be my focus in this chapter as I attempt to ground the instabilities of intraculturalism through specific negotiations of theatre language and translation in Karnataka.

TRANSLATION IN THEATRE

So far in this essay I have been assuming the purely verbal context of language in the literal sense of communication through words (spoken and scripted) in the dual contexts of politics and everyday life. 'Theatre language' opens up a totally different set of propositions and possibilities, in so far as 'the word' in theatre is never entirely literary, but mediated through the bodies and voices of actors in a specific *mise en scène*, wherein the meaning of a particular theatrical representation is shaped, enunciated, and embodied. Language in theatre exists only in a state of translation on the stage. This truism is what distinguishes the gestural, synaesthetic, syncretic, and concrete dimensions of theatrical representation from the logocentricity that continues to be affirmed in the 'dramatic text', which curiously survives the onslaught of deconstructive performative strategies, non-verbalism, physical theatre, invisible theatre, and a spate of non-textual activist interventions and infiltrations.

It is not my intention here to extend the critique against logocentricity – indeed, the 'spoken word' in theatre has been mindlessly marginalized in the post-Artaudian celebration of the body – but to call attention to theatre translation as 'the product, not of a linguistic but rather of a dramaturgical act' (quoted in Pavis 1992: 140). I shall attempt in the following section to elaborate on the politics of translation in intracultural dramaturgy, keeping in mind the earlier section on the politics of language in the Indian subcontinent.

I will begin by making the somewhat contentious suggestion that an access to the 'source-language' of a text does not necessarily imply an understanding of its 'theatre language'. I was alerted to this reality while working on excerpts from Chekhov's *The Seagull* in Hindi as part of an original, multilingual theatre piece called *Prakriya* ('Process') (Bharucha 1993: 248–249). While we were at work on this in Pune, where the primary language is Marathi, fortuitously I encountered a native speaker of Hindi from Benares, who also happened to be a professor of Russian literature and language. Unfortunately, this source of 'authenticating' Chekhov in Hindi was of no use at all, because the professor had no real feeling for theatre language. Indeed, his grammar was anti-theatrical, oblivious to Chekhov's echoes, whispers, and sentences left hanging in the air. Ultimately, it was left to the actress (Alaknanda Samarth) to translate the text from the existing Hindi and English versions of Chekhov.

While we were in a position in this particular case to have some access to both the 'source language' ('Russian) and the 'target language' (Hindi) of the text, this is not always possible in inter/intra-cultural circumstances of work, where the original text might be written in a totally inaccessible foreign language, or the mother-tongue of a particular Indian actor from another state can be isolated from the regional language of the performance site. Thus, while working on *Prakriya* in Pune with the Manipuri actor Heisnam Tomba, it was almost impossible to locate any responsible 'resource person' who would be in a position to provide a Manipuri text appropriate to the needs of the production. This limitation was at least partially responsible for the predominantly non-verbal, gestural interpretation of Abhimanyu (from the *Mahabharata*) that

Tomba devised, drawing on his own affinities to Manipuri martial arts and dance. While it was possible to explore some kind of interface between the Hindi text and other translations of Chekhov into Hindi, the isolation of Manipuri was, in contrast, virtually complete, alerting me to the indifference by which languages outside the mainstream of 'Indian' culture are systematically marginalized. Not only is there an absence of any infrastructure to support the translation of cultures from north-eastern states, there could be a more critical *absence of desire* in wanting to engage with these cultures in the first place.

In confronting such problems, one obvious response could be to avoid the demands of intracultural theatre altogether. One could easily make an issue of the fact that actors should not be 'decontextualized' from their locations, as indeed I have often argued in my critiques of the transportation of folk and tribal performers to New Delhi for the creation of political spectacles and *melas*. I continue to question this kind of arbitrary, cultural trafficking in the interests of 'national culture'. But it does not follow as a neat corollary that there should be no cultural exchange between Indian actors from different cultures in a third location, or on some common ground that is of mutual interest to them. To maintain that Manipuri actors can perform only in Manipur in their own language, or that Maharashtrians may perform only in Maharashtra in Marathi, can or may result in the worst kind of regional chauvinism, if not linguistic fundamentalism. One is not, I should emphasize, disputing the validity of a strong regional base in the construction of 'Indian' theatre, one is merely questioning the dangers of fetishizing its monopolistic control over other kinds of intracultural collaboration.

It becomes obvious that if we wish to explore different languages in theatre – not just at gestural, expressive, and kinetic levels, but through the immediacies and cultural histories of the spoken word as well – we will have to explore new structures and strategies of translation. While the institutional processes of such a task lie beyond the conceptual capacities of this chapter, I would like to focus on the ideological underpinnings of the 'translation of cultures' which I have assumed so far as some kind of imperative in the shaping of intracultural practice.

THE TRANSLATION OF CULTURES

The 'translation of cultures' has anthropological antecedents that need to be acknowledged if only to emphasize that the processes of translation in theatre are decidedly different. At a normative level, the concept of translation assumed validity in anthropological circles from the mid-1950s onwards as a means of avoiding the ethnocentric extremities of inferiorising other cultures on the basis of their incommensurable difference and of universalizing them on the basis of imagined family resemblances. Translation provided the means by which it was possible to accept that cultures and the languages embodied in them are 'different, but not so different as all that' (Leach 1973: 772, quoted in Asad 1986: 142).

At a more contentious level, there was the elaborate polemic around 'good' and 'bad' translations vis-à-vis anthropological attempts to either reveal or cover up the contextual minutiae (and limitations) of foreign cultures within the assumed norms of a western civilizational code of conduct. More pertinent to the Third World context of this essay, there is Talal Asad's more recent problematization of 'unequal languages' which demands a more vigilant negotiation on the part of the translator that was not anticipated in Walter Benjamin's now valorized position: 'The language of a translation can – in fact must – let itself go, so that it gives voice to the *intention* of the original not as reproduction but as harmony, as a supplement to the language in which it expresses itself, as its own kind of *intention*' (Benjamin 1969:79, original emphases; quoted in Asad 1986:156).

But are all languages ready to be used in this way? Attributing the somewhat fictitious quality of 'volition' to language in a self-conscious hypostatization, Talal Asad argues that 'the breaking down and reshaping of one's own language ... depends on the willingness of the translator's *language* to subject itself to this transforming power' (Asad 1986:157). Clarifying that the matter does not depend entirely on the individual skills of the translator but on the 'institutionally defined power relations between the languages/modes of life concerned' (ibid.), Asad emphasizes that Third World languages are more likely than their western counterparts to submit to 'forcible transformation' in translation because they are 'weaker' in terms of their negotiation of economic and global power. Emphasizing 'the asymmetrical tendencies and pressures in the languages of dominated and dominant societies' *as a fact*, Asad risks the obvious charge of determinism in his inscription of power in both the discursive *and non-discursive* dimensions of the translation of cultures.

Without resorting to the ambivalences that have become *de rigueur* in much postmodern revaluation of the imperialist legacy of anthropology, Asad specifies that in the ethnographer's construction of a text for a specific audience within the 'discursive games' of academic institutions, the purpose is to 'read *about* another mode of life', and not 'to learn to *live* a new mode of life' (1986:159). Tellingly, Asad acknowledges that the translating of another culture could be more effectively rendered and shared not through ethnography but through 'a dramatic performance, the execution of a dance, or the playing of a piece of music' (ibid.). Unfortunately, these translations would not necessarily be validated by most social anthropologists because they are qualitatively different responses to other cultures that 'enlarge cultural capacities, learnt from other ways of living, into our own' (1986:160). This is a clear case of overstepping the disciplinary norms of social anthropologists, who are 'trained to translate other cultural languages as texts', and, indeed, to regard translation as '*essentially* a matter of verbal representation' (ibid.).

In contrast, as indicated earlier in this section, theatre language works against the absolute demands of linguism. Even a purely verbal text with minimal or no movement at all is embodied ('lived') in performance. How it is 'lived', and what kind of 'life' gets transmitted through its presence on-stage, is open to being questioned, depending on the performative circumstances and training of the actors involved. Translation in theatre, therefore, is a more empathetic, variable, and psycho-physical act than the 'translation of cultures' in ethnography, whose performativity remains at best a rhetorical strategy in a reflexive representation of the Other.[4] While theatre is as 'enmeshed in conditions of power – professional, national, international' as the academic world that is the target of Asad's criticism, it negotiates these levels and agencies of power in significantly different ways. Along with capitulations to power in the practice of doing theatre, there are also transgressions and deviations in its exploration. Power may not disappear in the process of doing theatre, but it is subject to a different play of subjectivities and subversions.

PREPARING FOR INTRACULTURAL THEATRE

It is an axiom in theatre that an actor should 'prepare'. How does a director prepare if he or she is working in another cultural context without an adequate knowledge of its language? Perhaps, one needs to problematize one's limited access to the source culture, so that the acts of translation, adaptation, and dramaturgy can get grounded within the *uncertainties* of the intracultural encounter. To work with an acknowledgement of 'imperfect knowledge' could be the surest way of securing the trust of one's collaborators. It is also the most honest way of freeing one's self from the false obligation of having to make all the decisions.

Significantly, my need to do a particular play in an intracultural context has often emerged seemingly 'out of the blue', in a flash of illumination. Thus, the decision to do *Woyzeck* in the village of Heggodu emerged, as discussed later in the book, through an improvisation in which the archetypes of the play surfaced out of the 'communal unconscious' of the actors. Likewise, the transformation of a stainless-steel cup into a *saligrama* (sacred stone) in the course of another seemingly innocuous improvisation, catalyzed the dramatization of an episode from U.R. Anantha Murthy's novel *Bharathipura*. In contrast, *Gundegowdana charitre* ('The History of Gundegowda') was at one level a more pragmatic and pre-determined choice: to stage Ibsen's epic *Peer Gynt* in a contemporary Indian 'company theatre'. The Rangayana Theatre in Mysore, directed at that time by B.V. Karanth (who himself has strong creative links with the 'company *natak*' tradition of the Gubbi theatre), seemed an appropriate forum. But the actual realization of my need to do Ibsen in post-Ayodhya India became real for me only as Peer Gynt metamorphosed into Gundegowda.

Very briefly – to provide a preview of this 'need', I would acknowledge that Ibsen's hybrid monster of an epic has for many years pursued me in my dramaturgical dreams in my travels across continents and cultures. But the urgency to do the text was sparked by the specific political climate of India following the demolition of the Babri Masjid on 6 December 1992, after which the struggle to redefine secular identity has taken on a new significance.

One could justifiably argue that there is no particular need to turn to a 'foreign' text in order to confront a specifically Indian predicament. But this is precisely the point: *Peer Gynt* was never a 'foreign' text for me, even before it had been transformed into *Gundegowda*. After the events of '6 December', it became even more strangely and profoundly 'Indian', not just 'universal'.

I am not arguing here on the tedious, humanist ground, so tellingly critiqued by Homi Bhabha, that 'beyond individual cultures we all belong to the human culture of mankind' (Bhabha 1994: 36). My distrust of the universalizing tendencies in intercultural narratives like Peter Brook's *Mahabharata* is well known. In my critique of this celebrated production, I had taken issue with the premise that 'The *Mahabharata* is Indian, *but* it is universal' (Bharucha 1993: 70) and suggested that the 'but' was misleading; it would be more accurate to acknowledge that 'the *Mahabharata* is universal *because* it is Indian'.

With *Gundegowdana* I found myself engaging with a totally different set of dynamics in which the causalities of universal and national cultural identities were disrupted in favour of a more textured and reflexive dramaturgy. What concerned me were the multiple routes by which a European classic assumes a local significance that would almost seem to have been anticipated in the unrealized possibilities of the original text. As such the question of Peer Gynt's universality is a red herring for me, because, if I may put it somewhat provocatively, he was always already Indian.

But perhaps, he is not just 'Indian', but more specifically, a 'Kannadiga' (a resident of Karnataka) from the Gowda caste. By inscribing such a local detail from a specific regional culture, I am not necessarily celebrating the narrative of community in the anti-modernist, anti-enlightenment rhetoric of subalternist cultural theory; instead, I am questioning what constitutes a community in the first place through connections between 'local', 'regional', and 'national' identities. To what extent are these categories discrete or interdependent? Can they be collapsed into one identity? What would that identity be? Indian or Kannadiga, or both? If, as the production translator S. Raghunandan (hereafter, Raghu) has repeatedly insisted, there is 'more than one Kannada' – this was the guiding principle of his intervention in *Gundegowda* – can we essentialize Kannadiga cultural identity as an entity? Or do we see it as a textured fabric made up of internal diversities and differences?

Embedded within local particularities of culture, *Gundegowda* addressed national and global forces through a saga of the secular self. Caught between the forces of intolerance, fundamentalism, and bigotry, on the one hand, and the giddy, irresponsible, violent adventure of global capitalism on the other, the production narrativized a loss of the self, for which (in my interpretation, at least) there is no easy redemption. Countering the debased self-sufficiency of the trolls and the ruthless self-indulgence of capitalists, Gundegowda was less a person than an ensemble of energies, a contradiction of multiple 'selves', unresolved, yet open to being negotiated.

Tellingly, he was played by three actors: this was not just a strategy in democratizing the process of casting the play, it was also a means of improvising (and intersecting) the three *gunas* (states of being) – *sattva* (purity, light, truth); *rajas* (passion, desire); *tamas* (darkness, sloth) – by which human identity ('character') is constituted. In the opening image of the production, the identically dressed Gundegowdas emerged from one body, and in the final image, they were separated on-stage as three distinct beings, representing different points in Gundegowda's history. While two of the Gundegowdas seek comfort, one in the arms of a dead mother (Taiamma) and one in those of an abandoned wife (Gulabi), the third holds a minuscule spinning wheel in his hand – an inscription of Gandhi's faith in *swaraj* or 'self-rule' – which was offered metonymically as a possibility of significance rather than as a source of redemption.

As this concept unravelled in the course of rehearsing the play, I should emphasize that its contours were already visible in my mind's eye as a director, even before I had my first discussion on the translation with Raghu. At this stage, I had also edited the English version of the text drawn from at least three existing translations.[5] Raghu and I began with the assumption that since the Norwegian source-text of *Peer Gynt* was inaccessible to us, and since the play had not been translated to the best of our knowledge into any other Indian language, we had no other choice but to work with the multiple versions of the play in English, which became the derivative 'source-' and 'link'-language of the production. English, therefore, served to catalyse the reincarnation of a 'dead' Norwegian into the living idioms of contemporary Kannada.

RESOURCES OF FOLK CULTURE

In editing the text prior to the translation, I had already begun to shape a three-part narrative beginning with the pre-modern, rural, 'folk' world of Peer Gynt's youth and fantasies, culminating in his mother's death and his departure from home; the risks and jolts of capitalism, big business, tourism, and trade, which explodes in the violence of a madhouse; and finally, Peer's homecoming in which he confronts the emptiness of his multiple selves. Attentive to the disjunctive logic of Ibsen's sprawling text, which is more 'wild, reckless, formless' than the author himself had acknowledged, I made no attempt to elide the jumps in the narrative. All edits, therefore, were made *within* the scenes, not *between* the scenes.

The one major rewrite in the text occurred when Peer Gynt (who had not yet been transformed into Gundegowda) returns home. Instead of the Nordic gloom which pervades this part of the play, enshrouded in the slow lumbering disintegration of Peer's recollections of home, I inserted one of the central images of the production: a faceless 'community' watching television in a diagonal line that sliced across the stage, as Peer peels the proverbial onion. This was my way of situating the loss of self within the residue of global capital and the subsequent death of community. I should add that this image pre-figured the crystallization of the dramaturgy, indicating yet again the unconscious levels at which one articulates the archetypal dimensions of a text within the historical moment of a production.

All envisionings of a production are ultimately anchored within the cultural resources of a performance site. In a state like Karnataka, for instance, one continues to find contemporary theatre actors with relationships to living traditions of folk narrative. This does not mean that these actors are 'folk'; they are urban theatre practitioners, whose modernity cannot be separated from the folk resources constituting their memories of childhood, family, community, and tradition. It would not be accurate in this regard to claim any kind of 'authenticity' in this internalization of the folk in the actors' consciousness; indeed, the folk is fractured, romanticized, reduced to kitsch, and, at times, dismissed as irrelevant by the actors themselves. Even in their rendering of folk songs – and singing is the mainstay of B.V. Karnath's training of the Rangayana actors – one notes discomfitingly the kind of saccharine sweetness that characterizes the commodification of the folk: a gentrified voice-culture mediated by All India Radio and the appropriation of folk melodies for film music and in light classics.

Despite this softening of folk energies, which is also apparent in the cosmetic uses of pseudo-folk dance movements by urban theatre groups, in companies like Rangayana a relatively untapped repertoire of folk proverbs, epigrams, ballads, images, and metaphors can still be found. It goes without saying that these resources came in very handy while representing the pre-industrialist and pre-capitalist world of *Gundegowda*. The purpose here was not to reproduce folk resources – given the context of Ibsen's modernity and, indeed, the conflicting modernities of the actors themselves, this would have been entirely counter-productive. However, I cannot deny that there was a dramaturgical advantage in drawing on a folk context that is still alive in the actors' imaginations to evoke the world of agriculture, hunting, festivity, and wild flights of fantasy into the supernatural, which animate the first half of Ibsen's epic. Most western productions of *Peer Gynt* fall flat in the opening scenes because the folk is dead in European theatre cultures and does not even register, except in an ironic mode, where it is invariably reduced to kitsch.

It can be argued, of course, that the very absence of folk resources has led to some very inspired, if somewhat misleading, reinterpretations of Ibsen's key figures in European productions. Take the Button Moulder, for instance, the jocular emissary of Death who accosts Peer on the crossroads in the last moments of his hopelessly desiccated life. This bogeyman, who straddles the worlds of myth and quotidian reality, is quintessentially a folk character, sent to melt Peer into a button because Ibsen's hero is neither sinful enough to go to hell, nor good enough to be spared – a truly secular predicament. But how can such a seemingly anachronistic oddity as the Button Moulder exist in a postmodern, postcapitalist theatre production?

Inevitably, he is almost always transformed into a technocrat of sorts. The legendary Schaubühne production of *Peer Gynt* definitively represented him as an engineer masterminding a development and clearance project: 'all insignificant individuals [like Peer Gynt] ... as well as the entire retrogressive middle classes' would not be allowed to stand in the way of progress. Instead, they would accelerate the rate of progress by being reduced to 'the lubricating oil that keeps the wheels of our [West German] economy running smoothly' (quoted in Patterson 1981: 85).

While this transformation of the Button Moulder into an agent of collectivization was undeniably a dramaturgical *tour de force*, it somewhat missed the point in so far as the master engineer resembled 'the commandant of a labour camp' rather than 'the apostle of a new age' (Patterson 1981: 88). From the critical hindsight of a post-1989 political perspective, one is compelled to question the socialist credentials of this West German technocrat, who seems more like an agent of global capitalism than a catalyst of an anti-bourgeois social order. It does not come as a surprise, therefore, that he 'did not show any way in which the *petite bourgeoisie* might be won for the revolutionary cause' (ibid.). Clearly, this engineer's cause was not revolution, but progress in the interests of capital.

This ostensibly 'radical' reinterpretation, therefore, becomes all the more disingenuous when one remembers that in 1971 (when the Schaubühne produced *Peer Gynt*) that its director Peter Stein had openly declared that '[t]he theatre cannot be a means of realizing the ideology of the working classes' (quoted in Patterson 1981: 66). This conviction is what had inspired his critique of bourgeois individualism in the nineteenth-century figure and landscape of *Peer Gynt*. Stein's problem, however, was in finding a political alternative that was not ultimately subsumed by the global capitalist economy of the West German state – the very system, whose magnanimous, if not extravagant, funding of social democratic theatre companies like the Schaubühne, ultimately succeeded in neutralizing the critique of capital in their cultural practice. Tellingly, as it became evident from the 1980s onwards, the Schaubühne was reduced to culinary theatre, the repository of those very bourgeois values that it had set out to critique in *Peer Gynt*.

I have dwelt on the Schaubühne reinterpretation of the Button Moulder to highlight the contextual differences of his intracultural incarnation within the incomplete industrialization of modern India, where rural cultures continue to assert themselves with significantly different value-systems. In the Schaubühne production, the anti-individualist critique could not be sustained by a counter-reading of the liberatory possibilities of the self, but this was not the case with *Gundegowda* where it was possible to recognize the metaphysical significance of the Button Moulder's philosophy: 'To be one's self is to kill one's self'. In the Indian context, this statement cannot be dismissed as a moralistic maxim; indeed it continues to resonate within the philosophies of numerous seers who have speculated on the multiple levels of the 'self' – *atman* (the real self), *jiva* (the living inner being), *ahamkara* (the ego). These discriminations of the self are not merely spiritual categories; indeed, they animate some of the most critical questions on the 'politics of self', which are perhaps most radically confronted in neo-Gandhian modes of social and cultural activism.

Within this larger philosophical context of the resources of the self, it was not necessary to reinterpret the Button Moulder on the lines of the Schaubühne production. In *Gundegowda*, he could remain a 'folk' character with earthy wisdom. Nor was it necessary to project him into the past. As I saw him, this messenger of Yama, the God of Death, could be an ordinary vendor who might be encountered in the by-lanes of any Indian city – a locksmith jangling a ring of keys, a *kulumeyavanu* (literally a 'furnaceman'). The two directions that I gave the actor playing the role were: (1) to think of the sage Ramana Maharshi, and the liquid compassion of his eye; death does not have to be entirely grim; (2) not to waste the onion that Gundegowda peels and leaves on-stage. The onion is not just a symbol, but food to be eaten. The poor cannot afford to eat onions in India today.[6]

I mention these details to stress the multiple levels – the folk, the spiritual, and the economic – at which a character like the Button Moulder can be reconfigured in the Indian context. The irony that needs to be acknowledged here is that when Ibsen wrote *Peer Gynt*, the 'folk' was already dying in his culture. More than a century later, however, in a distant part of the world called Karnataka, which probably never entered the map of his mind, his play could assume another life in another language, precisely because the folk and epic resources in that context were in a position to negotiate and reanimate the archetypal dimensions of his text. The enigmas of this textual transmission become all the more striking when one emphasizes its mediation of a particularly troubled moment in the history of modernity that Ibsen's text anticipates, but whose contradictions have not yet been resolved in other parts of the world.

BETWEEN THE 'LINGUAL' AND THE 'SEMIOTIC'

After a dramaturgical frame for the production had been conceptualized, the actual translation process could begin. While Raghu focused on what Roman Jacobson has described as the 'interlingual' and 'intralingual' aspects of the translation (i.e. English–Kannada, and the negotiation of different idioms and dialects *within* Kannada, respectively), I worked with the actors on the 'intersemiotic' dimensions of the text through an exploration of its 'nonverbal sign systems' (quoted in Bassnett 1991: 14). This resulted in an autonomy of labour with Raghu agonizing in his study about the cultural geography and caste implications of Ibsen's characters, while I introduced the text to the actors not through a linear mode of improvisatory story-telling, but through exercises and compositions built around the primary motifs and gestures in the play.

For Raghu, the translator is a wordsmith, a myth-maker, who reworks the regional variations of a language into a modernist idiom. Significantly, his own language has been nurtured by his cultural affinities to border communities. Growing up in the border town of Ananthapur in Andhra Pradesh, he spoke Telugu in his early years; this language was used by his father's side of the family while his mother's side shifted between using Tamil and Kannada. This sounds like an Indian multilingual dilemma. Raghu himself was educated in English, but then, consciously, as a marxist and Communist Party (CPI) member, relearned Kannada while he was in university.

As a member of the upper-caste, Iyengar community, Raghu has continued to battle the ideological demands of brahminism and marxism, though he is no longer affiliated to any party. What seems to have resulted from these tensions is an extremely alert theatrical sensibility that celebrates the multivalent possibilities of language and identity. Indeed, Raghu is acutely aware that any theatre translation involving an *adaptation* of the location and names of a particular text has to be even more attentive to linguistic inventions. It is one kind of translation to have a character called Peer Gynt speak Kannada, but it is quite another matter for Peer Gynt to be renamed Gundegowda.

How did this come about? Quite literally through the strong associations between rural culture and the tilling of the soil (which are intrinsically part of Peer Gynt's background), and the agricultural community of the Gowdas. Names in the Indian context are intrinsically linked to the occupational identities of specific castes. It could be argued, of course, that there are many agricultural communities in Karnataka – for example, Havyaka brahmins – but can one possibly imagine Peer Gynt as a brahmin? This would require a suspension of disbelief that totally works against deeply entrenched associations with the cultural traits of specific communities and castes. These associations constitute a deeply internalized 'common sense' that cannot be entirely disregarded, even as their primordial constructions need to be questioned.[7]

The transformation of Gynt into Gowda was just one instance of the numerous choices that Raghu had to make in order to recontextualize the communitarian dimensions of Ibsen's text. Thus, for the rural scenes in the first half of the play, he finally settled for a Kannada spoken in the agricultural belt between Malavalli, in the Mandya district, and Mysore. This idiom was sharply juxtaposed to urban Mysore Kannada for the second half of the play, as Gundegowda gets gentrified. His business cronies (including Bofors Gajibiji and Los Angeles Burnaas) punctuate their city talk with a rendition of 'Kannada rap' as they sing out their capitalist invective against peace and ecology in the world.[8] Americanisms ('Hi Bob, how ya doin'?') also punctuate this NRI (Non Resident Indian) Kannada. For Moosa Baba, the oriental incarnation of Gundegowda, Raghu parodied the mythological rhetoric of the playwright Samsa. For the phantoms who appear in the last section of the play (Threadballs, Broken Straws, Sighing in the Air) he used *bhavageetha*, lyrical modern Kannada poetry, with onomatopoeic sound-patterns. The lunatic Rataratam (Ibsen's Huhu), who yearns for the absolute purity of the past freed from the culture of barbarians (*mlecchas*) and their heathen language (*mleccha bhasha*), used a very heavily sanskritized rhetoric that one associates with Hindu communal organizations such as the RSS (Rashtriya Swayamsevak Sangh).[9] In all these choices, Raghu was not just *reproducing* Ibsen's text; in Benjaminian terms, he was *reinventing* Kannada according to the impulses of the original text as they resonated within the dramaturgical framework of the production.

While Raghu was negotiating the intralingual resonances of the text, I was busy in the rehearsal room without a written text at all, drawing out other narratives from within the unconscious imaginaries of the actors in relation to the archetypal motifs of the play: homecoming, the death of a mother, cultural tourism, madness, masking, doubling, self-exposure. For instance, there are some totally unprecedented gestures in Ibsen's play, which are almost Artaudian in their shock-effect – the anonymous man who cuts off his finger with a sickle, or the madman who slits his throat with a knife that he imagines to be a pen. One of my tasks as the director was to explore such gestures in their primal intensities at a pre-linguistic, semiotic level. The purpose was not to decontextualize these gestures from Ibsen's text but to arrive at a new understanding of their context through different trajectories of intracultural interpretation.

Thus, when an actor explores a gesture like cutting a finger with a knife (without the director spelling out 'why' or 'which finger' or 'what kind of knife'), the discoveries that one can make in realizing the *potentialities* of the gesture are quite amazing. In the course of an improvisation, one can be opened to the mythic figure of Eklavya from the *Mahabharata*, who surrenders his thumb to his guru as a testament of his eternal devotion. More concretely, within the immediacies of contemporary modes of exploitation, the chopped finger can refer to a security hazard in a factory, or, more disturbingly, to an act of conscious self-maiming in order to receive financial compensation, each finger worth a separate sum. For an actress who rejects the institution of marriage, the chopped finger could signify divorce. In more intimate improvisations, the gesture can reveal a form of self-castration. The possibilities, therefore, of exploring the gesture at mythic and political levels are enormous so that when one finally confronts Ibsen's startling fiction of a man who cuts his finger in order to avoid being recruited in the army, one is deeply alerted to a recognition of that specific choice. Indeed, the recognition is enhanced by the accumulation of performative meanings that have gathered at semiotic levels, accentuating the primary motifs of the production.

At this stage in the rehearsal process, a performance text was already being created by the actors at very rudimentary levels through gestural, musical, autobiographical, kinetic, and rhythmic improvisations, while simultaneously, the dramatic text was being shaped by the translator. Inevitably, the challenge of our intracultural meeting materialized at very concrete levels when the linguistic and semiotic dimensions of the text were brought together. This was undeniably the trickiest and most harrowing of junctures in the rehearsal process where, as a director, I suffered silent breakdowns, misunderstandings, miscommunications, and the reason was critical: the *mise en scène* that had emerged in collaboration with the actors did not correspond to the *mise en scène* of the translator. At this point the actors became translators in their own right as they affirmed their own intuitive choices of the archetypal constructions of their characters, while the translator was reduced to defending 'his' text and the director in turn was compelled to relearn the text at the most basic linguistic levels – a truly humbling experience.

From this context, it becomes obvious that the translation process of intracultural theatre is decisively opposed to the norms of an ordered and omniscient discourse. At no point does it move in straight lines, as Patrice Pavis suggests in his overly determined trajectory of translation in theatre, which begins with the original text from the 'source culture' through the 'textual', 'dramaturgical', and 'stage' concretizations of the production, which are ultimately assimilated in the 'target culture' (Pavis 1992: 139). As I have already indicated, there can be a dramaturgical intervention between the reading of the original text (in another language) and the official translation, while there can be a renewed process of retranslation between the dramaturgical and stage concretizations of the text, which could be initiated by the actors themselves. One way or the other, the translation process is constantly being interrupted, reversed, and questioned from multiple angles, so that the determinisms of source and target cultures are subjected relentlessly to reflexive and collective scrutiny.

What Pavis fails to include in his neat formulations of theatre translation is the richness of dissent or disagreement. As he maps the territories and methodologies of cultural exchange, he does not sufficiently negotiate *difference*. This is what concerns me increasingly as a director, as I deconstruct the premises of my dramaturgical concept through an exchange of differences with the actors and translator, not just at linguistic but at ideological levels as well. I would like to elaborate now on these differences with particular reference to the representation of the trolls in the production.

REINTERPRETING TROLLS

In interpreting the trolls (*pishachi*) in *Gundegowda*, I had initially seen them as fundamentalists, a perspective to which Raghu had responded warmly with his strong secular commitments. What emerged, however, in his initial translation was a somewhat overly emphatic identification of the trolls with the extremist Hindu rhetoric of the RSS. The upper-caste actors were uncomfortable with the anti-brahminical subtext of the translation, which bordered at times on blasphemy. I was uncomfortable because the idiom seemed to reduce the complexities of the menace suggested by the trolls, who began to emerge in my reinterpretation as representing that silent majority of seemingly ordinary, middle-class people, respectable folk, who have voted Hindu communal parties like the BJP (Bharatiya Janata Party) into power in post-Ayodhya India. I, therefore, felt the need for 'mixed signs' in representing the trolls – on the one hand, fundamentalist (and specifically marked with the signs of Hindutva), but also bourgeois (which is how the trolls are normally typified in western productions).

With this clarification, there was some consensus on the representation of the trolls, but when I suggested to the company that the trolls could also represent a perverted form of 'ruralism', I realized that I had touched on a sensitive nerve because it seemed as if I was (with my metropolitan biases) ridiculing rural culture. My argument, on the other hand, based on specific images in Ibsen's text – the 'home-made', 'home-brewed victuals' of the trolls; their obsessive advocacy of a 'simple, homely way of living' and 'mountain-made clothes' – was an attempt to inscribe yet another layer in the communalization of the trolls. For me, they were not just like 'frogs in a pond' – an epithet used by Gandhi himself to designate the insularities of closed communities. These trolls were militant nativists in so far as they could be made to resemble a vast section of the Hindu Right that legitimizes its self-sufficiency by appropriating Gandhi's slogan of a *swadeshi* (indigenous) economy against foreign manufactured goods and industry. I felt that just as we needed to be critical about globalization – indeed, no one had problems with my lampooning of the corporate world as Gundegowda fraternizes with capitalist crooks in a Goa-like beach resort – we also needed to inscribe a critique of the ways in which the construction of 'village India' has been valorized in recent times as a rejection of Indian modernity. Significantly, this construction is not being endorsed by communalists alone, but by a great many secular activists and communitarian theorists as well.

Eventually, the ideological issues in the representation of the trolls got grounded when the designer Pushpamala, who is better known as a sculptor and installationist intervened with very specific questions: How do we *see* the trolls? What are they *doing*? Through renewed improvisations, where the political unconscious of the actors was stirred at very concrete levels, we arrived at diverse actions performed by the trolls: husking coconut, cutting betel nut, chopping roots, pounding grain, working out with traditional barbells, performing a Tantric puja. Slowly, the scene metamorphosed almost diabolically, acquiring a deep and strange sense of the primeval and the unknown, the overall metaphor of darkness punctuated with the menace of fundamentalism in India today. Through disagreements and multiple interpretations, therefore, the trolls emerged with mixed, syncretist intracultural signs, at once indigenous, middle-class, and fascist.

VERNACULARIZING IBSEN

The hybridity of the trolls was exemplified not merely in their appearance (a green half-mask, a sack-like, jute *dhoti*, and a tail) but in the actual shaping of their linguistic idioms. In the opening beat of the scene, in which I had attempted to capture the cacophony of a bad mythological serial on television, the Troll King is seen reading the Kannada daily newspaper *Prajavani*, which he interrupts by declaiming loudly: '*Shantam Papam! Thiga mucchikendiri ella!*' In these opening lines, we have a clash of languages – highfalutin' Sanskritized rhetoric ('Peace! Hear no evil!') and sheer profanity ('Shut the fuck up, you arseholes!'). Juxtaposing the abusive invective of the trolls – '*Avana andu kacchi bidtheene*' ('I'll bite his bum') – with the seemingly innocuous insertion of brahminic food preparations – '*Avananna beyisi kootu maadonavaa?*' ('Shall we boil him and make *kootu*?') – Raghu strategized his use of 'more than one Kannada' to produce a self-consciously stylized vernacularization of Ibsen.

In the process, he invented his own version of the 'cosmopolitan vernacular', to appropriate Sheldon Pollock's provocative category on the vernacularization of languages.[10] On the one hand, the capitalist incarnation of Gundegowda in the second half of the production was assertively cosmopolitan in its embrace of worldliness – an essentially urban condition which has been produced by the interventions of modernity and secularization. However, we were never allowed to forget the peasant origins of Ibsen's indigenized hero, even as he *became* cosmopolitan. This was most effectively theatricalized in the desert scene where he was shown, immaculately dressed in a white suit, conversing with insects:

A ontehula belagageddu, ekvagi ninthu
Devurge kaumugeetha ade, saganihula sagani valge
Rante hodeetha ade, kodathi hula neerin dari
Torusta ade; irvegolu pyate avarange
Satasata odadtha ave ...

That praying mantis, so early in the morning,
   standing straight,
Is praying with folded hands to God.
The beetle is ploughing up the dung, the dragonfly
Is showing the way to the water; the ants
Are scurrying about like city people ...

Even in this 'insect talk', which is steeped in associations from his rural childhood, Gundegowda cannot entirely forget the momentum of city life to which he is now addicted.

Surveying the empty desert, which inexplicably stimulates his entrepreneurial spirit, he speculates:

Joga Jalapathanodi
A Visveswararyya helida hage:
What a waste!

Like Visveswarayya said
After seeing the Jog Falls:
What a waste!

Here there is a conscious inscription of the name of Visveswarayya, an iconic figure in Karnataka, who was an eminent civil engineer and statesman of the erstwhile princely state of Mysore. It is said that when Visveswarayya saw the Jog Falls in all their natural splendour, he had remarked: 'What a waste!' Later, he went on to design an hydro-electric power station at the Falls, in addition to the Krishnaraja Sagar Dam, the Bhadravati Paper Mills, the Mysore Sandalwood Soap Factory, among other landmark ventures. Anticipating the modernist priorities of the Nehruvian nation-state, Visveswarayya was, not surprisingly, awarded the first Bharat Ratna, the most prestigious national award of the country. Tellingly, his name continues to be associated with the popular maxim; 'Industrialize or perish.'

Misquoting this maxim in the triumphant exit lines of Gundegowda in the desert scene, Raghu stretches the collision of different linguistic idioms to the limits of absurdity:

> *Nanage bekagirodu – Ondashtu bandavala!*
> *Amele kelasa hannada hagene! Ratnakara!*
> *Neenenage labhakara! Chal meri Luna!*
> *Modlu bandavala hudukona! Profit or Perish!*
> *Che, ondu kudure sikkibitre . . .*

> What I need is – some capital
> And then my work is done. Oh Lord of the Seas!
> You bring me riches! Let's go my Luna!
> Ah, to find some capital now! Profit or Perish!
> Shit, if I could only find a horse now . . .

These are 'exit lines' that need to be punctuated with histrionic gestures and kinetic rhythms. Instead of poetic resources, the actor has to work with different theatrical allusions and performative stances drawing on the rhetoric of company *natak* (*'Ratnakara', 'Labhakara'*); advertisement jingles of motor-bikes (*Chal meri Luna!*), and the Visveswarayya maxim in which the necessity of industrialization has given way to the immediacies of profit. Such a language with its hybrid inputs and chemistry facilitated the 'cosmopolitan vernacular' idiom of the production.

BETWEEN THE 'INTRA' AND THE 'INTER'

Having contextualized the social and political dynamics of intracultural theatre in the shaping of *Gundegowda*'s translation and performative strategies, I would like to end this account somewhat whimsically on what happens to the inter-cultural resources of a production in an *intra*cultural space. I cannot deny, for instance, that for all the vernacularization of Ibsen's text within the minutiae of Kannada culture, it was not possible (for me at least) to separate this reading from the western imaginaries of the play that I have internalized through the European production history of *Peer Gynt* as exemplified in the interpretations of Ingmar Bergman, Peter Stein and Patrice Chereau. It would be disingenuous to deny the directorial power of these interpretations, rooted in notions of bourgeois individualism, Christian salvation, and the ironies of enlightenment in a post-modern world. While I was not consciously influenced by any of these productions, I cannot entirely rule out the possibility that they may have catalysed my own deviations from the European hermeneutics of the text, as I recontextualized the play within the postcolonial location of an increasingly threatened secular culture in post-Ayodhya India.

In other words, while *Gundegowdana charitre* may well have been an entirely 'different' interpretation of *Peer Gynt* from any other in its western production history, I would not claim that it was definitively 'non-western'. In other words, I have no qualms whatsoever in acknowledging – and indeed, claiming – that the production has internalized 'the West', not merely in its use of the proscenium and adaptation of realist modes of acting, but in its very dramaturgic impulse to rewrite the text.[11] In one of my favourite moments in *Peer Gynt* – indeed, it is a paradigmatic intercultural encounter – Ibsen's protagonist surveys the Sphinx, and asks rhetorically. 'Who are you?' Promptly a voice from behind the Sphinx echoes Peer's question in German: '*Ach, Sfinx, wer bist du?*' In the Mysore production, Gundegowda's question in Kannada was echoed in English. This was a self-referential attempt to inscribe how our search for other cultures as Indians will invariably be mediated by English, if not ruptured by the mocking echoes of our Indian accents. Very solemnly, Gundegowda writes in his notebook: 'Echo in English – with Indian accent.'

From this scene, it becomes obvious that the re-envisioning of any text opens the critical issue whether cultures can be imagined autonomously in the first place. Can a specifically non-western imaginary of a play like *Peer Gynt* exist independently of its seemingly western origins? I would say that while the autonomy of the intracultural imagination can be so intense that one may completely forget Peer Gynt and think only of Gundegowda – indeed, this would seem to have been the dominant impression of the Rangayana production – there are other moments when a weird Norwegian spectre reminds us that Gundegowda would not have been possible without his earlier incarnation as Peer Gynt. In other words, the *inter*cultural resonances of the text continue to echo silently within its *intra*cultural imaginary, even if they do not always get embodied in the *mise en scène*.

There is a more private negotiation of the 'inter' and the 'intra' that cannot be easily generalized, so I will have to address my own specific predicament in directing the play. While supporting the vernacularization of Ibsen's classic, I was also aware that as a director I was silencing some of my own desires and fantasies that were specifically drawn from western cultural resources, which simply did not resonate in the actual intracultural constructions of particular scenes. For example, while directing the 'oriental' scene, where Gundegowda is transformed into a sheikh (Moosa Baba) and eventually stripped of his clothes and jewels by Anitra (who remained 'Anitra' even in her exotic Indian incarnation), I found myself consciously suppressing 'other' ways of playing oriental stereotypes. A feminist friend indicated that I had not sufficiently framed the irony of the scene; it was too much of a musical romp, drawing on Hindi film stereotypes, including a quotation from the *ghazal* tradition of romantic song. My critique of orientalism – or more specifically, 'reverse orientalism' – was missing, insufficiently attentive to the problematic of mirroring the exotic, non-western other in the subcontinent itself. In other words, I was glossing over the political risks of Indian actors playing 'orientals', and, in the process, the subterranean orientalism within Ibsen's imaginary was allowed to function as a source of entertainment rather than critique.

Undeniably, this position is valid, though I would claim that stereotypes can be played in different registers of fun in relation to different critical traditions of the Other. While Edward Said's perspective on orientalism was dutifully conveyed to the actors, they were more interested in playing with their own imaginary Orients. I realized, not without a sense of irony, that in criticizing orientalism, one does not necessarily have to suppress one's own fantasy of the Arabian Nights. This would be the surest way of denying ourselves an 'Orient', which we are in a position to laugh at. My problem with the direction of the scene, therefore, was not that it was politically incorrect, but that it was not true to my own fantasies of the Orient. The staging of the scene was ultimately the product of what 'worked' within the imaginative and technical resources of the company, but it was not revelatory of how *I* saw the Orient in that particular scene. The problem, therefore, had less to do with ideology than with fantasy: I was censoring my Orient.

I need hardly add that this is a strange confession to be making at the end of a politically contextualized reading of intraculturalism. But if I have to be true to my own subtext as a director, I would be compelled to draw on some of my earliest childhood memories in India which seem strangely connected to the fictionality of the Orient in *Peer Gynt*. There are blurred memories in my theatrical unconscious of a Russian(?) ice skating spectacle called *Holiday on Ice*, which I remember seeing in Calcutta as a child, and whose signature tune from the chorus of *Prince Igor* I later recognized as that enormously haunting melody from the 1950s – *Stranger in Paradise*. Along with this memory there is also the oriental kitsch of a piano piece entitled *In a Persian Market*, which begins with camels, moves on to beggars chanting '*baksheesh*', and then introduces a beautiful princess who enters the market-place with a flourish. There is also Federico Fellini's unforgettably seductive reconstruction of the Orient in *Amarcord* (1973), which I remember intensely.

In another production, in another location, I would be greatly tempted to deconstruct these memories of strangers in paradise, colonial piano pieces, and Fellini, which can be regarded collectively as nostalgic remnants of a residual cosmopolitanism. But in the specific intracultural incarnation of Gundegowda as Moosa Baba at the Rangayana theatre in Mysore, these images could not surface because of other cultural stimulations and rhythms, not least the hybrid musical compositions of B.V. Karanth himself that have drawn inventively on the repertoire of *company natak*, folk music, film scores, musical jokes and clichés. In this *khichri* (mixture) of cultural resources, it is possible to read yet another construction of the 'cosmopolitan vernacular' in the language of music, which contrasts sharply with my own memories of theatre that are perhaps less vernacularized and more derivative of western cultural resources. The point is not to dispute which imaginary is more authentically 'Indian' than the other, but to realize their different points of origin and possible trajectories of exchange in intersecting cultural histories. Intracultural theatre practice, therefore, can be regarded as the outcome of those intersections in differentiated imaginaries, which are at once autonomous and yet nebulously linked within the 'imagined community' of the nation.

No text is ever completely imagined in any one production. It can continue to be dreamed in different ways, with different people, at different times. This can be regarded as one of the central truisms of theatre. And yet, what remains enigmatic is not the multiple lives of a text, but the unknown lives that are concealed *within* it. Unknown to the author, these other lives have their own languages, which embody more than one history and more than one culture. As these languages return to different parts of the world – places from which they might have emanated originally – the life of the text is not merely sustained but renewed through other incarnations. Such was the case with Gundegowda who discovered himself in and through Peer Gynt, facilitating the intracultural reflections of this chapter.

4

TOWARDS A POLITICS OF
SEXUALITY

CRITICAL NOTES ON *SPIDER*
WOMAN AND *FIRE*

In this brief intervention, I would like to puncture the normative values of 'cultural diversity' in the Indian context by foregrounding one of the least interrogated elements in the conceptualization of identity in contemporary India: *sexuality*. On the enigmatic, often frustrating, silences relating to the vast spectrum of Indian sexualities that have yet to be addressed, I will not succumb to the hubris of even attempting a perfunctory mapping of the field. On the other hand, I would not like to valorize these silences by perpetuating their imagined mystique. Instead, I would assert tentatively that an emergent discourse on the politics of sexuality is beginning to infiltrate public culture in India, at times in unprecedented and even explosive ways. What I offer here are just two examples in the exploration of 'homosexual' and 'lesbian' identities drawn from my intracultural dramaturgy of a Hindi adaptation of Manuel Puig's *Kiss of the Spider Woman* and the much more powerful and widely disseminated phenomenon of Deepa Mehta's film, *Fire*. This film enables me to shift the boundaries of sexuality beyond my own experiments in theatre through the mediation of popular cinema into the public domain of contemporary India, where sexual identities are at long last being confronted, debated, and politicized within the larger conceptual parameters of secularism and national identity.

Without seeking any false synthesis in my critical notes on *Spider Woman* and *Fire*, I will call attention to the politics of naming sexual minorities that challenge not merely the conservative and fundamentalist orthodoxies of tradition and Hindutva; more critically, I am interested in questioning the implicit heterosexuality that underlies secular constructions of political identity – so implicit, indeed, that one could argue that 'our' sexuality in India is neutralized of any possible diversity or difference. This is one construction where not even lip-service is given to the nationalist mantra of 'unity in diversity', because sexual diversity as such has yet to be acknowledged as a viable reality.

While my subject-positions *vis-à-vis Spider Woman* and *Fire* are shaped by different functions – I am the director/dramaturge of the first text, while I am a citizen-spectator of the second – I would not underestimate the value of intersecting these narratives, even though their agendas are different. As I shall try to argue towards the end of this chapter, the cultural strategy of intersection could be the most viable means of imagining secular solidarities across different constituencies. With these preliminary remarks, I will begin my intervention on *Spider Woman* with the reminder that in this chapter I am not attempting any kind of synoptic perspective on minority sexual cultures. I am merely presenting a few notes on the instabilities of representing marginalized sexualities in India and their possible potency in stimulating a more inclusive and inflected secular cultural discourse.

MAN/WOMAN/SPIDER WOMAN

Written in 1976, Manuel Puig's novel *Kiss of the Spider Woman* defies its nostalgic aura through the provocative premise underlying its seemingly flippant, postmodern narrative: the meeting of a homosexual (Molina) and a revolutionary activist (Valentin) in prison. Fetishized as a gay text in many Euro-American theatre cultures, where marxism has clearly ceased to be relevant in a post-Cold War regime dominated by the market, the text resonates differently in India, not least because homosexuality has yet to be recognized as a valid presence in public culture, while marxism continues to survive not only as a rhetoric but ostensibly as a practice (the Left Front government in my home-state of West Bengal, for instance, has been in power since 1977). Within the specificities of the Indian political context, therefore, it was necessary in my dramaturgical intervention of *Kiss of the Spider Woman*[1] to undermine the overdetermined stereotypes of the 'revolutionary hero' (to which Valentin would subscribe), while inventing a homosexual imaginary for Molina in the absence of any contemporary conventions for representing 'homosexuals' on the Indian stage.

Significantly, I made no attempt to tell the story of Puig's narrative through an episodic, linear dramatization, focusing instead on a dramaturgical deconstruction of the text through a non-realist, fragmented juxtaposition of 'homosexuality' and 'marxism' as colliding languages and performative modes. A homosexual 'planted' in a prison cell to spy on a communist activist; their mutual antagonism and eventual bonding through sex; and the 'sacrifice' of the homosexual in the cause of the revolution, as he is framed and shot by the police: these 'facts' of the narrative were merely pretexts in my adaptation for dramatizing another story, another history.

Staged in an intimate art gallery, with the audience seated on four sides of a rectangular performance space, the opening moments of the production flaunted the hybridity of the adaptation. Molina and Valentin (whose names remained unchanged, and therefore sounded somewhat foreign in the Indian context) were introduced through their respective crimes, which were announced in a stentorian, official voice-over in Hindi. Simultaneously, three video monitors around the performance space projected sections of the Indian Penal Code in English. Valentin was linked to the notorious Terrorist and Disruptive Activities (Prevention) Act (TADA) – which continues to be invoked even after being rescinded by the State following the official admission that it has been blatantly misused by the police and the armed forces against alleged 'terrorists'. Molina's crime, on the other hand, was specifically contextualized within the parameters of 'unnatural offences' designated in Section 377:

> Whoever voluntarily has carnal intercourse against the order of nature with any man, woman, or animal, shall be punished with imprisonment for life or imprisonment of either description for a term which may extend to ten years and shall be liable to fine.[2]

The crime by this description is 'sodomy', not 'homosexuality', a discrimination that is undermined in the largely moribund legal culture of India, which has yet to decriminalize an anachronistic, colonial law arbitrarily misused by the police in their targeting of 'men who have sex with men'.

Within the framing of TADA and Section 377, which provided the essential 'footnotes' for the adaptation of the play in a contemporary Indian context, the oppositional politics of the production was made explicit. But it was also consciously blurred in the juxtaposition of different rhetorical registers that were used to identify – and intersect – the colliding (and interpenetrating) subjectivities of Molina and Valentin. Thus, the first half of the production was literally devoted to two narratives – a 'fantasy' in which Molina acted out his identification with the heroine in a Hindi-film-style adaptation of the Hollywood thriller *Cat People*; and a 'delirium' in which Valentin projected his inner turmoil in the form of an epic saga of violence and betrayal. The 'delirium' was performed in the 'interval' of Molina's movie.

The rhetorical modes of the 'fantasy' and 'delirium' were counterpointed by a 'love letter', in which I had attempted to inflect Valentin's machismo with a less masculinist idiom, cast in the language of romance – more specifically, the rhetoric of old Hindi films typified by legendary actors like Dilip Kumar. Here the purpose was to play against the stereotypes of the revolutionary hero by seeing him as a man in love. But who or what is this love? Marta, the upper-class woman and erstwhile comrade to whom he addresses the letter, remains a seductive absence, voiced as an echo by Molina, who transcribes Valentin's letter, and then reads it aloud in his own voice, filling her absence with his own femininity. This was the turning point in the narrative where Valentin recognizes 'woman' in another man, without realizing 'her' in himself.

Following the sexual intimacy of the men, which was suggested gesturally rather than enacted naturalistically, there was a more down-to-earth, matter-of-fact scene in which Molina and Valentin attempt to exchange their definitions of 'men'. This was my only inscription of realism in the performance text, and, somewhat predictably, it culminated in an impasse (to be described later). What did 'work' was the last section of the production which was staged in an operatic mode, with the voice-overs of the two men reporting each other's deaths. While Valentin narrates the last moments of Molina's histrionic death as he is pursued and shot by the police, Molina enters the morphine-induced dreams of a spider woman, who nurtures Valentin as he is tortured to mental oblivion. As these disembodied post-mortems are shared, the men embrace and finally part, suggesting a possible union in the future unmediated by the politics of the present.

An early directorial impulse was to merge the voice-overs of the men into a home movie, where the camera would follow the actor Molina leaving the theatre, who would then be shown hailing an auto-rickshaw on the street outside the theatre. The camera would then follow the vehicle through the cruising grounds of New Delhi in Connaught Circus, where the production would symbolically end. Unfortunately, this fantasy proved to be way beyond my budget, and we had to end the production within the physical space of the theatre itself, with the Japanese composer Somei Satoh's *Journey through Sacred Time* for solo soprano following the audience out of the art gallery into the rough anonymity of the Indian metropolis.

INVENTING A HOMOSEXUAL IMAGINARY

One of the central challenges in the production was to figure out the ambivalences of Molina's sexual identity, inflected by Puig himself. At different points in the novel, Molina is marked within the official language of the state as a 'prisoner' and a 'pervert', and as a 'queen', 'faggot', 'girl', 'homosexual', and 'gay' by his own self-definitions. While there was no problem in finding Indian equivalents for the dehumanizing language of the state, Molina's self-definitions in Hindi proved to be more tantalizing. Despite their derogatory associations, *chakka* and *gandu* are among the more popular terms for 'homosexual' in North Indian social contexts precisely because they are more graphic in their denotation of sexual acts than the sanskritized, antiseptic use of *samalingik* in formal speech and writing. While it could be argued that Indian homosexual argots exist for the categories of 'faggot', 'queen', 'transvestite', and 'butch', they are extremely diffused, and fail to be circulated even among homosexuals as a 'community', however scattered they may be in reality. As always, the multilingualism of the Indian subcontinent and the spectrum of its cultural diversities contribute to the problem of developing indigenous sexual categories on a 'national' basis, which would make sense to the men identifying with them.

In this confusion, where 'gay' remains a construct that would probably not be understood by large sections of Indian 'men who have sex with men', particularly from working-class backgrounds, I was almost tempted to opt out of this problematic of deciphering a contemporary sexual nomenclature by fictionalizing Molina as a *hijra*. This, however, would have been a real contradiction, involving a clash of cultural signs that would have exceeded what

I was prepared to confront in staging a Hindi adaptation of an English translation of a Spanish novel. Besides, the identification of Molina as a *hijra* would have been deeply inaccurate and even disrespectful.

The *context* of the *hijra* demands its own narrative. After all, it has a legacy with strong reference points in traditional Hindu mythology. At an epistemological level, s/he defies categorization within a western sexual imaginary, in so far as s/he could be a hermaphrodite; s/he is almost always a eunuch (i.e. a castrated male) and a transvestite (i.e. a man who dresses like a woman) permanently, or periodically. More critically, the *hijra* sees herself/himself as a 'woman', who is not entirely a woman (s/he is incapable of menstruating and giving birth to a child). While some *hijras* may work as prostitutes, others may value a ritualized notion of 'marriage', or a permanent relationship with a 'man'. With such variables of self-definition, it would be reductive to view *hijras* as 'man minus man' (O'Flaherty 1980) or 'man plus woman' (Nanda 1993), or even more normatively as 'homosexual' or 'gay': they are a 'third sex' in which 'man' and 'woman' are, at once, disfigured and hybridized.

To illuminate the interstitiality of *hijras*, a brief reference to one of their performative rituals would be useful. Serena Nanda (1993: 548) mentions a festival in Tamilnadu in which *hijras*, identifying with the god Krishna, become wives, and then widows, of the male deity Koothandavar. According to the myth, Koothandavar has to be sacrificed by his father in order to ensure victory in a battle. Before the sacrifice, however, the unmarried (and assumedly celibate) Koothandavar pleads for a bride who can satisfy him for at least a night. Not unpredictably, no woman comes forward to be widowed, and it is left to that divine experimentor of sexuality Krishna to come down on earth in the form of a woman and marry Koothandavar for exactly one night. One assumes that Krishna reverted to 'his' normal self the next day.

Fascinating as the myth is in its original form, with its numerous variations, its re-enactment by the *hijras* takes on a particularly powerful form of ritualized theatre. On the first day of the festival in Tamilnadu, the *hijras* are ceremoniously married to the deity, and on the second day, they enact the role of widows, beating their breasts, removing flowers from their hair, and, most poignantly, breaking the bangles on their wrists. This part of the ceremony can be analysed as a kind of psycho-drama, a ritualized group improvization of personalized grief. What should be remembered, however, is that in-between the 'marriage' and 'widowhood' of the *hijras*, there is a night in which every one of them can actualize a mythic state of ecstasy as a feminized 'Krishna' in the company of a surrogate 'Koothandavar'; the latter might be one of the growing number of visitors to the festival who use it as an opportunity to have sex with *hijras* and 'other men'. In short, there are many levels of same-sex intimacy that would need to be explored here which could reveal the contemporary fissures in the traditional mould of the *hijras* by which they renew their identities through numerous variations in their self-identificatory rituals and narratives.[3]

If Molina had been cast as a *hijra*, it would have been imperative to engage with the detail and cultural memory of their traditions. It would have been equally necessary to rupture these traditions with the dilemma of modernity that *hijras* confront on a daily basis as they are at once honoured and dehumanized by mainstream society. However, it was not just the ritualistic and social specificities of the *hijra* that compelled me to interpret Molina differently. There were other strategic reasons for seeking another sexual imaginary for his representation.

For a start, despite the cultural specificity of the *hijra*, or perhaps because of his/her marked characteristics, the *hijra* has become the most exoticized other of 'Indian men' (and I would include even a large spectrum of those 'men' who identify themselves, however nebulously, as 'homosexual' or 'gay'). Through the medium of commercial cinema, this exoticism has been somewhat domesticated, but the *hijra* remains outside of 'normal' society, an object of derision, if not a victim of fate.[4] If Molina had been a *hijra*, it would have been only too easy for the 'men' in the audience to distance themselves implicitly from the politics of 'his' identity. 'That's *not me*,' would have been a predictable defence. But by consciously blurring the 'feminine' identity of Molina, I believed, that such a distancing was somewhat minimized, compelling the spectators (both male *and* female) to figure out their own affinities to 'him'.

Molina's 'blurring' of identity in the production was epitomized at one critical point in the narrative when he 'talked back' to Valentin, affirming: '*Main chakka hun*' ('I am a homosexual'), while clapping his hands mockingly at Valentin, using the archetypal gestural sign of the *hijra*. This gesture was emphatically different in its cultural nuance from the tossing of the pink *chunni* (scarf) around Molina's neck, which the actor (Jitu Shastri) developed as a signature. In such juxtapositions, the contexts of 'gay', '*hijra*' and '*chakka*' were invoked to produce a hybrid sexual identity, one that I never consciously theorized, but which emerged during the rehearsals in collaboration with Jitu, whose fluid subversions of sexuality resulted in a *tour de force* of a performance.

What was needed, however, as I realize in retrospect, was a much closer attention to the shifts in language – not merely the sexual categories, but the indeterminacies of grammar which characterize Puig's 'voicing' of Molina. Within the category of 'woman', Molina *is* a woman, he *wants to be* a woman, and he is also *like* a woman. More ambiguously, after having sex with Valentin, he deconstructs himself through an almost unconscious, dream-like mirroring and dissolving of himself in the Other (Valentin). From the post-coital realization, 'I ... were ... you', to the lingering memories of 'feeling you', to the beginnings of doubt and separation – '*I* wasn't here: *it* was you', 'I wasn't *me*', 'I'm still *not me*', 'But then, I'm no longer *you* either', Molina arrives at a provisional self-illumination, almost *hijra*-like: 'I'm someone else ... neither a man nor a woman.'

THE POLITICS OF KISSING

This drift of a blurred identity within the contours of 'woman', moving towards a 'third sex', is precisely what contradicts Valentin's attempt at self-definition, when Molina challenges him to provide a definition of 'man'. All that the 'revolutionary' (in Puig's narrative) is capable of coming up with is utter banality: 'It has to do with not humiliating someone ... it's not letting the person next to you feel degraded, feel bad' (Puig 1980: 63). He does have the honesty, however, to admit: 'I don't seem to have the right words ... we can go back to it.' The point is that he doesn't because he hasn't begun to deconstruct himself as a 'man'; his sexual politics extends to his suspicion of monogamy and the contradiction of loving a woman from his own (upper) class, but it does not extend to any confrontation of his own masculinist/heterosexist assumptions of gender and sexuality.

At best, Valentin attempts to question 'male' prerogatives while countering the 'bourgeois' stereotypes of Molina as a 'woman': 'Look ... if it weren't for the fact that it must hurt a hell of a lot, I'd tell you to do it to me, to demonstrate that this business of being a man, it doesn't give any special rights to anyone' (1980: 244). The politics of penetration is obviously being questioned here, but not subverted. All that Valentin can imagine is a reversal of the Latino code of active/passive participants in the sexual act (Almagauer 1993, Alonso and Koreck 1993), but he cannot *undo* this code in the absence of envisioning other ways of being a 'man'. Unlike the creative promiscuity of Molina's shifting identity, he remains stuck in his dichotomies.

While the active/passive dichotomy can be regarded as a universal trope in homosexual practices across cultures, its 'oppositions may be partially subverted by the very desires they structure' (Cohen 1995a: 416). Besides, it could be argued that homosexuality should not be reduced to functionality. This point is finely discriminated by Lawrence Cohen (1995a, 1995b) who, on the one hand, is candid about the frequency with which Indian homosexual cruisers flaunt 'a negative language of using and getting used, of the law of the fishes: eat or be eaten' (Cohen 1995b: 281) – *karna* or *karwana* (doing or being done to); *lena* or *dena* (taking it or giving it up). Despite these very explicit sexual demands, by which certain cruisers can be identified in relation to what they 'do', there are other ways by which homosexual identity, friendship (*dosti*), and play (*khel*) are recognized. 'Doing and being done to', as Cohen points out, can be 'renegotiated as the play of a tryst shifts into the longer-range intoxication of *pyar mohabbat* (deep love)' (Cohen 1995b: 281). This, I would argue, is precisely Molina's preference, and therefore Valentin's somewhat pedantic defence that he would have 'allowed it to be done to him if it didn't hurt so much', is simply redundant. The man is clearly out of his depth.

In the production of *Kiss of the Spider Woman*, the politics of active/passive sexualities was not specifically addressed, but when Molina asked Valentin to define his masculinity, we arrived at the same impasse that Puig glosses over in his narrative. In the perceptible vacancy of the moment, the actor playing Valentin (Arjun Raina) intelligently attempted to strategize the breakdown in the dramaturgy through his own intervention by reading aloud a few lines of 'friendship' and 'revolution' from the diaries of Che Guevara. It was less an interruption then an awkward attempt to fill the silence, the void of being a 'man' without being able to find words to define what that means. Today, I would seize this most vulnerable point in the narrative and use it more subversively to problematize the hollow category of 'man', which underlies and reinforces the patriarchal constructions of gender in ideologies like marxism.[5]

But perhaps, it is not just patriarchy in which Valentin's masculinity is enclosed. There is also an unacknowledged sexism that surfaces most violently in his dreams. When women are inscribed in his unconscious, they exist as alluring absences or as subaltern allies, who are degendered and, at times, objectified with heterosexist self-loathing. This dimension which is totally overlooked in most adaptations of Puig's novel (notably Hector Babenco's film, which glamorizes the presence of Sonia Braga for obvious box-office reasons) can be traced in one of the most striking 'dream-fictions' that intersperse Puig's narrative. I interpreted this fiction as Valentin's delirium – a frenzied soliloquy, punctuated with staccato phrases – in which he fantasizes a 'revolutionary' (himself?) seeking revenge against his deceitful mother and comprador capitalist allies, in a banana-republic political saga. In this narrative, where archetypal figures flash like the rapid fire of a machine gun – 'the father', 'the mother', 'the classmate', 'the guerrillas' – a 'peasant woman' is marked not as an emblem of the revolution, but *as a girl*:

A girl with nubile flesh, a girl who lies there by his side, a girl whose breathing quickens, a girl who lets herself be taken in silence, a girl treated like a thing, a girl with whom you don't need to say nice things, a girl with an acrid taste in her mouth, a girl with a strong odour of sweat about her ... a girl to dump your semen into, a girl who's never heard of contraceptives ... a girl with whom there's no desire to caress after the orgasm.   (Puig 1980: 128–129)

Clearly, the violence of this language (which was even more uncomfortably sexist in the Hindi translation) is cast in the dehumanized, anti-woman stereotypes of machismo, from which Valentin is not free, for all his ideals of equality and emancipation.

The closest that Valentin ever comes to treating his machismo playfully occurs when he enters the fantasy of Molina's world and most flirtatiously describes Molina in their parting moments as a 'spider woman' (and not a 'panther woman', who cannot even be kissed because she would turn into a 'savage beast'). As for the kiss of the spider woman – or is it the kiss of the revolutionary? who is kissing whom? – it was necessary not to stage it either as a climax or as a compensation for Molina's decision to support the revolution. As I saw it, the kiss had its own autonomy, its own privacy that existed in and for itself. Staged almost like an afterthought, it was tentative, but real; non-theatrical, as opposed to the political embrace of Valentin and Molina when they become 'one' in the closing moments of the production, just before they separate.[6]

The politics of two actors kissing each other on the Indian stage cannot be separated from the politics of the 'public space' in which men are not free to kiss each other openly, even though they can hold hands. In the director's note to the production, I revealed one of the extra-theatrical events that had shaped the 'political unconscious' of my desire to stage Manuel Puig's narrative in the first place. Situating this event in what I described as 'our largely undocumented sexual history in India' – an episode which has acquired, for me, the 'reality' of fiction – I recalled:

> At dusk, in an open field, a crowd of men surround a vendor selling aphrodisiacs, whose sales-pitch provides the pretext for pornography. Gradually, the entire site becomes a masturbatory space. Two men are caressing each other, at first furtively, then more openly. Two ordinary men, not upper-class, westernized men, who are generally associated with the 'vice' of homosexuality in India. Just as these men begin to kiss each other tentatively, at that very moment, plainclothes policemen emerge from the depths of the crowd. They grab the men by the scruffs of their necks and drag them away to the local thana [police station].

What is the politics of kissing, of meeting through differences, beyond the privileged space of theatre in the prison-house we call life? How do we negotiate the articulation of one space with the silence of another? Is breaking the silence in areas of sexuality, for instance, politically expedient in the Indian context, in the absence of viable movements or languages to sustain the articulation of these silences?

As Judith Butler puts it memorably, with her deeply reflexive questioning of the politics of 'outness': 'Is there an unmarked class character to the demand for universal "outness"? Who is represented by *which* use of the term, and who is excluded? For whom does the term present an impossible conflict between racial, ethnic, or religious affiliation and sexual politics?' (Butler 1993: 227). While these questions are contextualized within the predominantly American framework of 'queer politics', they resonate strongly, to my mind, within the contradictory processes of representing emergent sexual cultures in India, where the challenge of affirming a secular identity, for example, has yet to incorporate the problematic of diverse sexualities. To elaborate on this problematic, I will turn now to Deepa Mehta's *Fire* which I will analyse not so much at the level of its fictional narrative,[7] but more in terms of the political controversy it generated in India, which can be read as a narrative in its own right.

THE POLITICS OF NAMING

At the heart of the controversy in *Fire* was the politics of 'naming' that extended beyond the provocation provided by Deepa Mehta in her representation of two Indian women – sisters-in-law in a middle-class joint Hindu family – whose lesbian relationship is affirmed in a strikingly open and sensuous way. But are these women 'lesbians' by their own self-definitions, or is this how they are being read? Conversely, to whom does it matter that they are lesbian? More critically, are there other components in the shaping of their sexual identities that are more problematic in the Indian context at political and religious levels? I will tease out some of the enigmas in these question as I proceed to analyse the larger politics of emergent sexualities in India and the censorship of the Hindu Right, which are strangely imbricated in their mutual opposition to each other's priorities and value-systems. The sexual politics of *Fire*, I would argue, cannot be adequately understood independently of the politics of the extremist Hindu communal parties and fundamentalist organizations like the Shiv Sena in Maharashtra and the Bajrang Dal, whose attack on the film has oddly served to enhance its radical potentiality.

At a normative level, one could affirm that sexualities in India will remain nebulous so long as they are not named. Without differentiating sexual identities that work against the grain of the implicit heterosexuality that pervades Indian cultural discourse, there can be no destabilization of the existing hegemonies of sexual culture. In this context, *Fire* can be regarded as an unwittingly subversive challenge to these hegemonies. I would stress 'unwittingly' because Mehta herself, whom I do not regard as the best spokesperson for her film, has vehemently reiterated in her numerous press reports that *Fire* is not a 'lesbian film'. Fighting the 'lesbian label', she has emphasized that her film can be more meaningfully read in the contexts of 'loneliness' and the making of 'choices' (quoted in John and Niranjana 1999: 582). The principal actress Shabana Azmi, who has brought tremendous grace and maturity to her performance as the older sister-in-law, has been even more circumspect in her assessment of *Fire*: 'The larger issue is that of empathy' (ibid.). It is worth remembering that Shabana was a member of parliament in the Rajya Sabha when the controversy raged.

If there is more than diplomacy at work here in this seeming marginalization of lesbians by the creators of *Fire*, the same cannot be said for the cultural commissars of Hindutva, who attacked the film primarily on the basis of the specific names of the lesbians in the film. Significantly, the attack was not directed against the naming of 'lesbians' as such, who were moralistically subsumed in the category of 'obscenity', and thereby 'normalized' within the legalities of censorship. Instead, the attack focused on the religious identities and cultural resonances of the women's names, notably Sita, the somewhat butch, younger daughter-in-law, who bore little resemblance to the apotheosis of Hindu/Indian womanhood in the *Ramayana*. Indeed, even before the Hindu Right had mounted its attack, the Indian Censor Board had prevailed on Deepa Mehta to change Sita's name to Nita. Curiously, the censors were not particularly concerned that the older daughter-in-law, who betrays her repressively celibate Hindu husband for another woman, is named Radha, the mythical lover of the god Krishna. The secularization of Sita, however, was too extreme for the agencies of the state.

The politics of naming took a more vicious turn with the perverse intervention of Bal Thackeray, the leader of the Shiv Sena, whose role in masterminding the communal riots in Mumbai following the demolition of the Babri Masjid has yet to be officially condemned.[8] Thackeray decreed that the

(Hindu) names of Radha and Sita/Nita should be altered to Shabana and Saira. Apart from the explicit Muslim identifications of these names, there are obviously autobiographical references here to Shabana Azmi herself, who has been a vocal and active secular activist, and to Saira Banu, the wife of the Hindi film star Dilip Kumar, whose patriotic credentials as a Muslim have recently come under fire following his admirable courage in supporting Deepa Mehta's film in public. Thackeray has demanded that Dilip Kumar should return the prestigious Nishan-e-Pakistan award that he had received from the government of Pakistan a few years ago, and thereby prove his 'Indianness'.

All these details (which could be redundant to the Indian reader of this chapter) are essential for an understanding of the larger communal dimensions surrounding *Fire*. We are no longer dealing with the indeterminacies of 'lesbian' identity as such, but with the cultural protocol surrounding 'Indian' identity, as determined by the self-appointed spokespersons of the Hindu Right. Now that the controversy around *Fire* has subsided – indeed, the censoring antics of Bal Thackeray only succeeded in whetting the curiosity of the Indian public to see the film – the question remains whether lesbianism catalysed a controversy in which it was ultimately subsumed and forgotten.

THE SECULARIZATION OF SEXUALITY

In her bold decision to use the names of Sita and Radha for the lesbian sisters-in-law in her screenplay, Deepa Mehta is not merely secularizing the names of quasi-divine figures, she is making a thoroughly irreverent and contemporary statement about the Great Indian Family Tradition. If there is anything that the audience has responded to in her film, I do believe it is the humour that is at once satirical in its attack on bogus Hindu religiosity and morality, but which is also intensely familiar in its grounding within the daily rituals of urban middle-class domesticity. This humour is most evident in the seeming normalization of lesbian desire, as, for instance, when a lugubrious morning *bhajan* (hymn) is sung slightly off-key, following the first kiss shared by the women; or when the older sister-in-law's celibate husband gloats with familial pride during a picnic, while his wife's feet are being sensuously massaged by her lover. My favourite moment involves Mundu, the family servant, whose punishment for masturbating to blue movies is nothing less than a compulsory viewing of the television serial of the *Ramayana*! Talk about shame and scandal in the family – this is 'Indian' with a vengeance.

The narrative of *Fire* is perhaps most subversive when it is least serious. In this context, I would agree with Ratna Kapur that the film is more effectively read not in terms of what it has to say about 'feminist politics', but in relation to the 'normative arrangements, sexual and cultural' within the context of a 'joint Hindu family household at the very moment when Hindu nationalists are in power' (Kapur 1999b: 1297, 1299). In this context, I would endorse Kapur's position that the film does not unequivocally assert 'sexual choice' as a 'sufficient

condition – indeed the sole criterion – for the emancipation of women'
(the position endorsed by Mary John and Tejaswini Niranjana 1999 in their
reading of the film). I would also concur that the erotics of the sexual interplay
between the women suggests an intimacy that exists independently of their
frustration as wives – in other words, this is not simply a matter of lesbianism
by default. None the less, I am still not entirely clear how the interrelation-
ships of the lesbian and Hindu/Indian agendas of the film can be most
effectively strategized.

Clearly, it is not sufficient here to simply broaden the agenda of the film
beyond its representation of sexual pleasure to include the 'larger ideological
struggle about who counts as part of Indian culture, and who is excluded'
(Kapur 1999b: 1299).[9] The more difficult challenge would be to see how this
struggle actually engages with sexual politics through different practices and
languages. In other words, the specificities of sexual diversities should not be
arbitrarily subsumed within the parameters of the 'larger ideological struggle' of
secularism. A more democratic process of secularizing any struggle demands a
recognition of its individual agencies and their capacity to question the premises
of this struggle at contradictory and perhaps conflictual levels.

In this context, it would be useful to hold on to the 'intersection' (as Kapur
describes it aptly) of the different issues generated around a film like *Fire* –
culture, freedom of speech, sexual practice, and minority rights. 'Lesbian rights
supporters or civil libertarians and others', as Kapur emphasizes, 'will only
succeed in their challenge [to the Hindu Right] if they recognize this
intersection' (Kapur 1999a: 19). At one level this intersection will have to work
towards the creation of new dialogic modes and structures cutting across secular
constituencies. This is not likely to be an easy task because secular groups in
India are not free of their own sectarian priorities and agendas. There is also a
puritanism that afflicts the cultural praxis of grass-roots radical organizations,
which often censor any kind of engagement with the politics of sexuality. Mary
John and Tejaswini Niranjana are entirely right in pointing out that gay and
lesbian groups in India have received 'too little public support from the
women's movement or other democratic organizations. Heterosexual feminists
in India show few signs of being aware of the costs and risks lesbians bear on a
daily basis both in their private and professional lives, nor of their complex
strategies of survival' (John and Niranjana 1999: 584).

The more difficult 'intersection' that would need to be acknowledged concerns
the contradictory terrain that secularists and feminists involuntarily share with at
least some communal activists on specific issues like the commodification of
women's bodies in beauty competitions and pornography in Hindi cinema
(John and Niranjana 1999: 583). Clearly, there are different rationales that need
to be discriminated here in what would appear to be a strategic solidarity for a
common cause. Instead of eliding these differences, which are often camouflaged
by their relatively unacknowledged class and caste inscriptions, we need to debate
them in public forums for the larger democratization of a secular political culture.

BEYOND A POLITICS OF IDENTITY

Having acknowledged the viability of intersecting different constituencies, there is nonetheless a legitimate fear concerning the representation of marginalized sexual identities in secular forums. Will their agendas be heard even if they are ready to be voiced? Returning to the political controversy surrounding *Fire*, one can say with critical hindsight that a possible sensitization to the discourse around lesbian desire has been prematurely smothered by the weight of a majoritarian secular agenda, which in turn has been determined by the monolithic threat of Hindutva. Secularism, as I will argue later in the book, cannot be determined by anti-communalism alone. Its future lies in the recognition of differences across a spectrum of cultural diversities. While we are now accustomed to defining (and sequestering) diversities within the established criteria of language, region, and religion, we need to enlarge this definitional spectrum by inscribing new diversities specifically determined by gender and sexuality.

While gender is increasingly a more politically correct criterion, not least through its opportunistic (and essentially rhetorical) use by political parties to guarantee a one-third representation of women in parliament and state assemblies, sexuality remains a non-issue, its diversities remaining largely unidentified and unnamed. There is not a single party in India that would dare to risk even an oblique reference to sexual rights even within the heterosexual domain. It goes without saying, therefore, that the task of naming and accounting for sexual diversities cannot be left to the political agencies of the state, which are increasingly obsessed with the mechanisms of reducing people to 'numbers' for short-term electoral gains. The more complex task of naming sexual identities and acknowledging their histories will have to be left to those much-maligned, independent ('elitist') groups in civil society for whom the compulsory heterosexuality and implicit Hinduization of male/female relationships are no longer adequate conditions for the larger secularization of Indian society at large.

Clearly, this task is not free of the obvious charge that can be levelled against the privilege of articulation, which is invariably monopolized by an English-speaking, westernized elite. Without denying the risks of valorizing a metropolitan subject-position, which can too easily be universalized for the secularity of Indian citizens at large, I would not underestimate the narrowness of those caste priorities that are so often disingenuously used by nativists to promote a fabricated notion of cultural authenticity. Indeed, what cultural norms can we assume to be authentically 'Indian'? And who determines these norms? These questions should not pander to the postmodern predilection for denying authenticity altogether, but they should challenge both the proponents of and the dissenters from specific cultural norms and identities to account for the partiality of their visions and the exclusions by which they are legitimized.

Following Gayatri Spivak's sharp injunction on 'the necessary error of identity', it is instructive to note here how Judith Butler has consistently refused to close the definitional indeterminacy of even the most valorized sexual identities. 'Every subject position', as Butler points out, 'is the site of converging relations of power that are not univocal'; in other words, no identity affiliation upheld by even the most marginalized of minorities, can 'fully describe those it purports to represent' (Butler 1993: 229). There will be internal diversities and exclusions in the self-assertions of sexual minorities, apart from unconscious erasures of other marginalized identities. While lesbianism, for instance, is one manifestation of sexual identity that encloses its own play of differences, there are other identities that may yet have to be named in the emergent politicization of other sexualities in India.

It could be argued that this vigilance in calling attention to the exclusions of other minorities within the vulnerabilities of asserting one's own difference is counter-productive to any struggle. And yet, there are lessons to be learned from other histories of sexual identity – not only the unacknowledged histories of subaltern sexuality in our own cultural contexts, but the more emphatically represented histories of anti-homophobic struggles in so-called developed societies as well. To assert with a false defensiveness that 'our' history of sexuality is essentially different, and therefore there is nothing to be learned across borders, can only reinforce the kind of cultural indigenism that is assuming an increasingly insular position in the anti-secularist debates in India today. On the other hand, there is every reason to assert that struggles around sexuality are inevitably articulated through different cultural trajectories and contradictions. There could also be discrepancies and time-lags between what actually exists in the untheorized dimensions of sexuality and what feminists and activists are prepared to articulate within existing struggles.

At one level, this lack of preparation can be linked to the problem of language and its tenacious norms of civility and decorum in determining what can be addressed in public and what must necessarily remain a private matter. The private, of course, is not necessarily silent. In our reticence, holding back from voicing its autonomy, we run the risk of repressing it altogether. This is where the catalytic power in the political phenomenon of *Fire* has to be acknowledged in so far as it challenges the under-theorized discourse of sexuality in India, which all too often legitimizes its silence in the surfeit of interpretations converging around public issues like gender justice and the Uniform Civil Code.[10] Contrary to what the creators of *Fire* might have intended, the controversy around the film demonstrates convincingly that sexuality in India can become a *public* issue in its own right. Not merely an adjunct to 'gender studies', or subject to feminist analysis within the confines of a few women's studies programmes, the film precipitated a national debate that extended beyond the educated middle class to more heterogeneous sections of the population, whose relative lack of acquaintance with a critical discourse on gender and sexuality did not prevent them from engaging critically with the dynamics of the film.

In the absence of sufficiently rigorous theories of reception in the emergent studies of popular culture in India, along with an acute dearth of reliable statistics in gauging the perceptual shifts in audience response across region and location, it could be argued that the massive public response to *Fire* cannot be homogenized. Pendulum swings need to be accounted for in the reception of *Fire* or other sexually controversial films, such as *Bandit Queen*; these films, on the one hand, reinforce heterosexist attitudes, but also, on the other, seem to challenge them at unprecedented levels. Therefore, it becomes eminently possible for *Fire* to be read at one level within a predominantly male, if not macho imaginary. C.M. Naim (1999), for instance, reports that at an afternoon screening of the film in Lucknow, six weeks after its release, the men in the front stalls vocally asserted their own sexual attributes and virility, while deriding the impotence of the male characters in the film; the spectators even urged the older husband to 'assault' the women while they were lying in bed.

Without undermining the violence of this reaction – indeed, the most vulnerable aspect of Mehta's film is that it does seem to contribute inadvertently to the fantasies of men in controlling women's sexualities – I would also stress that the heterosexist reaction to the film, as documented by Naim, cannot be essentialized. In my own observations of the film's reception in Calcutta, for instance, I was struck by the humour and empathy with which the audience responded to its sexual dynamics. At one level, it could be argued that Calcutta is not Lucknow, and that the Left Front government in West Bengal had succeeded in making a 'secular' issue out of the film by condemning the attack on the cinema halls in Maharashtra where the screening of *Fire* was temporarily disrupted. In other words, apart from engaging with the social dynamics of different film cultures in India, there is also the context of specific political cultures that needs to be emphasized in any reading of reception.

However, if I could risk making a somewhat more general observation on the tremendous popularity of *Fire* across cultural and political contexts in India, I would say that the film stimulated the growing curiosity and need among film spectators cutting across gender and class to encounter narratives celebrating adult sexuality. This does not mean that teeny-bopper romances and their numerous derivations are ever likely to go out of fashion in India. But there is also a growing demand for new 'stories', more closely imbricated in the unacknowledged salacious truths of everyday life. To my mind, it was not just the originality of the story in *Fire* that appealed to individual spectators; it was its plausibility (the fact that 'such things can happen', and indeed, *do* happen within the intimacies of our homes) that made it oddly pertinent.

And yet, I would acknowledge the difficulty of consolidating the sheer scale and polemical intensity of the reactions around *Fire* into a monolithic narrative. At best, one can draw some critical hypotheses from its volatile phenomenon in order to provoke the assumptions underlying our derivative discourses of sexuality borrowed from the West. Hypothetically, therefore, it is possible to assume that the sexual politics unleashed through films like *Fire* has the potential to cross the identitarian closures in which the more sophisticated narratives of sexuality in developed societies are irrevocably placed. For all their seeming transgressions, it should be remembered that the theoretical production around gay, lesbian, and queer identities in capitalist societies like the United States, for instance, does not necessarily get translated into political action. In contrast, the politics of sexuality in the Indian context, I would argue, is more likely to gain ground not within the redefinitions of sexual identity alone, but within the larger struggle to rearticulate what is 'secular' (i.e. worldly) in Indian politics and culture today. The very unformulated state of multiple sexual identities in India could be the stimulus for envisioning new intersections of sexuality with the language of rights and social justice, in whose moribund categories citizens are more often than not neutered of any subjectivity, sensuality, or possibility of deviancy.

The question remains: At what points (and through which interventions) in public culture can these intersections be realized? How can we not just envision but activize the interpenetrations of the public and the private, the imaginary and the real? How do we secularize sexualities within the ongoing struggles for democracy in India? Instead of positing a utopian point of synthesis, we need to work through our existing contradictions and silences in order to undo the dominative modes that inhibit our attempts to shape new sexual nomenclatures and narratives of struggle.

Perhaps, these narratives are not likely to emerge from the constraints of our disciplines alone. Indeed, the irony of drawing a politics of sexuality from a film like *Fire*, following my more tentative explorations in inventing a homosexual imaginary in *Spider Woman*, is not lost on me. Nor would I undermine the specific mediation of lesbian sexuality in igniting the larger inderminancies of homosexualities in India. Indeed, it is somewhat harder to imagine the lesbian couple of Sita and Radha substituted by the gay partnership of a fictional Rama and Krishna. Notwithstanding the censorship to which such male sexuality would be subjected, the point is that if such a partnership can be imagined, it is because its possibilities have already been stimulated by a different struggle of representation in *Fire*, whose protagonists challenge rather than exclude the possibilities of representing same-sex intimacies between men.

More than at the start of these notes, when I had expected nothing more complicated than a dramaturgical reflection on how a gay Spanish text can be adapted in a contemporary Indian secular context, I have been opened through the controversy of *Fire* to the gaps and slippages in the instabilities of representing sexuality in my own search for new narratives in theatre. On the borderlines of my discipline, therefore, I am, indeed, positioned at that critical juncture when theory has interrupted my practice in unsettling ways, but I am not yet sure how this emergent theory will be interrupted in turn by a different kind of practice.[11] Interruptions in theatre cannot be determined by the mediation of one's subjectivity or initiative alone, still less by the reassurances drawn from critical theory. Other social and political affiliations in the public domain are needed to push the boundaries of representation beyond theatre into the politics of everyday life. In this interregnum, when reflexivities break down, one may have no other choice but to renegotiate those silences in which the languages of sexuality are unproductively privatized. By insisting on the legitimacy of sexuality as a critical element in articulating the secular, one may be in a better position to reimagine the art of the possible, both within the domain of cultural practice and beyond, thereby stimulating the formation of new cultures of struggle across diverse constituencies of change.

5

PHANTOMS OF THE OTHER

FRAGMENTS OF THE COMMUNAL UNCONSCIOUS

In this chapter, I will focus on a few manifestations of the Other within the larger communalization of politics and culture in India today. Without assuming the clarity of an evolved theory of communalism, I choose to speak through what Edward Said once described as 'disorientations of direct encounters with the human' (Said 1979: 93). It is through these disorientations, these violent shifts in space and time, that I would like to problematize how the Other gets internalized, questioned, and performed in contemporary theatre practice in India, along with its more glaring (and inexplicable) manifestations in public culture. Inevitably, I will seek refuge in fragments, because what I have to offer is no master narrative, but an assemblage of aberrations, enigmas, and moments of violence that I have encountered in a range of seemingly indiscriminate representations: improvisations in theatre; 'defences of the fragment' in the historiography of communalism; police reports on caste violence; excerpts from interviews by the survivors of Partition – in short, articulations of the communal unconscious at different levels of critical reflexivity and accountability.

While the fragment has been valorized in recent subaltern historiography, its vulnerabilities have yet to be fully encountered. More often than not, the fragment becomes a strategic compensation for not being able to deal with the enormity of any event, or else it is simply a theoretical catch-word for dealing with 'minor', relatively undiscovered or marginalized resources in any field. At times, fragments are no different from the component parts of a missing narrative, but the implication is that these disconnected parts can always be reconfigured to form another whole, yet another narrative. I am not free from this tension to link a fragment to a narrative, as will become evident in my description of certain improvisations in theatre that have been sparked by pre-existing narratives. But I am also aware that the most disturbing fragments are those that resist the hegemony of any clearly articulated text. Resolutely, they will defy assimilation into any cognitive framework. Without seeking a point of return to any state of coherence, the fragment remains unconstituted and seemingly detached from any referent.

SOMEBODY'S OTHER

I will begin my exposure of the communal unconscious with the somewhat provocative conjecture that it is linked to the construction of Somebody's Other. Containing two unknowns – a 'somebody' and an 'other' – these components seem to be linked through a relationship, bound by a possessive clause. Locating myself in relation to this construction, I am compelled to ask if I am an absence or some kind of recalcitrant element, another 'unknown' hovering around its periphery. As I confront the hidden agenda of its dynamics, I realize that I have no other option but to view myself as a 'third' element and that I am obliged to intervene.

But how does one intervene? As I problematize Somebody's Other, its enigma yields to the immediate pressures of the *realpolitik*, as the Other acquires a face, a name, a history. Theoretically loaded, politically charged, it becomes inextricably linked to the spectre of communalism by which entire communities are being differentiated, ostensibly on the grounds of religion, which has become a pretext for unleashing all kinds of violence in an increasingly fascist mode. As this 'banality of evil' enters our everyday lives, the mechanisms by which entire communities are othered are becoming increasingly more explicit. No longer enigmatic, somebody's other has become disturbingly real.

Almost as a survival instinct, one could qualify at the very outset that somebody's other need not be mine. But there is also a small, taunting voice that reminds me of another, more grim possibility that *I* could be somebody's other. Therefore, it becomes expedient not merely to negate the construction of somebody's other on politically correct grounds. One may have to oppose it for one's own survival and for the protection of a secular sense of history and identity.

Is there a way out, however, in which one does not have to problematize being othered in such an embattled context? Can the construction of somebody's other be dismantled through a blurring, if not dissolution, of its polarities? I would like to believe that this is not just desirable but necessary. Quite simply, if we had to constantly define ourselves in opposition to the constructs of otherness thrust on us, then this would be the surest way of othering ourselves. The moment we allow ourselves to be subsumed within predetermined categories of otherness, we automatically empower what we are set against, and in the process we fail to call attention to the differences in our own history and culture and to alternative paradigms of defining cultural identity.

THE COMMUNAL UNCONSCIOUS

Within the conceptual framework of 'Somebody's Other' as outlined above, I would now like to complicate the reading by describing in some detail this chapter's first fragment: an improvisation on violence conducted at the Ninasam Theatre Institute in Heggodu, Karnataka. Improvisations are perhaps even more fragmented than rehearsals. Indeed, they cannot be determined prior to enactment. More often than not, improvisations disintegrate or scatter into random images that do not add up to anything. The more 'successful' ones, however, are sustained invisibly by an inner chemistry of energies, out of which a provisional grammar unfolds that holds the improvisation together. Tellingly, I find the less 'successful' improvisations more potentially illuminating not least because their vulnerabilities are more intense. Unlike rehearsals, which develop a certain pattern through the ritual of repetition, improvisations offer a psychoanalytic site in which the most evanescent glimmers of an actor's unconscious can be revealed, if not painfully exposed.

Inevitably, these improvisations (which I associate specifically with the state of pre-acting) are 'private' interactions between the actors and the director. Even more so than rehearsals, they are rarely 'open' to public viewing, which makes any description of their happening a necessarily partial and incomplete representation. I should emphasize at this point that what I am about to describe – the communal unconscious – is very much my reading of what I was privileged to see. I can claim no criterion of authentication or verifiability beyond what I describe in words of what was essentially a non-verbal experience.

While the duration or modalities of improvisations can almost never be determined, it would be illusory to imagine that they are entirely 'free' of directorial intervention. There are sections in an improvisation wherein one can enter a state of 'flow', where the very momentum and volition of the actors' interactions seem to merge of their own accord, rather like a soccer match in its final moments when you can no longer see who is passing the ball to whom. During such durations of 'flow', a director becomes an observer of an improvisatory process that totally circumvents what may have been intended through an exercise or a warm-up or an exploration of a motif. Thus, there is no apparent link between the stimulus of an improvisation and its execution.

In one particular improvisation with the Ninasam actors, I set the rules of a particular 'game': one actor in the group had to invent a non-verbal language, while the other actors had to attempt a dialogue with him in their mother-tongue (Kannada). Somewhat self-consciously, I had explored this exercise during an earlier work-process on *The Tempest* in Heggodu, where I had wanted the actors to explore a process of colonization through language. In the second improvisation, I had no such intention in mind. In fact, if I have to be frank, it was a 'filler' in a workshop session, an almost unconscious slippage on my part in which I had merely wanted to see how the improvisation would work out its own logic.

To my horror, what I saw emerging before my eyes was unprecedented in its eruption of violence. More clearly than in any of the histories of communalism that I had been reading in the febrile political atmosphere that had anticipated the demolition of the Babri Masjid, and more vividly than any of the images of communal atrocity that I had seen on television, I was made to confront a construction of the communalized Other. In this scenario, the non-speaking actor was differentiated as he was ridiculed, teased, humiliated, animalized, made to perform like an animal, poked, prodded, stamped on, violated, othered.

Concretized in the psycho-physical language of theatre, this process of othering was made all the more painful through the eyes, the gaze as it were of another actor, who did not participate in the improvisation but who chose to remain on its periphery. Almost quizzically, he watched the action with a slight smile as if he were recognizing something very familiar to him. Was it a coincidence that this actor happened to be the only person in the entire neighbourhood who belonged to what we in India euphemistically describe as 'the minority community' (i.e. Muslims)? In retrospect, it took time for me to accept that I was the other member from 'a minority community' (Parsees) – a community that has had the privilege of not having to think of itself in minoritarian terms, but perhaps for not too long. As I saw my otherness unconsciously mirrored in the eyes of this actor, whose own condition seemed to be shaped in front of – and between – us, I was deeply moved by the intimacy of the moment. I was seeing the other in my self.

But this is not all. As I was watching this communal scenario unfold through its own volition as it were, I also began to see the 'unconscious' of another narrative from a different history, culture, and time. In very emphatic terms, I began to encounter the archetypes of a primal play from which practically every movement in 'modern drama' has emerged, a radical text whose playwright had the genius and the courage to place an ordinary man at the very centre of his vision: Georg Buchner's *Woyzeck*. From this intensely fragmented play, we know how this most simple and downtrodden of protagonists is ruthlessly peripheralized, as he is made to stand outside of the enlightened norms of Reason, Civilization, Morality, and the Law, which are assumed by the other characters in the play. At no point in time was the reality of Buchner's common man more painful for me, his otherness acquiring a strange intelligibility in the communal context of contemporary India.

This is not the place for me to describe how the production evolved. What concerns me is the convergence of two constructions of otherness from different points in history, from two seemingly incommensurable cultural contexts, within the structure of an improvisation. Through the cracks in these intersecting narratives, which I could see in my mind's eye, I was also coming to terms with the mirroring of my unacknowledged otherness in the actor who was unable to participate in the improvisation, and who continued to hover around its periphery.

In retrospect, the consciousness of this moment alerted me yet again to the enigma of fluctuating times in theatre, whereby different languages, histories, and cultures can meet at unconscious levels. It also made me confront, not unlike *Gundegowdana charitre* described in an earlier chapter, how the archetypes of a 'foreign' text can actually accentuate the immediacies of the historical moment in another cultural context. In this sense, the inter/intra-cultural possibilities of theatrical intervention need not be regarded as necessarily exclusive or antagonistic activities so long as they find a common ground within the 'political unconscious' of a particular group of actors in a specific context.

And yet, there are some deceptions in such formulations that should not be allowed to pass without critical qualification. For a start, it would be reductive to assume that there is a direct link between 'violence' in everyday life and a particular 'structure of action' in theatre. If the archetypes of *Woyzeck* surfaced for me in the pattern of actions played out by the actors in the course of the improvisation, it would be necessary to emphasize that this was my *interpretation* of a particular criss-crossing of images and memories in theatre at a particular point in time. It is necessary, I believe, not to essentialize such connections, but to submit their archetypal illumination to the scrutiny of particular facts in history. In the process, the archetype can be disturbed, if not obliterated, by the sheer intransigence of a moment of violence in real life that defies representation.

OTHERING *DALITS*

Such was the interruptive power of a photograph in a newspaper that I had encountered a few months after the improvisation in Heggodu. The image: a *dalit*, a landless labourer from a scheduled caste, tied to a stake, with a shit-smeared *chappal* (slipper) shoved into his mouth. One cannot invent such brutality in theatre; it is a reminder of the ceaseless legacy of cruelty by which the lower castes have been systematically dehumanized by their upper-caste oppressors and accomplices. This dehumanization follows a predictable pattern as is evident from the growing number of activist reports on the atrocities inflicted on *dalits* (Sitaraman 1994, Pinto 1994).

Invariably, a particular *dalit* is marked for an alleged misdemeanour that is transformed into a crime that is aggravated by his 'foul' language, 'drunken state', and generally 'uncivilized' behaviour. Subsequently, he is tortured, not infrequently by being beaten and made to eat his own shit. Eventually, when he gets to a police station in a neighbouring village, he confronts yet another cycle of violence, where he may be actually blamed for the atrocity inflicted on him. The 'atrocity' by this time has become an unavoidable, though somewhat excessive, 'punishment' that had to be inflicted on him so that he could behave himself. By this time, the Theatre of Cruelty, of which the *dalit* is the primary protagonist, has become a Kafkaesque Theatre of the Absurd, where the violence is systematically bureaucratized and reduced to a series of investigative reports (some of which may even be discussed in Parliament with upper-caste politicians weeping crocodile tears). Under the semblance of restoring 'order' and 'peace' to a 'troubled area', the *dalit* in question is *absented* from the public discourse that emerges in his name, with official pieties bringing the 'unfortunate incident' to a platitudinous end – 'Therefore, for reasons of social betterment, proper action should be taken against those involved in fabricating this story. ... Nothing worthy of record and action [needs to be further reported]' (Sitaraman 1994: 1445).

To return to the image of the *dalit* tied to a stake with a shit-smeared *chappal* shoved into his mouth, I was compelled to confront with some difficulty that this particular atrocity had taken place not very far from Heggodu. I was alerted to the contradictions of caste underlying the seemingly secular structure of theatre that I had assumed as a norm in my investigations of cultural difference. Consequently, as I began to rehearse *Woyzeck*, I realized that there were two *dalits* among the actors who were subtly differentiated not through any process of inferiorization, but rather through a false sense of 'privilege' by which minorities in so many different contexts are patronized and kept in their place. The 'privilege' in this particular case alluded to the tremendous singing abilities of the two actors. But can they *act*? I asked their mentors. No, they can sing.

Indeed, their singing was full-throated and abandoned, particularly when they sang the revolutionary songs of the political activist Gaddar from Andhra Pradesh. I noticed, however, that they invariably shut their eyes when they sang, and after two or three songs, Gaddar would become a kind of drug. It was at this point that I felt a need to intervene. But how was I to intervene as a 'third element' without disrupting this connection with Gaddar? How does one intervene in any intracultural encounter without becoming coercive or violent through the force of an assumed enlightenment? Not to intervene, however, could only perpetuate the 'primitivization' of Third World actors, whose 'instinct' and 'spontaneity' have been valorized for so long (and particularly by interculturalists) at the expense of acknowledging their consciousness.

Ultimately, I did intervene through the language of theatre by asking the actors to improvise basic actions relating to everyday life, simulations of labour in which the very *context* of Gaddar's songs is grounded. The *dalit* scholar-activist Kancha Ilaiah has reminded us in this regard of the material, productive bases underlying *dalitbahujan* culture in which 'song is an integral part of labour. If any *dalitbahujan* is not involved in work, such a person is known as *panii paata leenoodu* (a person without work or song)' (Ilaiah 1996: 110). As the actors discovered the intensities, durations, and energies of their simulated actions – digging, cooking, stitching, chopping wood – it was during this process that I intervened yet again and suggested that they sing Gaddar while *doing* the actions. What resulted was a clash in the minds of the actors that compelled them to confront their deeply entrenched cultural conditioning as singers. Out of this 'clash' emerged a new vitality and alertness in relating the song to its economic and political realities.

I would suggest that in any work with actors from 'other' cultures, and, more specifically, from deprived socio-economic contexts, the point is not to use their 'indigenous' skills or resources in order to authenticate them, but, in a catalytic process, to ignite what has been submerged so that the critical consciousness of the actors can be heightened. And yet, there are instances of violence relating to the everyday lives of these actors and their communities that no text or improvisation can seem to approximate or confront adequately. Thus, the image of the *dalit* tied to a stake with a shit-smeared *chappal* rammed in his mouth, was not something that I could represent within the immediacies of its violence. It was too *real* to be represented. None the less, if such moments of violence challenge the language of theatre, they are points of reference that compel us to inscribe our difficulties in attempting to represent the unrepresentable. As vulnerabilities infiltrate our imagined modes of expertise, we have no other choice but to acknowledge our distance from the violence in question, and, thereby, to explore new proximities to its echoes and repercussions.

THE REPRESENTATION OF MINORITIES

It would be useful to interpolate in the discussion at this point some political perspective on the representation of 'minorities' in India today. Designated as 'permanent entities, with fixed and definite empirical manifestations', the 'official' minorities of India include 'the Muslims, Christians, Parsees, Buddhists, and Sikhs' (Gupta 1995: 2205). There is an obvious irony in this notion of 'permanent' minorities because they were officially identified as such by the State from 1993 onwards. Prior to that the Parsees, for instance, who have never clamoured for minority status, were marked as a minority, while the Sikhs were more justifiably included in this category following the 1984 anti-Sikh riots in New Delhi after Indira Gandhi's assassination. Even if one accepted the two most obvious criteria for the selection of minorities – 'numerical weakness' and 'socio-economic' deprivation (Bilgrami 1997: 18) – there are any number of variables and contradictions within and across these categories that make it almost impossible to determine an adequate set of criteria to connect communities as seemingly diverse as Buddhists and Christians.

There is also a need to account for differences *within* these homogenizations of 'religious community'. When dealing with Christians, for instance, are we concerned with denominational discriminations relating to Roman Catholics and Protestants, or are we concerned more specifically with the recent spate of Hindu fundamentalist attacks on Christians from *dalit* and tribal communities? Within the minoritarian designation of Christians, there are casteist discriminations, just as, in the seemingly majoritarian status of certain upper-caste Hindu communities, there can be acute economic disparities. So *where* and *how* does one draw the line between 'majority' and 'minority'?

Perhaps, the only sensible approach to the problem is by accepting the necessity of 'a highly localized and criss-crossing set of defining criteria for minorities' (Bilgrami 1997: 18) that would need to be ceaselessly reassessed in relation to the ground realities of exploitation, discrimination, and the denial of social justice to any disadvantaged section of the population. Merely upholding the rights of minorities through a political 'game of numbers', where the necessary intervention of reservations is reduced to a tokenistic exercise in controlling minority votes, can only succeed in deepening the process of 'minoritization' (Gupta 1995: 2206).

In a succinct article entitled '*Mukti* [freedom] from the "Majority", "Minority" *Mantras*', the political philosopher Akeel Bilgrami has called attention to a number of traps that are inherent in these categories. Without brushing them aside by advocating a normative reading of equal citizenship, he calls attention to the paradoxical complexity of Dr. Ambedkar's opening remarks as the Chairman of the Drafting Committee of the Constitution: 'In this country both the majority and the minority have followed the wrong path. It is wrong for the majority to deny the existence of minorities. It is equally wrong for the minorities to perpetuate themselves' (quoted in Bilgrami 1997: 18). While it would seem that Dr. Ambedkar himself was entrapped within the majority–minority paradigm, his own seminal contribution to the articulation and realization of the rights of the downtrodden (*dalits*) remains a model of critical vigilance in negotiating the status of minorities *vis-à-vis* 'the universalist and individualist tenets of a liberal and secular state' (ibid.).

How does 'the majority' deny the existence of 'minorities'? Bilgrami suggests that the *inclusionary* rhetoric of 'You must be like us and give up your alien cultural attitudes and customs' is not essentially different from the *exclusionary* rhetoric that declares, 'You cannot live here as equal citizens with full advantages that citizens enjoy' (1997). The 'threat' underlying both these propositions can be expressed as follows: 'If you want to live here as full and equal citizens *then* you must change your ways and cultural habits' (ibid.). 'Disenfranchisement' and 'deculturalization', as the historian Gyanendra Pandey has pointed out, are the fundamental tenets of the dominant Hindutva slogans that have emerged in recent years:

Hindustan mein rahna hai, to hamse milkar rahna hoga.
If you wish to live in Hindustan, you will have to live like us.

Hindustan mein rahna hai, to Bande Mataram kahna hoga.
If you wish to live in Hindustan, you will have to raise the slogan – Bande Mataram – Victory to the Mother.   (Pandey 1991: 567)

This rhetoric would hardly seem inclusionary, and yet there is at least the provision of a conditionality here that leaves the possibilities of assimilation open for the Other. There is no such illusion of reasonableness in the following slogan, which is more of an exhortation: *Babar ki santan, Jao Pakistan ya kabristan!* ('Descendants of Babar, Pakistan or the grave, take your choice!') (Pandey 1991: 18). While these are among the many strident examples of how the majority denies minorities any existence outside of its fixed perspective on their inherently degraded status, there are more subtle overtures that are made by the more 'refined' upholders of Hindutva. These representatives of the upper castes would like minorities to believe that they are under no threat because Hinduism, after all, is an intrinsically tolerant religion.

If the intolerance of the majority to the minorities would seem to be a truism in the increasingly communalized political culture of post-Ayodhya India, the second part of Dr. Ambedkar's statement ('It is equally wrong for the minorities to perpetuate themselves') raises some more complex questions. Apart from calling attention to Dr. Ambedkar's very consciously inscribed time-frame for the reservation policies that he had pioneered and his tacit postponement of any imposition of a uniform civil code, Bilgrami conceptualizes the problem of the self-perpetuation of the minorities around the distinction between a 'normative' and a 'descriptive' understanding of communities (1997: 19). While a 'normative' reading of community would somewhat uncritically endorse the community's inherent traditional qualities that need to be preserved – this would seem to be the position of a growing number of anti-secularist, anti-modernist communitarian thinkers like Ashis Nandy and Partha Chatterjee – there is also the descriptive *fact* of community that has to be acknowledged. Bilgrami rightly takes his fellow secularists to task for succumbing so resolutely to the 'phobia' of community in their defence of the secular state that they would almost 'eliminate it as an analytic and descriptive category' (ibid.).

Wisely, Bilgrami emphasizes that 'it is very important to make a descriptive acknowledgement of community wherever it exists in the mentality of a people *because that is the first step in democratizing that people and that community*' (ibid.; emphases in original). Whether or not this process of democratization can or should be deepened by liberal initiatives within the community or by the agencies of the State – Bilgrami's own faith in the capacities of the State to be 'improved' reveals an optimism that I cannot readily share – the more difficult issue concerns the perpetuation of the minorities by the minorities themselves through their own increasingly defiant self-assertions.

At a surface level, it would seem that such minoritarian identifications are counterproductive in so far as they uphold an essentially nativist identity that works against the modern and secular polity that Dr. Ambedkar had endorsed. And yet, within the immediacies of the *dalit* struggle in India today, this normative stance can be read as a necessary affirmation of *dalit* identity, which has yet to be fully respected and acknowledged on its own terms.

Thus, in his audaciously defiant celebration of what he describes as *Dalitbahujan* culture, Kancha Ilaiah contextualizes the idealized ethnography of his seemingly pan-Indian community around the polemic of 'Why I Am Not a Hindu' (1996). Unavoidably, this raises the problematic issue of the self-perpetuation of the minorities; more critically, it compels one to examine *how* this process is actually endorsed and rhetoricized. 'Why I Am *Not* a Hindu' is different in effect from saying 'Why I *Am* a Dalit'. Through his scathing critique of brahminic Hindutva at just about every level of history and culture, Ilaiah does not – perhaps cannot – at any point free himself from the brahminic stranglehold that has othered his sense of identity. Even in his concluding clarion call to 'Dalitize India', in reaction to the fundamentalist agenda of 'Hinduizing' India, there is no possibility of dislocating the Hindu–Dalit epistemic structure in which Ilaiah's polemic is bound. At best, there is a reversal of power but the paradigm remains intact: 'We must shout "we hate Hinduism, we hate Brahminism, we love our culture and more than anything, we love ourselves"' (Ilaiah 1996: 132).

Arguably, this is an emphatically essentialized liberationist rhetoric that consciously endorses an almost atavistic celebration of community. And yet, can its political urgency be denied? Here it becomes necessary to highlight what Akeel Bilgrami has emphasized as the 'location' from which a particular position is made, whereby 'the same idea can seem to be both worthy and wrong depending on its location ... in an ongoing situation of social relations in a specific political context of power' (Bilgrami 1997:18). From a non-*dalit* perspective, 'Why I Am a Hindu' could be as provocative as Ilaiah's 'Why I Am Not a Hindu'. The point is: Who is speaking for whom? And in what circumstances? At what cost? If one critiques a normative affirmation of minority rights, can one deny one's own privilege in doing so? On the other hand, if the articulation of minority rights cannot be freed from the spectre of the majority culture that has branded its minoritarian status in the first place, is there any hope of defining one's 'self' independently of the strictures of being othered?

'WHY I AM NOT A MUSLIM'

I would now like to shift the discussion to yet another denial of cultural identity, which is entitled 'Muslims and I' (1997) but which could more accurately be described as 'Why I Am Not a Muslim'. This is an autobiographical account made by the famous contemporary Indian playwright Vijay Tendulkar, who attempts to articulate an anti-Muslim prejudice through an analysis of his own 'communal unconscious'. What concerns me here is not the amateur and perfunctory attempt made by Tendulkar to question, somewhat disingenuously, why the only Muslim character in his *oeuvre* happens to be a friend of the iconoclastic macho Hindu protagonist of *Sakharam Binder*. The treatment of this *minor* Muslim character is far too gratuitous to warrant serious critical attention. Indeed, what Tendulkar needs to question is the relative *absence* of Muslims (and other minorities) in his arguably uninterrogated upper-caste affinities to Hindu secularism. What does interest me, however, about Tendulkar's 'Muslims and I' is his description of the Hindu Maharashtrian cultural background that has fed his anti-Muslim prejudice.

To his credit, Tendulkar is candid about his restrictive socialization with Muslims. As he puts it in forthright terms:

> I did not get an opportunity to meet any Muslim or even see one in real life and from close quarters till I was over 12-years-old. Not many from the white-collared middle class got to meet and know a Muslim on a personal level, not even in the normal course of growing to be an adult in the so-called cosmopolitan city of Mumbai. One was only aware of a Muslim presence in another part of the city [particularly during communal riots] and inherited some stray ideas about them while he or she grew into an adult.   (Tendulkar 1997:2)

This is a chastening reminder of how the myth of multiculturalism in India is built so glibly on notions of the interactivity of cultural diversities that does not, in actuality, exist. Indeed, so valorized are the multicultural underpinnings of 'Indian culture' that 'culture' itself has been envisioned as a repository of resistance to the communalization of politics in India today. Ironically, 'culture' could be the deepest source of legitimizing the absence of social interaction across communities. Indeed, so tenacious are the norms and taboos of upper-caste Hindu cultures that they continue to prohibit the most basic levels of socialization across communities and castes. It is not surprising, therefore, that even an upper-caste non-brahmin like Tendulkar should admit that he did not even 'see' a Muslim in real life till he was over twelve years old.

Significantly, the first 'Muslims' that he actually encountered were characters in a Marathi play, who were predictably stereotyped as Mughal villains. Within the hagiography of Maratha history emblematized by the militant figure of Shivaji, the political icon of the Hindu communal party of the Shiv Sena in Maharashtra, the Muslims in these plays were invariably demonized as violent, unscrupulous, and lecherous rapists and criminals. Such was the power of these stereotypes that the figure of that infamous Mughal emperor Aurangzeb was clearly marked as an 'enemy' in Tendulkar's imaginary as a child: 'He was painted in loud colours, a religious fanatic, a ruthless tyrant, an obnoxious figure with a long white beard on a crooked face, wearing garish costumes and shouting swearwords supposedly in Urdu and Farsi . . . [i]n short, he was like the villain in any commercial Hindi masala film of today, alternately comic and repulsive' (Tendulkar 1997: 2). While it has become somewhat fashionable in the theorization of Indian popular culture to reduce the political menace of stereotypes to the play of postmodern pastiche, the unsettling reality is that these stereotypes underlie and occasionally catalyse communal narratives at very debased levels of violence, perpetrated on others and at times inflicted by the victims on themselves.

Indeed, the entire process of othering entire communities in the communal scenario in India today cannot be separated from the stereotypes by which communities have been demeaned and internalized in everyday life. In other words, communalism is not exclusively a political phenomenon engineered by political parties and fundamentalist organizations; it is also culturally deter-mined by the more seemingly non-political interventions of the school, the neighbourhood and the family. Tendulkar is right to point out that while the 'weird' and 'twisted' images of cultural stereotypes 'can change over time, I doubt whether they disappear entirely from one's psyche' (Tendulkar 1997: 2).

In this context, the violence of popular expressions by which the Other is rhetoricized continues to stimulate the rhetoric of communalism, whereby 'the Muslim' is marked in terms of his 'aggression' and 'unbounded sexuality' (Pandey 1991: 566). While this violence can be camouflaged through a filter of fun and teasing, it continues to sting, as in the popular expression from Tendulkar's childhood – *Manoos ahes ka Musalman?* ('Are you a human being or a Muslim?'). While this would seem to be a communal witticism from another time, the more violent reference to Muslims as *laandya* (literally 'an animal whose tail has been cut, generally a dog'), which first became popular shortly after the Partition, resurfaced with disturbing frequency after the demolition of the Babri Masjid. Once again, the Muslim was marked by his circumcised penis, as indeed by his beard and generally unclean appearance: these would seem to be the primordial traits of his community.

The Muslim also continues to be marked within the narrative of betrayal. In this context, Tendulkar is compelled to confront the anguish of his close Muslim friend, Amar Sheikh Shaheer, the revolutionary bard in the cultural squad of the undivided Communist Party of India. Amar Sheikh raises a pertinent question: 'Why as a Muslim am I regarded as a traitor?' To which Tendulkar attempts an answer:

> Because we were brought up that way. We, Hindu children, with casual remarks like *Manoos ahes ka Musalman?* ...
>
> Because of the biases knowingly and unknowingly sown in our minds at an early age by presenting and teaching us our history ... in a wrong light.
>
> Because of the experience of the Partition of the country through its portrayal by the mass media and of the preceding years of Hindu–Muslim relations as they percolated to us through the attitudes of our elders.
>
> And, most of all, because of the total lack of contact, the wide chasm between us and the Muslims among us, as people. Yes, I am aware of the games politicians have played among us. But those games would not have succeeded ... if we had grown together from our childhood as one community, rather than two separate worlds within one nation, within one city. (Tendulkar 1997: 8)

It is rare that the anti-Muslim prejudice is confronted so directly within the cultures of everyday life. Increasingly, there is a tendency in the growing body of theoretical work on communalism to work against the grain of economic and instrumentalist explanations of violence. The ambivalence of human agency is more readily accepted, but there is still a curious incapacity among historians to relate violence to the structures of everyday life. The roots of violence are perhaps more enigmatic than we imagine if we are prepared to accept that they have been sown unknowingly within the 'narrow domestic walls' of our own homes and communities. Such a reading challenges the increasing idealization of the 'narrative of community' that is invariably posited against the narrative of the State and its administrative machinery, which have undeniably manipulated communal tensions for electoral purposes. However, what tends to be disingenuously denied is that communities could be implicated in the very narrative of communalism that victimizes them.

VOICING VIOLENCE

I will at this point make a sharp cut to yet another fragment, an interview of a Partition survivor, who, in a far deeper and more harrowing context of suffering, echoes Tendulkar's position on the absence of a real meeting across communities. The pain deepens as one learns from this testament how diverse communities did interact in the pre-Partition days, except in the seemingly trivial area of inter-dining which was an unquestioned taboo. I will quote from sections of this interview, drawn from Urvashi Butalia's ground-breaking *The Other Side of Silence: Voices from the Partition of India* (1998), to address the sobering reality that the violence in the subcontinent was not an atavistic upheaval of primordial forces, or the result of colonial machination, or a combination of vested interests; rather, it was the explosion of a deeply internalized process of othering communities that had received the sanction of tradition and good living over the years. This othering was all the more virulent when it involved differences that would seem to be so small that they could hardly be said to exist.

In this context, it is useful to remember Freud's prescient observation that 'the smaller the real difference between two peoples, the larger it looms in their imagination ... [I]t is precisely when external markers point towards the absence of any major differences that people act as if they are deeply divided' (Bhargava 1999: 33). Such is the case with the testament on the Partition that I would like to quote, which focuses on the seemingly trivial – yet dehumanizing – codes of inter-dining across communities:

> Such good relations we [the Sikhs] had that if there was any function then we used to call Musalmans to our homes, they would eat in our houses, but we would not eat in theirs, and this is a bad thing, which I realize now. If they would come to our houses, we would have two utensils in one corner of our house, and we would tell them, pick these up and eat in them, and they would then wash them and keep them aside and this was such a terrible thing. This was the reason Pakistan was created.
>
> (Butalia 1998: 221).

What is astonishing about such evidence is the immediacy of the voice, which enables the speaker (Bir Bahadur Singh) to make a connection between the violence embedded in the protocol of eating and the fact of Partition itself. This kind of connection – more precisely, a slippage – would be improbable in more conventional modes of historiography, where one would be obliged to work out certain causalities and patterns between the social context and the act of violence. But the evidence of the voice is more volatile, as it shifts back and forth between the memory of another time and its re-living in the present moment.

Continuing to think aloud on the shameful ways in which Muslims were treated in his village of Thoa Khalsa in the district of Rawalpindi, Bir Bahadur Singh does not spare his memories the backlash of his bitter criticism. Relating the purist constraints on the eating habits of his community to the restrictions of caste, he reflects:

> Brahmanism was there in Sikhi also, it was there and we were all caught in this dharam kanta, this dilemma that was why the hatred kept growing. ...

Brahmins have cast such spells, bound people in such devious webs that perhaps for the next hundred generations to come we will have to suffer this punishment they have made for us.   (1998: 224)

Confronting his epic sense of rage and grief with a more resigned acceptance of his own complicities in violence, Bir Bahadur acknowledges:

We were not capable of living with them. All the punishment we have had at their hands, the beatings they have given us, that is the result of all this. Otherwise real brothers and sisters don't kill and beat each other up ... [T]o hate someone so much, to have so much hate inside you for someone how can humanity forgive this?   (1999: 225)

Once again, the voice challenges any neat fixing of its interpretation, as it eddies in a vortex of memories, some of which have been articulated before, while others are surfacing for the first time.

It is to Urvashi Butalia's credit that she does not delude herself about the construction of these voices; they are not the unmediated manifestations of 'raw experience'. On the contrary, they are intensely personalized, and perhaps, at a certain level, even fictionalized accounts of 'what happened'. The task is not to retrieve an authentic 'truth' in the voice, but to examine its infinitesimal changes and contradictions, its quirks and sudden lapses into silence. *How* people remember is almost more important, and illuminating of a moment of violence, than *what* they remember. Without assuming that oral narratives can replace history, Butalia convinces us that they are capable of offering a different way of looking at history, wherein our own consciousness is shifted ever so slightly into confronting the 'moment of violence' that historiography invariably circumvents.

In his 'defence of the fragment', the subaltern historian Gyanendra Pandey has acknowledged how the history of violence in India is dutifully 'written up' as *aberration* and *absence*: aberration in the sense that 'violence is treated as something removed from the general run of Indian history', and absence in so far as 'historical discourse has experienced very great difficulty in capturing and representing the moment of violence' (Pandey 1991: 559). While Pandey attempts to push the borders of subaltern historiography, by acknowledging its singular incapacity to confront areas of pain and suffering, he is not fully prepared to betray the prerogatives of his discipline. Too restrained to acknowledge his own pain, Pandey attempts to hold on to a semblance of equanimity by avoiding, on the one hand, the extremities of 'sensationalism' and 'over-dramatization' in representing the victims of communal riots, and, on the other, the academic penchant to 'sanitize' violence, and, thereby, to 'make bland and rather more palatable what is intensely ugly and disorienting' (ibid.: 563–565).

The result is a somewhat predictable self-lacerating critique, where the 'fragments' of unacknowledged subjects are offered as an alternative to the master narratives of history determined by the state. Significantly, Pandey continues to valorize the 'fragment' in terms of what is *written* as opposed to what is *spoken*; he is more confident of drawing historical verification from, say, the poems written by a college teacher in Bhagalpur during the riots in 1989, rather than from listening to the voices of the riot victims. Unlike Butalia, who has an uncanny capacity to listen to the most harrowing oral narratives on a one-to-one basis, Pandey seems to seek refuge in the 'ritualized' renditions of a 'collective memory or record' which do not 'narrativize' suffering so much as they call attention to 'authorized accounts' of particular losses of property and destruction of homes during the riots.

Pandey, if I may venture to say, is uneasy with what I would describe as the performativity of suffering. Undeniably, this is a problematic category in so far as it would seem to aestheticize what is a profoundly painful experience that may resist any articulation in words, on the part both of the victims and of their representers as well. It is my contention that while historians are beginning to confront the discursive limits of their expertise in addressing areas of madness, pain, suffering, unreason, and while feminist writers like Butalia are opening new sensitivities to 'voice' in their rejection of impersonal, omniscient histories that seem, in Roland Barthes's words, 'to write themselves', there are still more elusive areas of psycho-physical evidence that need to be incorporated into the rewriting of history.

The gestural, the expressive, the somatic, and the kinetic dimensions of the ways in which people address their histories are what I would include in my understanding of the 'performative'. Here the point is not to seek some authentication of 'facts', but to observe the ways in which they are communicated (and dissimulated), which could very justifiably involve histrionic registers, even melodrama. The trap here is to dismiss the 'performance' of victims as 'sensational' escape-routes, instead of accepting that it is one more version of an unassimilated (and, perhaps, unassimilable) reality. One is not denying 'reality' in the process; one is merely alerting one's self to the multivalence of its construction, and to our own complicities in registering its existence.

THE PERFORMATIVITY OF SUFFERING

In positing the performativity of suffering in areas that lie outside of the confines of theatre, it is obvious that I am pushing the existing definitions of 'performance' as it registers in the Indian context. While there is a tacit acknowledgement that most politicians are actors – indeed, some of them have been film stars with a mass following – there is still a tendency to demarcate the boundaries of the 'private' and the 'public', the political persona of an actor and his or her screen image. Notions of performativity are still restricted to particular modes of histrionic representation – a rhetorical style of delivering speeches or gesticulating a particular set of signs. While this relatively 'safe' area of performativity in politics has yet to be seriously researched beyond profiles of star politicians like 'NTR' and 'MGR' (the erstwhile legendary Chief Ministers of Andhra Pradesh and Tamilnadu), there is an almost total void in addressing the performativity of public culture, and, more acutely, the ruthlessly marginalized demonstrations of grief and anger by the victims of the communalization of the state. Here again the media will call attention to, say, the public self-immolations of upper-caste students protesting against reservations – the lurid photographs of burning bodies contribute to good cover stories – but they are relatively silent about how the poor represent themselves outside of the stereotypes that have been thrust on them.

For evidence of this most difficult exposure of pain and suffering, I will turn to two fragments from the pioneering research of the sociologist Veena Das, who has investigated the rehabilitation processes of Sikh refugees recovering from the traumatic violence that was inflicted on them during the 1984 New Delhi riots. Following Indira Gandhi's assassination by two (Sikh) security guards, there was an almost immediate outburst of manipulated violence in which *gurdwaras* (Sikh temples) were attacked, Sikh houses were looted and burned to the ground, Sikh men were humiliated by having their hair cut off and beards shaved, and Sikh women were molested and raped (Das 1996: 165–166). For survivors of this frenzy of violence and for many other anguished spectators, this was the resurfacing of Partition from the seeming oblivion of its silenced memories. Now the issue was no longer the incarceration of a mass communal unconscious, it was communalism itself that was on display, flaunting its menace and threat with an almost demonic energy.

In the vast spectrum of events that constitute this outbreak of violence, there are moments of such acute pain that they defy not just the act of representation, but the very acknowledgement of their existence. One is grateful in this regard for the courageous interventions of Veena Das, among other social actors and activists, which acknowledge the 'opacity' of what is seen in the sites of rehabilitation, where fragments of communal violence continue to manifest themselves in disturbing ways.

In the two fragments that I will quote at length, the disturbance lies precisely in the dimension of performativity that Das by her own admission cannot fully fathom. While the first fragment deals with a demonstration of grief in a state of pollution that functions at the level of protest, the second is a re-enactment of violence by the survivors themselves. If in the first instance, the women reclaim their fractured subjectivities as they refuse to be 'othered', the second instance reveals an even deeper process of othering where the victims become their malevolent 'others' in a fictional state, and thereby violate themselves one more time.

FRAGMENT 1

As long as their suffering was not acknowledged and addressed, [the women] insisted on sitting outside their ruined houses, refusing to comb their hair, clean their bodies, or return to other signs of normality. Here the somatic practice drew deeply from the Hindu tradition of mourning and death pollution ... I am not claiming that this discourse was explicit – it functioned rather as an unconscious grammar, but fragments of it were evoked when the women insisted that the deaths of their men should not go unavenged. I remember one instance in which there were rumours that Mother Theresa would visit the colony. X [a politician from the Congress Party] ... implor[ed] the women to go back to their houses, to clean up the dirt and to return to some normality. They simply refused, saying he could himself sweep the remains of the disaster if that offended him.

(Das 1996: 201)

There are at least two motifs here to which Das astutely calls our attention. On the one hand, there is the collective display of bodies in a state of 'pollution', which recalls at a mythic level (and not as a 'model of imitation', as Das correctly emphasizes), the violated figure of Draupadi from the *Mahabharata*. On being violated, Draupadi refuses to remove the 'signs of pollution from her body', notably her dishevelled hair that is invariably used as the central sign of her anger (as in Kathakali performances where the hair is constantly tugged as a reminder of what has been done to her). The women described by Das are not grieving widows and victims; they are not doing what we expect them to do, as demonstrated in documentary reportage and the television news, which capitalize on the grief of others.

On the contrary, there is another kind of decision-making at work here which relates specifically to how the women wish to be seen in the eyes of the law, which in turn would prefer *not* to see them in that state. In this process, Das correctly emphasizes that the 'passive display of pollution' is so 'terrible' at one level that 'it could not even be gazed at', but this very difficulty (if not assault on the eyes) converts the 'female body into a political subject that forcibly [gives] birth to a counter-truth of the official truth about the riots' (1996: 201). The body, therefore, is not just a source of pollution; it becomes a site of political evidence.

FRAGMENT 2

[W]hile walking back we found many men in the street enacting a spectacle while they were in fits of laughter. These were the Siglikars whose kinsmen had been butchered a few months ago. The men appeared drunk and as we stood and watched, it seemed they were enacting scenes of death with snatches of dialogue from Hindi movies. The dialogue of the film *Sholay* with an angry Gabbar Singh [the villainous dacoit character] looming over his fallen victim was being enacted. A child was standing on the periphery. He said casually that the men took drugs (*goli*) every day and that they were repeating what some of the killers had said. In one particularly gory enactment, they would surround a man and poke him with a *lathi* (a wooden pole) and say, come Sardarji dance – you must have seen many dances, show us how they dance in Muscat. (Das 1996: 198)

This is the kind of evidence relating to communal violence that historians and social scientists cannot readily interpret. It is not just the inadequacy of language that is the issue here, but a fundamental lack of emotional preparation on the part of the researcher to encounter such devastating reassertions of violence, where the overt performativity actually heightens the seemingly displaced 'moment of violence' through its choreographed immediacy. Das says she was too 'terrified to stay' and watch the outcome of this performance, and she cannot be blamed, but the source of the terror as I read it is not just in the enactment of *Sholay*, which is after all a highly familiar narrative (Gabbar Singh, as played by Amjad Khan, is an oddly lovable villain). No, the source is more inexplicable: the men who are enacting the scene have been familiar to Das on a day-to-day basis in her work at the resettlement colony; now, all of a sudden, they are 'unrecognizable' (ibid.).

I can empathize with this shock of recognizing the Other in somebody you had imagined to be familiar. Even in the seemingly protected, illusory world of theatre, where transformations are part of the game, one can be shocked into recognizing total strangers, and at times menacing ones, that can emerge from the seemingly innocent bodies of actors. Thus, to get back to the image of the Other that I had described in the theatrical improvisation at the beginning of this essay, where the isolated non-verbal actor was also prodded and poked with manic glee by a horde of fellow actors, it was not possible for me to see this violence after a point. I had to stop the improvisation. This, I believe, is the significant difference between enactments of violence in theatre and in everyday life. You can stop the first; you are more likely to run away from the other.

I would not underestimate the preparation required to 'stop' communal violence even in its simulations of 'what actually happened'. Das is unable to deal with the problem, but as she puts it honestly, she is learning to confront its 'opacity'. In the process, she throws out some possible avenues of interpretation with her characteristic intelligence and analytic rigour:

Why did the bodies of the survivors reenact the somatic and speech patterns of the perpetrators? And what shall we make of the bodies of men becoming 'possessed', as the women claimed, by the fate of their dead kinsmen? And the further possession of the body by the script of a film?

(Das 1996: 198)

In Freudian terms, the scene lends itself to being interpreted through 'an identification with the aggressor'; in cultural-historical terms, it can be seen as 'an attempt to invent the symbolic order that has been lost'; and in social-experiential terms, it could illuminate the transformation of 'bodily practice from the receptive side of experience to the active side' (ibid.). While these interpretive possibilities can be regarded as an overkill of theoretical hypotheses, they can also be read as attempts to camouflage the silences that continue to resound loudly in our failure to come to terms with violence.

THE SECULAR IMAGINARY

Within the limited parameters of my theatre work, where I have never consciously sought to work with 'victims' of any particular social group, I am nonetheless struck by the embeddedness of violence in the biographies of the actors that I have dealt with in workshop situations. Most of these actors, I should stress, have been 'non-actors'. A few have been social workers by profession, who are compelled by the constraints of their academic discipline to view people as 'disadvantaged' or 'marginalized' or 'oppressed', without ever once considering that they too could be disadvantaged, marginalized, and oppressed in their own right. In my brief interactions with developmental activists and social workers who have discovered the liberatory possibilities of theatre workshops, which are invariably instrumentalized for social agendas, I have been struck – and indeed, shocked – by the staggering hiatus that exists between the sheer emotional density of the participants' interactions in slums, remand homes, prisons, orphanages, refugee centres, and their refusal to acknowledge the intimacies that colour (and complicate) the dynamics between facilitators and victims. These participants, I have realized, are professionally disabled from confronting the emotions in themselves. They are their own censors.

Within the more circumscribed area of theatre practice, where one does not consciously attempt to relate an improvisation or game to the explication of a larger problem like communalism, the irony is that one can inadvertently stumble on to some very elusive truths. The very fictionality of the theatrical idiom facilitates an illumination of some unbearably ugly realities. It is no wonder then that the theatre should be the most fertile ground for sharing secrets. In one such experiment, which emerged almost playfully during a blackout when a candle was the only source of light in the room, with the crickets and the other sounds of night in the countryside providing a somewhat eerie background to the human voices, I was taken aback by the secrets that the actors were prepared to share: first-person accounts of suicide attempts, social ostracism, divorce, a search for a lost mother in a cancer ward, even an admission of wounding a friend in a fight which could have resulted in his death. This was more than I was prepared for when I had suggested to the actors that we explore secrets, calling attention to the *trust* that we had established as a group in the course of our workshop. There is something humbling about what we sometimes receive in theatre, but it is equally necessary that we return this gift with a gesture that can approximate the specific dynamics of sharing a particular process of pain.

I would like to end this chapter by sharing one particular experience in which, I believe, there was a genuine dissolution of the dichotomies that shape the communal constructions of 'Somebody's Other'. Without celebrating the narrative of community in a mindless way, this experience resulted in a very tentative, yet concrete, realization of a secular consciousness that was viable precisely because it was not pre-determined; indeed, it emerged from out of the fragments of the communal unconscious that had surfaced in the course of the exercise.

The improvisation took place in a large room in a deserted schoolhouse in Heggodu. In one corner of the room, there was a container of water with a stainless-steel cup from which we all drank when we were thirsty. Absently, I began an innocuous exercise – a mere pretext for an intervention that I could not predict – in which the cup was transformed into other objects, such as a telephone, a microphone, a bomb. It was then that I interrupted the exercise – suddenly, inexplicably – by asking the actors whether they could believe that the cup was a *saligrama*.

What is a *saligrama*? A narrative had surfaced from my political unconscious in which I recalled one of the most potent episodes from the novel *Bharathipura* by the renowned Kannada writer, U.R. Anantha Murthy. In this fiction, a brahmin socialist, educated in England, wants to free the untouchables in his village by making them enter the temple, which is prohibited ground to them. Before doing so, however, he embarks on a secular ritual of 'de-casteing' himself, by taking out of the house a *saligrama* – a fossil-like stone, embodying the godhead, which represents the household deity. Addressing the untouchables who have assembled in the courtyard, he orders them to touch the *saligrama*. They flinch in terror because of the deeply entrenched taboo that is being challenged. Ironically, the more he attempts to convince them that the *saligrama* is merely a stone, the more its sacred aura is enhanced. Finally, in exasperation, he commands them to touch the stone, whereupon they do so – after all, for all his socialism, his feudal power cannot be questioned. As they flee in terror, he is left momentarily confused, staring at the *saligrama*, which he throws into the darkness.

'Can you believe that this cup is a *saligrama*?' In this question, I was compelled to confront the contradictions and coercive possibilities of my own intervention as a director. Through the gestures of the actors, I was exposed to an entire gamut of vulnerabilities, privileges, inclusions, exclusions, fears, desires, ecstasy. While some of the actors caressed, anointed, and genuflected before the '*saligrama*', others wanted to touch it but were unable to do so, while still others retreated from it altogether. Inevitably, the silences of caste were broken and articulated, not just through gestures but also by the revelations of biography that followed in which the low-caste actors acknowledged instances of social ostracism, humiliation, shame, and violence.

Needless to say, the 'imagined community' of the actors was shattered. Now I felt another need to intervene, but through my own fiction this time, not Anantha Murthy's. As I entered the improvisation as an actor in my own right, I thought aloud: 'This was a cup that we took for granted. We didn't even see it. Then it became a telephone, a microphone, a bomb. Then it was transformed into a *saligrama*, in which some of you believed and others didn't or couldn't. But now, when I see the cup, I realize that it is merely a container of water, which we can all share.' As we shared the cup of water in a ritual of our own making, I was compelled to ask: 'Is the cup the same as it was when we started the exercise, or is it different?' Everyone felt it was different. Having absorbed the multiple lives, histories, and above all the caste differences of the actors, the cup – and more specifically, the act of drinking from it – was charged with another, secular significance.

If this experience sounds somewhat too rhapsodic, I should add that the shadow of Somebody's Other is never entirely absent in any seeming resistance to its violence. Such was the case with the *saligrama* experience when I realized that, in another room of the seemingly deserted schoolhouse where I was working, another class was taking place without my knowledge. Another process of indoctrination was being initiated through pedagogical modes that were antithetical to what I was trying to explore in the secular space of theatre. The local boys of the village were being exposed to the extremist Hindu nationalist ideology of the RSS (the Rashtriya Swayamsevak Sangh).

It would be falsely utopic, if not downright foolish, on my part to imagine that the theatre workshop could have been shared with the RSS. Somewhere along the line, we need to protect ourselves through boundaries, both imagined and real, but perhaps, we should not allow these boundaries to harden into barriers. Rather, we need to open ourselves to other, like-minded, yet distinct frames, in whose overlapping spheres we can find those blurred spaces that bring us together. While we may not be able to entirely dismantle our constructions of the Other, we may find other ways of stretching the limits and assumptions of our secular selves.

6

THE SHIFTING SITES OF
SECULARISM

CULTURAL POLITICS AND
ACTIVISM IN INDIA TODAY

I would like to present here a series of disjunctive reflections on the relationships between cultural politics and activism, in the larger struggle and search for secularism in the increasingly communalized political context of contemporary India. I would stress the disjunctive nature of these reflections, which have emerged out of the shifts in the sites of my critical inquiry. At one level, these shifting sites reflect my need to theorize secularism with as many differences as possible – differences that are related not merely to the contentious realities of religion, but to the variables of class, caste, community, gender, and language that constitute any consideration of culture as an ideology, practice, and process of social interaction. Religion, I would contend, is one factor in the negotiation of secularism in the Indian context, but not its determining criterion.

I did, however, begin my secular journey by reflecting on 'the question of faith' (Bharucha 1993), which was my first intervention in the post-Ayodhya debate around secularism. In questioning the enigmas of faith, I was primarily interested in countering the monolithic and homogenized constructions of Hindutva, thereby challenging the right assumed by Hindu fundamentalists and communal politicians to interpret matters of religion for their own communities and for society at large. My strategy was to 'meet them on their ground' through a reading of the ambivalence, multivalence, and contradiction to be found in varied Hindu religious sites and experiences. While this strategy continues to be valid, it is incomplete and somewhat reductive, in so far as it risks the false universalization of an essentially tolerant Hindu faith, in which all differences can be accommodated.

Today, there has been a shift in my thinking since I wrote *The Question of Faith*, and I now feel that it is equally necessary that 'they' should meet 'us' on 'our' grounds as well. But what are these grounds? And how can we speak of them as 'our' grounds, when secular constituencies are known to be not just differentiated, but divided and even sectarian in their individual orientations, agendas, and struggles? These are some of the questions underlying my most recent critical intervention *In the Name of the Secular* (Bharucha 1998), which attempts to historicize different readings and practices of secularism within the framework of cultural activism in India today. Instead of summarizing the argument of this book, my purpose here is to risk articulating what did not get theorized in its mapping of the secular – precisely those shifts and disjunctions in an emergent secularist discourse and practice that are not easily accommodated within the established categories and agendas of secularism. As one pushes the boundaries of what remains unnamed and unwritten about secularism, one is alerted to the task that lies ahead in theorizing secularism not merely as a political ideology but as an everyday critical life-practice.

Let us begin with some contentions and working propositions around secularism, which can help us to think through some of its imbrications within the larger narratives and realities of communalism, multiculturalism, and globalization.

POSITIONING SECULARISM

1

While secularism is pitted against communalism – this opposition cannot (indeed, should not) be diffused – secularism should not be equated with anti-communalism, because that would be the surest way of allowing its possibilities to be determined and reduced by the Other. Instead, I would suggest that the concept of secularism needs to be opened to include those components of everyday life relating to the respect for, if not toleration of, differences. There is an obvious risk here of dilating the concept of the secular, but this risk is worth encountering in order to democratize the discourse around secularism, instead of allowing it to close in on itself. Secularism needs to be interrogated from several vantage points, instead of being hegemonized within any one constituency. The concept needs to be filled, fleshed out, embodied, with different investments and languages, before one can hope to arrive at any distillation of its meaning(s). The challenge is to sustain one's critical inquiry into the secular without allowing it to be reduced to an essentially defensive reaction to the communal threat. Secularism, in short, should not be othered by communalism.

2

I often ask myself: Before I became politicized as a secularist, what was I? Was I not secular? Indeed, I was so secular that I never once had to think about it. Such was my privileged amnesia. Instead of functioning as an ideology, this nascent secularism was, at best, an attitude to the worldliness of everyday life that celebrated, at very unconscious levels, the diversities that constitute the multicultural society of India. This attitude may have been naive, ensconced within the cosmopolitan privileges of class, education, and culture, but it was not without its uses. Today, I ask myself: How does one retrieve critically, politically, and not just nostalgically, those components of worldliness in one's earlier assumptions of the secular?

This retrieval of worldliness necessitates a more inflected reading of multiculturalism in the Indian context, which is more often than not taken for granted, assumed as a norm rather than investigated as an ideology or practice. No reading of secularism in the Indian context can afford to ignore the subtleties, gradations, and densities of cultural differences in the Indian subcontinent. What is urgently needed in this context, as indicated earlier in the book, is a sustained critique of the politics of diversity upheld by the state, which has mindlessly propagated an aura of multiculturalism in India, while regimenting and dividing cultures on regional grounds, more often than not with the active support of a regional, brahminized, patriarchal elite. Diversities, which are invariably invoked to conjure a mythic 'unity', cannot be assumed to constitute a plurality. Our secularism in India has to work towards a more interactive plurality, instead of seeking an essentially illusory comfort in our eminently quantifiable, if insufficiently mobilized, diversities.

3

Secularist discourse in India has been interrupted through the incursions of globalization. Polemically inscribed within critiques of development, without being sufficiently analysed at cultural levels, globalization is associated almost synonymously with the new economic policies of the Indian government, which are attempting to promote a notion of liberalization under the dictates of the World Bank, the IMF, GATT, and TRIPs. This is one agenda, as I have indicated in Chapter 1, that has the potential to bring together the most diverse secular groups and activists in opposition to the anti-democratic agencies of global capitalism that are working against, if not destroying, the possibilities of social justice in underprivileged contexts.

While social justice remains the primary principle around which political secularism is being propagated in India today, it should inform cultural practice as well. A dialogic base for the propagation of secular culture can emerge only through an engagement with the diverse struggles for social justice, which should not be reduced to a mechanistic and essentially opportunistic slogan to promote vested interests in the name of protecting minority rights. Secularism, in short, cannot be separated from the systematic erosion of social justice and human rights through the invasion of global capitalism in India today.

SHIFTING THE GROUNDS OF SECULARISM

With all these multiple narratives and realities of communalism, multiculturalism, and globalization, which jostle, collide, and occasionally converge on one another, it is not surprising that the sites of secularism as outlined in this chapter should be dispersed. Instead of attempting to synthesize the rifts *between* the sites – a falsely utopic endeavour – I have focused on the shifts operating *within* them. I have come to regard these shifts as tremors, the unconscious manifestations of the instability inherent within the concept of secularism itself, in so far as it is possible to posit *an* entity like 'secularism' within the larger spectrum of its contradictions and confusions, vulnerabilities and possibilities.

The instability of secularism in India today should not be regarded as a limitation of its political pertinence and efficacy. Rather, it can be viewed more accurately as a point of departure for articulating those emergent meanings and practices of the secular that lie outside of the moribund prescriptions provided by the state – notably, *dharmanirapeksata* ('impartiality to religion') and *sarva dharma sama bhava* ('equal respect for all religions'), which seem to have displaced an earlier, more literal, yet open usage of 'secular' – *laukik* ('of this world'). Retrieving the connotations of worldliness in this word, I would like to reinflect the dominant categories of secularism, by consciously shifting my sight away from the overdetermined political sites of secularism in order to call attention to those areas of everyday life in which the secular is beginning to resonate through what is fragmented, emergent, processual, ordinary, and unnamed. These are my key-words in the search for the secular.

Why these key-words? Why this shift in sight? This may sound grandiose, but if India has survived '6 December' and the worst communal riots engineered since Partition, this cannot be attributed entirely to the constitutional inviolability of secularism, precious as it may be as one of the primary foundations of the Indian nation-state. There is no point in being falsely reverent about the abuse of secularism by politicians across parties, particularly by the votaries of the Hindu Right who have had the audacity to condemn the 'pseudo-secularism' of others. If India has survived '6 December', as indeed it has, one should acknowledge that the basic principles of secularism as a life-practice, involving the respect for and toleration of differences, have been internalized by a vast spectrum of its citizens, perhaps at very inchoate, inarticulate, unconscious, yet concrete levels, independently of any knowledge of the Constitution. And these principles are being practised and activized in the most communally afflicted neighbourhoods, by the least recognized citizens of the Indian state. If these gestures of ordinary people are not always acknowledged in theories of secularism, this is not the fault of secularism as such, but of the strictures determining its official and academic agendas and criteria.

NAMING SECULARISM

Ironically – and tellingly – it is in the locations most marked by division and violence, that one can find emergent sites of what is euphemistically described as 'communal harmony' by the agencies of the state and a wide spectrum of activists as well. Here one confronts the enigmatic reality that the actions conducted in these sites may not be named as secular. Indeed, the indeterminate relationship between the activization of secularism and the naming of it, contributes to the larger instability of its conceptualization. When one learns, for example, of Hindu and Muslim slum-dwellers in the aftermath of the Mumbai riots, engaged collectively in rebuilding the damaged homes and shrines of their neighbourhood, it is difficult not to describe these interactions as secular. And yet, it could be argued that these interactions may not be conceptualized or named as secular by their agents.

This situation compels one to question whether concepts always have to be named before being realized. Or can they not, as in the case of *satyagraha*,[1] for example, follow a specific practice? The name can almost become, in such instances, an arbitrary appendage. Moving away from the philosophical problems of such a conjecture, I would emphasize that the political task of naming concepts like secularism cannot be indefinitely postponed. At the risk of essentialization, one is compelled to name a concept around which a struggle has emerged, and without which it cannot be sustained. This is not merely a case of 'strategic' essentialization, as in Gayatri Spivak's (1985) critical endorsement of the category 'subaltern'; nor is it entirely a matter of 'arbitrary closure', without which the 'articulation' of politics is not possible, as Stuart Hall (1986, 1988) has forcefully pointed out in his resistance to the postmodern deferral of meanings, and its now predictable capacity to reduce all reality into discourse.

Naming secularism, as Pradip Datta has emphasized within the contradictions of the post-Ayodhya political context, is no less critical than 'the struggle for the authorization of its use' (1997). Within the chaos of the appropriations surrounding the rhetoric of secularism, the accusations and counter-charges of 'pseudo-secularism' and 'genuine' secularism, accompanied by the multilingualism of secularism that has yet to be accounted for in the hegemonic uses of English and Hindi as the dominant languages of secularism, the task of naming secularism is fraught with the deepest tensions, presumptions, and risks. The silences around practices that have yet to be named as secular add further dimensions to the epistemological complexity of the problem. Indeed, one can safely assume that there can be no 'ontological purity' (ibid.) attached to the naming of the secular after '6 December.'

And yet, it would seem politically necessary to embrace the tensions of naming secularism, however imperfectly, instead of surrendering to the vacillations of being neither secular nor communal. At one level, this apparent no man's land, marked by the hyphen in the secular-communal question, would seem to accommodate ambivalence, but it can also be used to legitimize anti-secularist acts, which assume a semblance of normalcy, as they are forgiven, forgotten, absorbed, and incorporated within the contradictions of everyday life.

To assume, for instance, that the assailants who had participated in the destruction of the Babri Masjid are essentially 'misguided youths', the kind who do not come across as communal in everyday life, is to legitimize the most seemingly 'spontaneous', yet insidious, violence, on the grounds that its determinants and agencies cannot be fixed. To argue further that there can be no divide between secularism and communalism, because no one is entirely secular or communal, or, conversely, that we are all capable of being communal and secular at the same time, does not remove the responsibility of identifying some fundamental distinctions between 'secular' and 'communal' in the first place. Some borderlines need to be posited whereby, despite prejudices and even intolerances of other communities, which could be racial, religious, or cultural, the violation of anyone's person, interest, or sentiment that is perceived to be culturally inferior, invasive, or threatening, should be identified as communal. The fact that this perception of other communities could be a *mis*perception, engineered by communal and fundamentalist agencies, does not erase its violence.

As an aside, it would be useful here to draw some cross-cultural insights on the discriminations by which 'racism' is now identified in multicultural discourse:

> To see the world through the lenses provided by one's own culture is not necessarily racist, nor is it racist simply to notice physical or cultural differences, or to detest specific members of a group, or even to dislike the cultural traits of specific groups. What is racist is the stigmatizing of difference in order to justify unfair advantage or the abuse of power, whether that advantage or abuse be economic, political, cultural, or psychological.   (Shohat and Stam 1994: 22)

While the borderlines between 'racism' and 'communalism' are very fine in the Indian context, contextualized within specific social contexts and religio-cultural histories where minorities and foreigners are marked in distinct ways,[2] it is useful to regard the 'stigmatizing of difference' as the ground on which 'communal' and 'racial' discourses can meet. Whether the target is another 'race' or another 'religious community', the violence ultimately lies in a demeaning of the Other. This process of inferiorization, however, may not always be explicit. As Stuart Hall (1981) has pointed out, racism can also be 'inferential', consisting in 'those apparently naturalised representations of events and situations ... which have racist premises and propositions inscribed in them as a set of unquestioned assumptions' (quoted in Shohat and Stam 1994: 23).

Likewise, communalism can be inscribed or implied or suggested in the most seemingly secular of situations. The challenge is to identify its violence through the masquerade of normalcy. If implicit communalism has not been a priority in the numerous studies of communal violence in the Indian context, the reason may be that the dominant narratives of communalism have focused, not unjustifiably, on the 'big events' – riots, insurrections, killings, pogroms, the manufacture of rumours. It is a truism, however, to acknowledge that when a riot subsides, communalism does not disappear. Rather, it goes underground, it becomes invisible, it enters other realities through subterranean passages, it infiltrates the most ordinary of conversations. For example:

'You have a beard. You must be an intellectual.'
'Well, actually, I've been mistaken for a terrorist.'
'Ah ... It's a good thing that you haven't been mistaken for a Muslim.'

The uncanny swiftness by which an 'intellectual' can metamorphose into a 'Muslim' via the mediation of a 'terrorist' – all in the course of a perfectly light-hearted conversation in which my beard was the subject of conversation – indicates the interstices of the communal unconscious at work. I would now like to elaborate on these interstices within the larger social context of Site 1.

SITE 1

The location: *Calcutta.*

The place: *A neighbourhood cinema hall, frequented by a predominantly male, working-class community and unemployed youth. This is an intimate secular space where the spectators assert their right to feel entirely 'at home' – they can stretch their legs on the seat in front, chew paan (betel leaf), spit, eat, talk, fight. This is also a space where they have paid hard-earned money to dream, fantasize, and 'time-pass'.*

The provocation: *A documentary on the Lai Haraoba, one of the most ancient and vibrant of religious festivals celebrated in Manipur, which brings together a rich conglomeration of fertility rituals, agricultural rites, shamanic trances, ancestor worship, enactments of the origins of creation, etc.*

The situation: *Barely minutes after the film starts, there is a restlessness in the audience – at one level understandable, given the unfamiliarity of the material. One would expect whistles, comments, and generally rowdy behaviour. This restlessness is different: it gets consolidated in an extraordinarily swift passage of time into a collective derision – a derision that is directed not against the film, but more specifically, against those funny-looking, slant-eyed aliens in the film, whose mongoloid appearance and strange language are subjected to racial abuse. The situation becomes so charged with resentment that the entire hall is transformed into a site of communal violence: 'us' against 'them.' If the man-agement had not stopped the film, the audience (now beginning to function like a mob) would have vandalized the theatre.*

Any such fragment of experience is vulnerable to critical scrutiny. I am aware of the partiality and the subjectivity of my description even through the cryptic objectivity of its idiom. It could be argued that I am strategically withholding information – for example, the religious constitution of the neighbourhood – for the simple reason that I resist the description of any collectivity in a secular space like a cinema hall in terms of 'religious community'.[3] It could even be suggested that I am inventing a fiction here, something that did not really happen. The site is entirely made up. In answer to these charges, I will not attempt to defend my 'truth', but will try to problematize the issues emanating from the site, which I would like to use as a take-off point in order to reflect on the failures of secularization and the resistances to the sharing of cultural differences in India today.

First of all, the transformation of the cinema hall into a site of violence, needs to be contextualized within codes of spectatorship in cinema. The fragment I have described would seem to reverse all conjectures relating to 'spectatorial schizophrenia' (Shohat and Stam 1994: 347). This condition has been specifically related in multicultural film studies to those colonial situations where 'we' (in the former colonies) have empathized with those figures that are the products of racist and orientalist strategies. (The problematic affinities of young black audiences in the Antilles to the archetypal figure of Tarzan, as indicated by Frantz Fanon, and Bertolt Brecht's admission that his 'heart was touched' by the Indian traitor Gunga Din, are just two archetypal examples of how 'cultural aliens' can become subjects of identification. This process of identification, however, can be ruptured within the politics of a different location. A black spectator, for instance, is less likely to identify with Tarzan in a cinema in Paris than in a movie theatre at home [ibid: 348, 351].)

The situation of the fragment discussed above, however, is radically different, in so far as the 'aliens' in question are functioning within a national imaginary (more specifically, within the documentary space of an Indian News Review), and they are being *rejected* through a process of being othered. What we have here is not a demonstration of 'schizophrenia', where the audience is 'split' and therefore compelled to negotiate dual value-systems through a dialogic process, but rather, an affirmation of monoculturalism ('our' culture) that ultimately rejects seeing the Other: therein lies the violence of the encounter. The 'refusal of empathy' by which racism is legitimized (Shohat and Stam 1994: 23), need not be restricted to colonial situations of struggle and oppression, where the underdog is denied sympathy. In a neo-colonial nationalist context as well, one can refuse to empathize with another culture's joy, and that can be a violence in its own right.

This is one dimension of the site that can lend itself to being interpreted within a cinematic context. But there is more that needs to be probed in a wider social context, not so much in relation to *why* it happened, but *how* such situations are actually made possible *by default* through the failures of secularization in India. I believe that this is a more viable way of approaching the problem of 'communal behaviour', instead of surrendering uncritically to a primordialist reading of a lumpenized mass, in whom the demon of communalism always lurks. Countering such readings, we can now draw on an increasingly wide and authoritative body of research on communalism, in which we learn how extremist right-wing organizations like the RSS have systematically hegemonized a 'common sense' around the basic principles of Hindutva since the mid-1920s (see Basu *et al.* 1993 for a fuller description). Clearly, communalism is not an arbitrary upsurge of inexplicably irrational feelings directed against other communities. Hindu communalism in particular has been built, constructed, inscribed, rhetoricized, consolidated, in and through the political and civic structures of everyday life.

In contrast, the processes of secularization in contemporary India would seem to be more arbitrary, if not chaotic. By 'secularization', I am referring here primarily to those measures adopted by the State and civic institutions in relation to education, health care, gender justice, democratic and accountable decision-making at local levels, that function independently of religious hierarchies, taboos, and priorities. Sadly, after fifty years of independence, these processes have proved to be diffused, disparate, contradictory, and incomplete to the extent that one needs to acknowledge that secularization's failures contribute to the upsurge of communalism, and not (as anti-modernist, anti-enlightenment, anti-secularist critics would like us to believe) that secularism itself is responsible for communalism through its innate insensitivity to the indigenous cultures and value-systems of people.

At the risk of generalization, I will now outline four areas of failure in the larger process of secularization.

FAILURES OF SECULARIZATION

1

The sense of belonging to a larger entity called the nation cannot be assumed. It has to be nurtured through processes of communication across different ethnicities and cultural groups. Instead of being marked, sealed, bordered, hierarchized, and regionalized, our cultural diversities need to be mobilized and exchanged on an ongoing basis. Then only is it possible to circumvent insularity, chauvinism, and an exclusionary sense of difference that works against the interactive and dialogic possibilities of a secular culture.

Returning to the site described earlier, I would venture to hypothesize that there was nothing in the world of the audience rejecting the Lai Haraoba that enabled them to have access to any knowledge or information about this festival. In the absence of any symbols, images, experience, or interaction relating to Manipur, this audience, I would suggest, had no frame of reference by which they could displace their construction of these imagined 'aliens', who are, in actuality, our neighbours and fellow-citizens from the north-eastern state of Manipur, which has a distinct cultural, religious, and linguistic legacy. Underlying this hypothesis is the undeniable fact that the State has failed to provide its citizens with a basic knowledge of other cultures within its borders. I would take it further and make a more provocative allegation that the State has failed to imagine the nation in all its multicultural diversity. The 'nation' that has been supposedly imagined has excluded a wide range of 'other' cultures, which have been merely slotted within the map of Indian cultural diversity, without being respected for their intrinsic particularities. In fact, some of these 'other' cultures are marked as 'lesser' cultures, their border status aligned with the political realities of secessionism and insurgency.

In the absence of adequate infrastructures for what I have described in the earlier chapters of this book as 'intracultural' exchange – the exchange of cultures between, within, and across regions in the larger framework of the nation – and in the total indifference to the activization of the 'translation of cultures' in a rampantly multilingual society, the state's assumptions of 'diversity' have atrophied within the spectre of an assumed 'unity', resulting in divisiveness between cultures.

2

One of the primary agencies of secularization in any society is education. In fact, the fundamental principle on which Benedict Anderson (1983) has built his influential, though to my mind relatively uncontested, thesis of the 'imagined community' of the nation, rests on the propagation of print-capitalism, by which people across regions within a particular geographic space develop bonds that transcend local commitments. There are some empirical lacunae in Anderson's thesis that restrict its applicability in the Indian context.

Print-capitalism assumes 'the power of mass literacy and its attendant large-scale production of projects of ethnic affinity' (Appadurai 1997: 28). In a country like India where *illiteracy* remains the reality for more than half the adult population, can the nation be 'imagined' when the act of reading (individually and across groups) cannot be assumed, when the collective experience of belonging to a larger entity called the nation remains fractured at sub-nationalist, if not secessionist, levels? Calling attention to the dismal failure of basic education in India, at levels which can only be compared with the poorest of countries in sub-Saharan Africa, the economists Jean Dreze and Amartya Sen (1996: 109–139) have made a powerful case for its relationship to the deprivation of 'social opportunity'. Indeed, the activization of social justice, as advocated by the proponents of political secularism in India, remains severely restricted for millions of people, notably two-thirds of the entire population of women, who are unable to read their own land deeds (*pattas*) or ration cards, or to identify the number on a bus. Not only does this illiteracy undermine their participation in the decision-making processes of democracy at ground and state levels, it continues to ensure their dependency on upper-caste/class patriarchies and religious orthodoxies that would prefer to leave them in a state of ignorance.

At a more complex level, one would need to question whether 'the nation' can be imagined through the multilingual trajectories of several print-cultures that are sharply contextualized within specific ethnicities that collide rather than merge into a framework of affinities. Anderson's underpinnings of print-capitalism, it should be noted, are intrinsically monolingual. In contrast, the politics of multilingualism in India has persistently contradicted any attempt by the state to impose one language, so much so that the turbulent debates around Hindi-Hindustani-Urdu in the pre-independence struggle, and the anti-Hindi assertions of Tamil-speaking groups, for example, in post-independence India, totally counter the neat thesis of imagining the nation through any one language. Apart from the very real complications of working through as many as eight dominant scripts in India, there is no collective will to adopt the national language as a mother-tongue, as was the case with *bahasa Indonesia* (which was self-consciously invented and disseminated as the national language of Indonesia in 1928).[4]

In India, such a process has not emerged and is not likely to evolve, even with the increased dissemination of Hindi as a national language through the mass media. The process of secularization has obviously worked through multiple linguistic tracks, which exist almost independently of each other, with little or no translation of the differences underlying the specific secularizations of Indian languages, which have developed at very different speeds and intensities. This is a massively uninterrogated area in secularist research, to the extent that the very word 'secular' has vastly different significations within the spectrum of Indian languages. In the absence of an interlingual reading of secularism, the use of English and Hindi as the dominant languages of secularism has now been hegemonized – a reality that has greatly estranged a great many users of the so-called 'regional languages' from the concept of secularism itself.

3

If the State has failed to activate intracultural understanding across diverse communities, this can be directly linked to the abdication of its right and responsibility to secularize society through a democratic control of the media. The ideals of the late 1960s in instrumentalizing the process of development through television never got off the ground. Despite the implicit nationalist context of the promotion of satellite technology for television in 1969, spearheaded by one of the pioneers of India's space research programme, Dr Vikram Sarabhai, followed by the institution of the Satellite Instructional Television Experiment (SITE) in 1975 – see Rajadhyaksha (1990) for a trenchant contextualization of India's burgeoning television culture in the mid-1970s – we have seen in recent years a most abject surrender of the State to, if not a collusion with, the global television networks. Before a national television culture could develop with adequate funding and expertise, it has been decimated, to my mind, by the State itself, so that today we have to seek national credibility and representation through the mediation of global media agencies, for whom India is not a priority.

Clearly, when the commodification of First World imaginaries is being disseminated by foreign television networks to audiences who continue to be denied the basic necessities of life, we have come a long way from the early promises of Dr. Sarabhai. As a nationalist, he had envisioned television as an ideal means of disseminating information to 'the broad masses of people, particularly to the illiterate section of the population' on subjects like 'new fertiliser, seeds, insectidices, cropping patterns, new technology, new findings and discoveries in all fields, new goods and services, new living patterns' (quoted in Rajadhyaksha 1990: 35) – in short, basic resources and modes of knowledge applicable to the secularization of a 'developing' society at ground levels.

What we have today on television are imaginary utopias (see Bharucha 1998: 168–171) that are at once unaffordable and decontextualized from the realities of people's lives. The primary critique of the 'cultural invasion' by the foreign networks should not be based, to my mind, on the fear of contamination; rather, it should be rooted in an awareness of the disruption of social ecology and the fundamental injustice relating to the global dissemination of information in the world, at the expense of heightening a knowledge of local cultures within a national context. What we confront today on the foreign networks is nothing less conspicuous than our *absence* as a people in the map of the world, except in the context of disasters, plagues, riots, and the occasional miracle. In the meanwhile, our knowledge of the life-styles relating to *Baywatch* or to the developments of the European Union increases, but we continue to remain ignorant about what is happening at cultural levels in our neighbouring states or within the boundaries of our own state.

This manufacture of ignorance, legitimized by the State in its liberalizing affinities to the global networks (despite its occasionally sanctimonious affirmations of 'our' autonomy), has contributed decisively to the growing indifference to 'other' cultures *within* the boundaries of India. And 'indifference', as I shall indicate below, has a communal potential that should not be ignored.

4

If the state, the education system, and the media have not succeeded in mobilizing a knowledge of other cultures through a respect for cultural differences, one cannot fall back on the narrative of community to compensate for the failures of the state. Suffice it to say at this point that the narrative of community is invariably so self-enclosed and self-referential that it is the least likely resource to provide a knowledge of *other* cultures. When anti-modernist/ anti-secularist critics like Ashis Nandy (1988) have turned to traditional cultures to retrieve non-sectarian, universal values of tolerance and coexistence, uncontaminated by the hegemonistic categories of science and the state, they invariably fail to *account* for the *a priori* claims of universality and eternal wisdom assumed by cultural traditions. Javeed Alam puts it accurately when he claims that the pluralist claims of religious traditions, as interpreted by anti-secularists, do not stand up to external, democratic critical criteria, because they are 'embedded in a mode of questioning that is wholly *internal to the presuppositions of the tradition*' (Alam 1994: 24). While 'tradition' within a society can be marked by 'diversity', 'pluralism' is a 'post-enlightenment result born of struggles for democracy' (ibid.: 23).

To present a more inflected resistance to the narrative of community, let us consider the possibility that a certain degree of indifference to other cultures, particularly in a society as prodigiously diverse as the Indian subcontinent, may be a perfectly viable way of conducting one's life. Indifference to other cultures is not necessarily anti-secularist. Indeed, it could be argued that it is neither necessary nor desirable to interact with all the cultural diversities within our respective locations, something that is, indeed, a practical impossibility. Moreover, one could argue in a nativist mode that this thirst for other cultures can be attributed to a certain culturelessness, a rootlessness, that seems to afflict westernized, metropolitan seekers of cultural diversity, whose eclecticism is a mere mimicry of the kind of narcissistic interculturalism that I have critiqued in my earlier writings on theatre, as well as a surrender to the more disturbing manifestations of 'cultural tourism'.

Having acknowledged these tendencies, it is necessary not to make a virtue out of cultural self-sufficiency, which has become the norm in certain readings of 'Indian culture', where the assumed commitment to pre-colonial, non-western, indigenous, local – therefore, authentic – cultures, more often than not serves as a masquerade for upholding the vested interests of a regional, brahminized elite. The hegemony of 'regional culture', in which tribal and *dalit* cultures are conveniently subsumed with no adequate representation, is justified on the grounds that it is resistant to the homogenizing influences of nationalism and globalization. Perhaps, the situation is more contradictory than nativist critics are prepared to acknowledge. One should emphasize that there is a very thin line between upholding cultural self-sufficiency and legitimizing regional parochialism (what Gandhi himself, the greatest advocate of *swaraj* ['self-rule'], characterized as 'frogs croaking in a pond'). Likewise, there is a tenuous border between accepting indifference to other cultures as a secular mode of life and developing an implicit intolerance for any culture that does not correspond to one's assumed norms.

With these programmatic comments on the failures of secularization at the levels of the state, education, the media, and community, we can now address some of the more recent incursions of globalization in the field of culture, and return to the residual hold of patriarchy in the communitarian structures of traditional cultures. The difficulties of articulating secularism in India today cannot be fully grasped without a surrender to the clashes of several contexts. It would be an axiom in this regard to say that in India we live in several times, but these times (of globalization, and of surviving pre-modern cultures) are imbricated in deeply turmoiled, emergent processes of disruption and change. Let us turn now to Site 2 in which some of these processes can be traced.

SITE 2

The location: *A neighbourhood in Imphal, Manipur.*

The occasion: *Lai Haraoba.*

The performance space: *An open courtyard.*

The event: *The 'secular items' in the Lai Haraoba. Inserted in a prescribed space within the larger rituals of the Lai Haraoba, they are watched by the*

entire neighbourhood, which comes together to enjoy a variety entertainment
programme that combines an informal community get-together with a local
talent contest.

The first item is performed by a young girl, who is dressed not as the
Vaishnavite saint Chaitanya Mahaprabhu (which is one of the most auspicious
roles for any young female performer in Manipur), but more like the Hindi
film star Madhuri Dixit. The girl regales the audience with a dance-rendition
of Choli ke peeche kya hai? ('What's behind the blouse?'). The number goes
down well, and there are no problems whatsoever with its sexist content.

The provocation: *A young man enters the performance arena dressed in blue*
jeans and T-shirt. He bows formally, and then, to a deafening blast of Michael
Jackson's 'Beat it', he begins to dance with a vigorous, uninhibited, secular
assertion of energy that is not just sexual, but driven by anger and defiance.
The underlying self-affirmation of the young man's dance is perceptible, and
the crowd is with him.

But – *censorship prevails. All the organizers of the Lai Haraoba, middle-aged*
or old men, interrupt the performance in a flurry of white dhotis. They are like
fussy old hens, clucking with disapproval. In the spirit of secularism, there are
loud demands from the audience for the dance to continue. 'Beat it' is resumed,
only to be cut for the second time. And this time there can be no negotiation as
the organizers stop the show with formal announcements on the microphone.
The secular items are abandoned, and the spectators disperse, revealing an
empty site.

There are a number of 'takes' on this fragment, which are at once imbricated
and yet distinct. History has obviously intervened in the traditional and
sanctified space of the Lai Haraoba, which has been opened to the dual processes
of modernization and secularization. This opening has emerged not through a
process of organic evolution, but through the popular demands made on the Lai
Haraoba by its spectators, who are also the participants and the producers of the
festival, in so far as it is through their support and donations that the festival can
continue its seemingly ageless legacy. This kind of secularization of religious
festivals is, perhaps, even more marked in the metropolitan locations of India,
whose political cultures influence and condition traditional festivity in specific
ways – for example, the 'saffronization' of Shiv Jayanti or Ganesh Chaturthi in
Maharashtra (see Bharucha 1998: 149–150, for some glimpses of Shiv Sena
religiosity), or the Pujas in Calcutta, which continue to draw on social themes
appealing to the sentiments of *bhadralok* (gentrified) marxism.

The process of secularization in the specific site of the Lai Haraoba
mentioned above, however, is not merely fed through local needs and regional
politics; it is also stimulated by the seemingly arbitrary 'flows' (to use Arjun
Appadurai's term) of global cultural traffic. Hence, along with the inscription of
Madhuri Dixit from the national imaginary of commercial Hindi cinema, one
also encounters a simulation of the ultimate icon of global entertainment,

Michael Jackson. Why the pre-pubescent impersonation of Dixit should escape censorship while the Manipuri 'Jackson' is interrupted, could reveal deeply complicated layers of sexual hypocrisy in the transmission of Indian popular culture, where obscenity in cinema can pass as family entertainment. My purpose here is not to probe these particular layers, but, as in my earlier analysis of Site 1, to contextualize a fragment of experience within the larger problematic of the secularization of cultures in India today. In this site, I will focus on the heated agenda surrounding the globalization of 'Indian culture' – its economic dimensions and relationship to nationalism, its effects on the production of new subjectivities; and, more tangentially, on the continuing stranglehold of patriarchy in regulating the process of secularization at local levels in the preservation of traditional cultures.

CONTEXTUALIZING GLOBALIZATION

Any perspective on the globalization of 'Indian culture' would need to be contextualized within the specific immediacies of a postcolonial nation-state, which has celebrated a mere fifty years of independence, at a time when the nation-state is being dismissed as a redundancy in a state of 'terminal' crisis (Appadurai 1997: 169). As diasporic intellectuals in the First World are increasingly drawn to 'transnations' and as yet undefined states 'beyond the nation', a construct like post-nationalism is perhaps only valid within the emergence of 'diasporic public spheres', as represented in the cultural theory of Arjun Appadurai (1997). Within the fractious contradictions of political society in India, post-nationalism is at best a utopic construction. With all the failures, oppressions, corruption, and inefficiency of the nation-state, we may have no other option but to work within *and against* its parameters.

This is precisely the point that has been made forcefully by Partha Chatterjee (1997) in his critical response to the post-national thrust of Appadurai's dismissal of the nation-state as 'a viable long-term arbiter of the relationship between globality and modernity' (Appadurai 1997: 19). Chatterjee calls attention to the emergence of 'political society' in postcolonial India (as opposed to 'civil society' in the colonial period), in which all kinds of mobilization are at work through parties, movements, and non-party political formations, out of which 'new democratic forms of the modern state' are being articulated and debated outside the post-enlightenment paradigms of the 'secularized Christian world' (Chatterjee 1997: 33). In this context of the ongoing struggles by large sections of the population, and not just by marginal representatives of the urban elite, the 'proposals to move "beyond the nation"', as Chatterjee emphasizes, can only 'strengthen inequalities and defeat the struggle for democracy the world over' (ibid.: 34).[5]

Tellingly, the critique of globalization in India is compelled to work through the contradiction of retaining, if not defending, the epistemological terrain of the nation-state, while fighting its tyrannies and complicities with global agendas. Activists of people's movements have been compelled to negotiate more than one tactic or strategy in this regard *vis-à-vis* the State: from outright opposition; issue-based collaborations on specific projects; pressurizing the State to fulfil its promises; distancing oneself from state agendas; marginalizing the State through one's own agendas. In all these manoeuvres, the State is never entirely erased from the processes of struggle, and certainly, it would be facetious, if not downright arrogant, to place one's commitments 'beyond the nation', when the nation itself is in such peril, if not vulnerable in its making.

As a construct, therefore, post-nationalism is best viewed as a particularly privileged reading of the diaspora, whose links to the agendas of global capitalism are unproblematically assumed. Thus, in the exhilarating, yet numbing sweep of Arjun Appadurai's diasporic field of vision, one is struck by the ease with which the predicament of refugees, for instance, can be placed within the same 'post-national order' as 'transnational, philanthropic movements', 'international terrorist organizations', and even 'international fashion' (Appadurai 1997: 167). This mode of juxtaposing the displacement of refugees with the 'transnational assemblages' of the world of fashion is not simply a matter of 'disjuncture' (as Appadurai would stress); it is in effect another homogenization of conflicting realities, in which the struggles of one reality (refugees) and the fiction of another (fashion) are flattened out, leaving little or no trace of the economic and political *contexts* of difference.

At an economic level, Appadurai uses the concept of 'disjuncture' without any confrontation of the violence of global capitalism in relation to mass unemployment, the marketing and patenting of biodiversity, the destruction of natural resources and environments that I had indicated earlier in the book. This erasure of such extreme realities in the economic propagation of globalization reduces the concept of 'disjuncture' to a liberalizing, if somewhat chaotic principle of cultural interaction. Appadurai would have us believe that 'the new global cultural economy has to be seen as a complex, overlapping, disjunctive order that cannot any longer be understood in terms of existing centre–periphery models; nor models of surpluses and deficits, consumers and producers' (1997: 33). What exist instead are symptoms of 'disorganized capitalism' (Lash and Urry 1987), from which it would seem as if the new economic global order is not that hegemonistic after all.

The realities of global capitalism in India reveal that it is a lot more organized, centralized, non-negotiable, and hegemonistic than earlier modes of capitalism. In the sober estimate of one of India's leading economists, C.T. Kurien, we learn:

Global markets are not free; global prices are determined by those who control resources and markets; many of them set prices to suit their own interests with very little relationship to the cost of production. There are many barriers to entry into markets and into production; knowledge and information are not widely diffused – they are controlled, distorted, and hidden to promote one's advantage and profits.   (Kurien 1994: 90)

Keeping in mind Kurien's sound advice that the world around us is not necessarily 'what some theories want us to believe', it needs to be stressed that the inequalities of global capitalism cannot be dissociated from those determining global cultural 'flows'. This is a fundamental axiom that should inform any study of the cultural dimensions of globalization in the Indian context.

MICHAEL JACKSON: SIMULATION AND REALITY

With this axiom in mind, let us turn now to the figure of Michael Jackson, as it was simulated by the young Manipuri dancer in the context of the 'secular items' in the Lai Haraoba. At one level, it is possible to read his 'body-culture' as a search for a new subjectivity: a subjectivity that needs to be viewed within the context of an oppressive present, to which he is linked, to which he is resistant, and out of which he wants to find another language to express himself. One of the most searing sights that any *mayang* ('foreigner', 'outsider') from India is likely to encounter in Manipur – the irony that a citizen of India can be regarded as a foreigner in one of its states should not be lost here – is the ubiquitous sight of young male rickshaw-drivers, with their faces swathed in cloth, sporting bandanas or sports caps, occasionally accentuated with dark glasses. This seemingly subcultural fashion, which would be considered 'cool' in diasporic multicultural circles, is, in actuality, a dissimulation of shame. These young men do not want to be *seen* by others, notably by members of their own community. They other themselves. It is out of this reality, to my mind, that the abandon and dignity of the Manipuri 'Michael Jackson's' performance needs to be viewed, countering the very pervasive and moralistic propaganda against Michael Jackson as a source of decadence and corruption.

This reading, however, of a specific internalization and embodiment of global influence within an individual's body and attitude, would need to be situated within a larger process of indigenization, which Appadurai rightly emphasizes is often forgotten in critiques of globalization that concentrate exclusively on 'homogenization', 'Americanization', and 'commoditization' (Appadurai 1997: 32). 'Indigenization', however, does not imply an absence of disjuncture – when something is indigenized, the foreign influence is never fully incorporated; there can be all kinds of fissures and cracks in the process of incorporation. Nor should indigenization be regarded as some kind of authentication of globalization. If one 'indigenized' McDonalds, the product would not necessarily be 'better', or 'purer', or more 'acceptable' than the real McDonalds. Even if one acknowledges the production of new, more hybrid subjectivities through global cultural influences (as would seem to be the case with the Manipuri 'Michael Jackson'), one cannot valorize here a narrative of self-realization.

The paradox of indigenization is that while it can appear to empower its agents with the aura of the other culture, this seeming power does not readily remove the vulnerability of the agents in *not* being able to change the larger realities of their lives. The Manipuri 'Michael Jackson' has a very truncated life, not only because he is interrupted while performing, but because he has to go home, in all probability, to a world of poverty and no future. Here one encounters a violent clash between two different processes of secularization: the first, on the one hand, fuelled through global cultural flows in the form of new performative roles, sexualities, meta-languages, and an illusion of worldliness which is cast in the image of 'the West'; the second, on the other hand, an arrested, if not failed, secularization at a national level, in terms of economic subsistence, education, employment, cultural choices, and alternative faiths.

There are other situations relating to the dissemination of global culture that function as masquerades of indigenization, which merely reiterate, if not deepen, the existing inequities of power. The search for exotic locations in Third World countries to host international beauty competitions, for example, is one such site of cosmetic exploitation.[6] With all the organizational hype surrounding 'getting to know the culture of the host country', supplemented by the increasingly strenuous rhetoric that beauty is also about 'personality' (which would include some social consciousness for the poor of the world), the entire framing, marketing, advertising and televising of the event follows a totally non-negotiable course of First World cultural production. In such a situation, the indigenization provided by local spectacle – for example, the Kathakali dancers and elephants, dance numbers from Hindi films and the Indian pop hit 'Made in India', in the 1996 Miss World Beauty Pageant in Bangalore – is so blatantly packaged in its regimented choreography, that it becomes almost impossible not to revert to a critique of globalization in terms of homogenization and commoditization. The indigenization is literally part of the package.

There is a more serious dimension in the *realpolitik* relating to the globalization of culture that is tellingly mediated through the figure of Michael Jackson himself, though he must be blissfully unaware of it. In what must be one of the most weird illuminations of the conflation between globalization and communalism, we have the almost fictional encounter of the 'real' Michael Jackson being sponsored for a live concert in Mumbai by an organization with close (indeed, familial) links to the upper echelons of the Hindu communal party of the Shiv Sena.[7] Is this an entirely arbitrary coincidence? Even if one resists the unearthing of a 'sinister plot' in the coming together of Jackson and Bal Thackeray – the world's most famous performer and an Indian politician who has no difficulties in legitimizing the pogroms of Hitler in his own marking of minorities in Mumbai – the sheer ease of the meeting is what is so chilling. Here we encounter not disjuncture but the most uncanny flow, the 'natural' collusion as it were of the most consummate agencies of communalism and globalization.

THE PATRIARCHY OF COMMUNITY

From these reflections on the cultural fall-out of globalization in the Indian context, we return to the site of the Lai Haraoba to draw on a more familiar discourse relating to 'community'. I draw attention here to the significant detail

that the 'Michael Jackson' performance was interrupted and later disbanded by
the organizers of the festival, who are instrumental in both facilitating and
controlling its process of secularization. To elaborate on this detail, using it as a
take-off point for a larger theorization of the patriarchy in traditional social
structures, I would like to shift the rhetorical moorings of this text, derived from
(and directed against) the language of global diasporas, and turn instead to a
very different, theoretical idiom articulating an intensely communitarian
reading of a 'symbolic site'.

The reading I have in mind has been provided by the French-Moroccan
ethno-economist Hassan Zaoual (1994), who in his intercultural critique of
development, has evolved a theory of the 'symbolic site' that could serve as a
critical point of reference for the rearticulation of community in Indian secular
contexts. Drawing on the universalist premise that 'there are as many sites as
there are cultures or shared views on the world' – a site could include such
diverse empirical realities as an ethnic community, a social group, or an
NGO – Zaoual builds his notion of the site on the foundations of what he
describes as its 'divinities', 'symbolic software', 'mythical complexes'; these
intangible elements constitute the 'invisible but unique stable core' of the site,
whose tensile integrity enables it to 'adapt all foreign incoming elements to
itself' (Vachon 1994: 28). The key assumption here is that 'the human being
[placed within the site] is not a placeless being, that he [*sic*] is always rooted in a
concrete culture, that cultures are not simply conceptual systems and signs, but
also invisible symbolic realities' (ibid.). Within this 'ethics' of the site, it is
possible to resist both the 'universality' of science and the 'debris' of development, which, for all the mess that it creates within the site, is ultimately
absorbed through a series of 'accommodations' (Zaoual 1994: 23). With 'many
tricks in its bag', as it were, the site 'adapts, changes in order not to change':
therein lies its 'intelligence', its 'collective unconscious', its 'soul' (ibid.: 15).

Not a language that one associates readily with economists? One should
qualify that, for Zaoual, 'the economy is not primarily an economic problem but
a cultural one' (Vachon 1994: 2). Locating his reading of the African economy
within the 'magico-religious' substratum of people's conceptual systems in
Senegal, Zaoual resolutely avoids the exposition of any facts, data, or statistics.
Instead, he thinks through indigenous proverbs – 'Man is a remedy for Man';
'Unlike mountains, human beings meet' (Zaoual 1994: 18). Unfortunately,
these symbolic verifications of people's belief-systems are universalized through
the construction of an intrinsically unified and harmonious 'Africa'. ('In African
sites, there really are *no anonymous* individuals. All African individuals are *persons*,
embedded in relationship to each other ... Everything seems to be *linked*
together, including what comes from outside' [ibid.; emphases added]).

Apart from these totally idealized premises of communitarianism, which
border on unreality, the problem with Zaoual's site is that it circumvents the
possibilities of being questioned or disrupted from within its boundaries by any
form of dissent or disequilibrium. Following the sociological premise that
'society precedes inter-individual agreements' (1994: 13), Zaoual would say

that the 'values of the site are anterior to its institutions, its organisation, and its forms of inter-individual coordination' (ibid.: 12). So there can be no tolerance of any deviation from the primordial *ethics* of the site, which 'constantly watches the individual's behaviour'. Its unspoken credo: *'The facts must obey the patriarch, not vice versa'* (ibid.: 21; emphases added). Herein lies the subtle, indeed sinister, disclosure of the patriarchy underlying Zaoual's symbolic site. The fact that it is not an issue in his argument at all – it is literally a slippage, a quotation in a footnote – reveals the depths at which the most communitarian, anti-Eurocentric, anti-development, anti-secularist discourse can conceal its own patriarchal biases.

Anti-secularist discourses in India as well, which draw their credibility from the 'narrative of community', are not free of a total oblivion to the role and function of women, for instance, in relation to the sites in which they have been placed. In a totally different rhetorical mode, one encounters in the communitarian and nativist strains in Indian political theory the same implicit faith that Zaoual has expressed in the site's innate integrity and resilience: 'communities will work things out among themselves', 'they don't need mediations', 'they have their own inner resources', 'they don't need to give reasons for being different'. Within the context of these non-negotiable premises, the minimal demands of secularism relating to representation, accountability, and democracy are elided under the illusory spectre of toleration that communities are assumed to embody, even though they may not always put it into practice.

In this context, it is expedient to call attention to Kumkum Sangari's powerful feminist critique of the communitarian assumptions underlying Partha Chatterjee's (1994b) strenuous plea for toleration, which is based on the voluntarist premise that 'religious groups can generate internal, political processes separate from the wider polity' (Sangari 1995: 3307). Contextualizing her position within the fractious debate around the formation of the Uniform Civil Code in India, Sangari questions 'where and how women will become agents in the internal transformation of religious groups' (ibid.). Challenging the unconscious conflation of religion, culture, and patriarchy in Chatterjee's support of communities, Sangari exposes the traps in assuming the existence of inherently homogenized communities with fixed religious identities, whose cultural rights are inextricably linked with personal laws, which in turn are assumed to be inherently 'pluralist' (ibid.: 3300 – 3301). (The same assumptions are uncannily at work in Zaoual's reading of the site, which is on the one hand intrinsically homogenized and yet 'pluralist' through the sheer assertion of its ethos.) Why, as Sangari rightly questions, should the essentialisms of religious communities not be questioned? Or are we to accept that they are protected in a 'male sanctorum', which becomes ironically 'the privileged site of cultural diversity' (ibid.)?

With this feminist inflection, we have obviously entered a very different politics in the reading of sites, which does not draw on a nationalist imaginary of 'cultural diversity', or on the multicultural celebration of difference through the emergent hybrid identities of the global diaspora, or on the assumedly eternal and tolerant values of religious communities. Through Sangari's feminism, we are alerted to the emergent articulations of secularism in a more directly activist mode, rooted in and against the communalizing tendencies of the *realpolitik* in contemporary India. This would be an appropriate point, I believe, to turn to Site 3, in which I will begin not with fragments of experience, as in the earlier two sites, but with a more concrete site of secular activism in contemporary India – the *mohalla* (neighbourhood) committees of Mumbai – which will serve to catalyse the shifts in the concluding discussion of this chapter.

SITE 3

While secular sites are being systematically communalized, from the most august institutions of Parliament, the courts, and universities, to the most informal meeting places in civil society, a renewed process of secularization is beginning to emerge in some of the most communalized neighbourhoods in metropolitan cities. I am thinking in particular of the *mohalla* committees that have begun to gain ground in the aftermath of the Mumbai riots following the demolition of the Babri Masjid. These committees, which are located in the slums of Dharavi, Ghatkopar, Jogeshwari, and the innermost recesses of the city, should not be viewed as 'symbolic sites' – Zaoual's primordial grounds of an eternally resilient community. Nor are they organic sites, the spontaneous manifestation of the people's will rising collectively to combat communalism. Significantly, the idea of such a committee was first initiated by the Deputy Police Commissioner Suresh Khopade in 1990, while he was stationed in the small industrial town of Bhiwandi outside Mumbai, at a time when the BJP leader L.K. Advani was conducting his *rath yatra* throughout the country.[8] To circumvent the possibility of communal violence, which the town had previously experienced in 1970 and 1984, Khopade mobilized both Hindu and Muslim communities in Bhiwandi to form *mohalla* committees, which can be regarded as the smallest micro-structures of neighbourhood itself, the most concentrated nuclei of affirmative secular action.

Obviously, the most contentious element in the structure of the *mohalla* committee concerns the presence of the police as active partners in a dialogue with religious communities. Militant secular activists would question the credentials of the police to foster a dialogue on communal harmony, when they themselves have been the most deadly agents of communal violence. More often than not, this violence has been triggered through the calculated indifference of the police to rumours, threats, and provocations that have frequently exploded into communal situations. Indeed, the inaction of the police has *produced* violence on many occasions. In this context, one cannot entirely rule out the possibility of the police using the *mohalla* committee as a front to legitimize their own complicities in communalism.

A more sceptical view of *mohalla* committees would resist the tendency to homogenize the entire police force as intrinsically demonic. The proponents of this view would question not just the strategic presence of the police in the *mohalla* committees, but the modalities of power that are negotiated within its structure: if the police could learn to listen, for instance, to how communities represent themselves to each other, then perhaps there could be some hope for their re-conscientization. This involvement of the police in everyday matters of particular neighbourhoods could lead to a more heightened awareness of their responsibilities as guardians of the law. On the other hand, if the police are merely going to use the *mohalla* committees to further empower themselves, then this strategy can result only in the deepening of a totally undesired surveillance, masquerading as protectionism.

Perhaps the most open attitude to *mohalla* committees would be cast in the language of pragmatic activism. It would draw on the undeniably positive fact that while large areas of Mumbai, even in the so-called 'secular' neighbourhoods, were violently affected by the riots in December 1992 and January 1993, Bhiwandi remained relatively peaceful, its simmering tensions controlled and negotiated within the larger context of communitarian coexistence that had been prepared in advance by the *mohalla* committees. This fact cannot be written off as mere coincidence. The *mohalla* committees in Bhiwandi had obviously prepared the ground for dialogue between its volatile factions. Even if they could not entirely eliminate violence, they could contribute to its deterrence. From this example in Bhiwandi, we learn how the activization of secular culture can never be assumed; it has to be worked at.

Today the idea of the *mohalla* committee has travelled from Bhiwandi to other sites in Mumbai, notably to Dharavi, the largest slum in Asia, which has sometimes been described as a 'mini-India', layered with the most differentiated contexts of cultures, languages, classes, castes, religions, and ideologies. It is in such sites that we are witnessing the emergence of what I am tempted to describe as inter-faith citizenship at grass-roots levels, where members of diverse communities are learning to live together not through the pieties of religion, but through the actual task of rebuilding each other's homes and sacred sites that have been damaged, if not destroyed, in the riots.

In Dharavi, for example, communities were mobilized after the riots to collect building materials instead of money in order to renovate at least twelve damaged religious structures. What is being demonstrated here, perhaps, is not the self-conscious affirmation of religion – 'I am doing this for you because you are a Muslim, and you are doing this for me because I am a Hindu' – but a far more fundamental sense of belonging to a working neighbourhood that cuts across blood-ties and primordial bonds.

A process of citizenship is in the making here, intensified not only by the communitarian ties of neighbourhood but by a sense of belonging to a larger city called Mumbai. This allegiance may not necessarily be defined in metropolitan terms, although it would be useful to ask why the much-maligned 'metropolis' in anti-secularist discourse should be equated so reductively with the 'westernized elite', when millions of working-class communities and migrants regard this metropolis as their home. This metropolis is also the centre of global capitalism in India, a fact that is not lost to the millions who keep this city going, from scavenging in its garbage to providing its basic services in labour, transportation, and industry. This growing awareness of being marginalized by a capitalist system, from which they are the least likely to benefit, is resulting in the emergence of new political identities and assertions. Countering the communalization of political culture, these identities and assertions are resulting in an intensely differentiated yet vibrant awareness of citizenship that is being negotiated through resistance at ground levels.

'HUM SAB EK HAIN'

From the site of the *mohalla* committee as a grass-roots political structure, I would now like to shift the focus to specific cultural practices emerging from these structures. The Dharavi Mohalla Committee, for instance, has facilitated the articulation of new cultural idioms drawing on local processes of production that have contributed to the imagining of communal harmony. While these idioms may be cast within the existing nationalist imaginaries of calendar art and street posters, which more often than not reinscribe the patriarchal biases of Indian society, one significant counter to the commercialization of these idioms has been made by a tailor called Waqar Khan from the Dharavi Mohalla Committee. His image is cast in the form of a sticker depicting a photograph of four young boys dressed as priests, representing four distinct faiths – Islam, Hinduism, Christianity, Sikhism. The boys face the camera frontally, with the colours of the national flag emblazoned in the background, and a slogan '*Hum Sab Ek Hain*' ('We are all one') printed below. At a very purist, ideological level, one can question the conflation of religious and cultural identities in the figures of the boy-priests; one could also question the exclusion of the girl-child. But these are niggling issues relating to political correctness: the reality is that the image 'works' through a very concretely realized form, and the disarming aura of its boy-actors.

Hypothetically, one could argue that if an advertising agency had duplicated this image, as part of the recent anti-communalist campaign in the media (which can be more appropriately read as a means by which corporations can enhance their public relations), the effect would not have been the same. The four young boy-priests would have in all probability been reduced to kitsch. But it is obvious that kitsch with its metropolitan play of irony and stereotype is not part of Waqar Khan's vocabulary. What a public relations expert would render as kitsch is the most vibrant evidence of inter-faith solidarity in Waqar Khan's 'technicolour secularism', consciously drawn from the local resources of a neighbourhood photographic studio.

Such was the communicative efficacy of Waqar Khan's image that it proved to be enormously popular with local communities, who used his emblem of a 'secular India' to adorn the entrances to the Ganapati *mandals* (pavilions) during the religious festival of Ganesotsav (Barve 1996). One cannot claim here any counter to the saffronization of Ganesh by the Shiv Sena, but at least a more naive celebration of the coexistence of diverse peoples and faiths counterpoints the communal appropriation of religion. The plurality being celebrated here is cast in a totally different idiom from the more self-consciously defined secularism of metropolitan activist organizations like SAHMAT (Bharucha 1998: 52 – 74), or the more monolithic nationalist propaganda of the Indian state conveyed by slogans like *Ekta* ('oneness', 'unity') and *Mera Bharat Mahaan* (literally 'My Bharat [India] is great'). At a denotative level, Waqar Khan's slogan *Hum Sab Ek Hain* is equally tendentious, but the visual gesture accompanying it is light; it even has an element of fun that secularists could learn to incorporate in their somewhat self-righteous approaches to politically correct imagery.

And yet – as always a note of caution underlies my seeming retreat into an uncritical celebration of subaltern culture – Waqar Khan's image has also 'worked' with the police force, who have offered to print several thousand copies of the image for mass distribution. Once again, in a very graphic way, we can see how the site of an image can change, thereby challenging any notion of the ontology of its construction. From the site of Waqar Khan's imagination, where the image was fantasized; to the local photographic studio where the image was actually shaped, shot, processed, and manufactured; to the Dharavi Mohalla Committee which served to distribute the image to other community centres; to the office of the Mumbai Police Commissioner R.D. Tyagi, who sits under a large laminated blow-up of the image; to its reproduction in an article on the Dharavi Mohalla Committee in the activist forum *Communalism Combat*; and finally, to its inscription in this chapter on secularism: we cannot fail to be struck by the multiple sites of the image's transmission, reproduction, and resignification.

Nonetheless, the predominant circuit of the image remains regional, if not local (Dharavi, Mumbai, Maharashtra). It is a telling fact that, despite some exposure of the *mohalla* committees at a national level through daily newspapers, it remains a predominantly Mumbai phenomenon. This is characteristic of many other initiatives that have been undertaken in the vast spectrum of cultural and political activism in India today, in the fields of environment, law, education, literacy, health, gender justice, and the right to information. While some of these agendas do get disseminated at very wide levels, so that the struggle around the construction of a dam in Narmada, for instance, has spread beyond its location in Gujarat through the activism of the Narmada Bachao Andolan to far corners of India and the rest of the world, the daunting reality is that the majority of social and cultural movements in India today remain unknown outside of specific linguistic regions; or else, particular movements get so tightly networked within specific frames of development that there is no linkage whatsoever to other contexts outside these frames.

The question here is not simply one of secular sectarianism, a charge that has often been raised against activists by leading supporters of the civil liberties movement in India, such as Rajni Kothari, who has been very vocal in his critique of 'the exclusivist notion of identity and struggle in grass-roots, struggle-oriented movements on the Left' (Kothari 1994: 1594). Arun Patnaik has been even more scathing in his condemnation of 'self-arrogating' discourses:

> The people's movements are not simply too numerous but too sectarian, disunited and unrelated to each other. An agrarian struggle frowns at the birth of a *dalit* movement and treats any critique of caste as a divisive force in the course of the class struggle. A *dalit* movement dismisses feminism as an urban middle class women's problem as if the latter do not have material interests in women's questions. ... A women's movement raises the critique of patriarchy, as if it does not have anything to do with the struggles of ryots and coolies.   (Patnaik 1995: 1202)

While these are valid charges that need to be contextualized within the partisan ideological moorings of social movements in India today, deepened through their linguistic and regional specificities, what is almost never addressed by political theorists in the Indian context is the dearth, if not absence, of the 'technologies of interactivity', to use Arjun Appadurai's category, relating to what he describes as the 'production of locality. This is yet another uninterrogated area in the dissemination of secular culture, with the specific challenges of translation, as indicated earlier in this chapter, remaining unresolved in the absence of multilingual/intracultural infrastructures of communication.

It is not just the nation-state that has tacitly prevented the emergence of such infrastructures; the initiatives for such interactivity across specific regions have not been forthcoming from the regional cultural hegemonies determining local processes of production. There is a complex history to be written here on the resistances to interactivity at cultural levels within the nationalist imaginaries of specific regions. As I have indicated in my essays on intraculturalism in the Indian theatre, the desire to encounter other cultures within a culturally diverse national space need not be reciprocated. In my experience at least, I have realized that 'language, blood, soil, race, and kinship', which Appadurai (1997: 161) believes are falsely 'naturalized' categories propagandized by right-wing nationalists, are in actuality the most tenacious categories of the residual narrative of community, which refuses to die, even as it is in the process of being fractured by very contradictory processes of citizenship. While I would not fix or valorize this narrative in the mode of certain anti-secularist strains in subaltern and communitarian theory (Chatterjee 1994a, 1994b), I would none the less acknowledge the determining hold of this narrative on the imagination of diverse communities out of which identities continue to be shaped and negotiated within *and against* predominantly local and regional cultural hegemonies.

The tantalizing task for any cultural critic in India today is to figure out the increasingly indeterminate relationships between the local, the regional, and the national. These shifts demand an infinitely more complex cultural vigilance than a mere demonization of the nation-state cast within the overdetermined, Foucauldian categories of discipline, regimentation, surveillance, and the policing of borders, by which citizens are constructed (Appadurai

1997: 189). For secularists in India today, the most immediate political task is to counter the Hinduization of the Indian state through a relentless critique not merely of Hindutva but of the failures of the 'secular state' itself. The purpose here is not to undermine the state, but to challenge its duplicities and abdication of responsibilities, by calling attention to the democratizing impulses and agendas of multiple movements addressing the needs of underprivileged and marginalized communities in an emergent political society. The future calls for 'more – not less – government activity and public action', as the economists Jean Dreze and Amartya Sen have stressed in their recommendations for India that go 'well beyond liberalization' (Dreze and Sen 1996: 203).[9] We do not have the privilege, as I have stated earlier, to imagine ourselves beyond the nation.

VIRTUAL AND ACTUAL SITES

Within the repressive machinery of the state, Appadurai nonetheless concedes that neighbourhoods represent 'anxieties' for the nation-state; they are a 'perennial source of entropy and slippage', in so far as their spaces cannot be fully disciplined by the 'techniques of nationhood (birth control, linguistic uniformity, economic discipline, communications efficiency, and political loyalty)' (Appadurai 1997: 189 – 190). Countering this anti-statist perspective, I would say that the 'anxiety' faced by millions of people in India is not that the state is denying them their subjectivity, but that it is depriving them of the most basic public services that are expected of citizens in any self-respecting democracy. The problem does not lie with the violent efficiency and non-negotiable disciplinary procedures of the state (as in Singapore, for example, where, as Appadurai rightly points out, spitting on the streets can be regarded as a crime). In India, it is the total collapse of public services relating to the most basic necessities of life – drinking water, sanitation, transportation, and health services – that is of critical concern, particularly in those areas which have been totally neglected, if not abandoned, by the state. Secular activists have to demand these public services from the state agencies by mobilizing neighbourhoods at street levels.

Instead of seizing the sources of 'slippage' and 'entropy' within *actual* neighbourhoods as potential resources for public resistance, Appadurai seems more enamoured of the liberatory possibilities of *virtual* neighbourhoods on the sites of Internet and other electronically mediated forms of communication. Once again there is a dissolution of conflict in his theory as he cautions against dichotomizing virtual neighbourhoods from 'highly spatialized' ones, in so far as the former are able to 'mobilize ideas, opinions, moneys, and social linkages that often directly flow back into lived neighbourhoods' (Appadurai 1997: 195). Admittedly, these global flows are not entirely utopian; they could also include dystopic agendas facilitating, for instance, the sale of arms for local nationalisms, and propaganda for terrorism and secessionist movements. Of late the Internet has become a virtual battleground for the most juvenile forms of Hindu and Muslim communalisms, hate-speech, and the most potentially inflammatory rumours.[10] While Appadurai attempts to soften the intensity of this violence by claiming how the electronic networks were 'exploited equally' by expatriate Indians in the United States, positioned on opposite sides after the demolition of the Babri Masjid on 6 December 1992, one would need to know whether this free-for-all 'exchange' of views has ultimately contributed to the secularization of political culture in India, or whether it is not indeed feeding the hegemony of the Hindu Right. The neo-liberal approach of tolerating 'both sides of the debate', with no demand for moderation or regulation whatsoever, reveals a political indifference that is totally at odds with the actual struggle of sustaining a secular movement in India today.

While acknowledging the emergence of 'a more complicated, disjunct, hybrid sense of local subjectivity' (Appadurai 1997: 197) through the mediation of the electronic networks, one would need to differentiate this production of new subjectivities in the diaspora from the emergent subject-formations in Third World contexts, as in India, within actual neighbourhoods and political movements. It is not as if the nation-state is destined to produce only 'compliant national citizens' (ibid.: 190); other subjectivities, caste mobilizations and new ethnicities are at work through multiple political investments that are challenging, stretching, rejecting, and yet working within the premises of the state.

Virtual struggle, I would contend, can be described as the voyeuristic stance of a privileged global intelligentsia, who can afford to surf the possibilities of resistance transmitted from the trouble spots of the Third World into the padded cells of First World intellectual production. Appadurai himself acknowledges that 'electronic communities' do not 'directly affect the local preoccupations of less educated and privileged migrants' (1997: 197). The critical authority on cyberculture Olu Oguibe has put it even more sharply by calling our attention to the irrevocable condition for entering cyberspace – namely, the possession of a 'computer or digital interface', along with 'computer literacy' which presupposes 'the ability not only to read and write, but to do so functionally' (Oguibe 1997: 49). Not only are these conditions unavailable to millions of people in the Third World, who may be more concerned with the availability of drinking water, but cyberspace forecloses the geographies of the dispossessed. '[N]ot the new, free global democracy we presume and defend', it can more accurately be related to 'an aristocracy of location and disposition, characterised, ironically, by acute insensitivity and territorialist proclivities' (ibid.: 50).

The irony deepens when one contends with the activist euphoria surrounding cyberspace, particularly by those elitist NGOs who, in recent years, have valorized the availability of Internet facilities, for example, to indigenous communities. Not only is the availability of electricity in the dwellings of such communities in India a moot question, but one would need to confront the linkages of technologies with new modes of conscientization. More often than not, 'electronic communities' are linked in the subcontinental context to religious narratives and phenomena, like the national television serials of the *Ramayana* and the *Mahabharata*, and the more short-lived 'Ganesh miracle' that was catalysed by the media and communal organizations across the world.[11] The communities that emerged through these phenomena, assuming mythic dimensions overnight (as in the 'Ganesh miracle'), cannot be separated from the intricate propagandist machinery of Hindutva – a fact that would not be denied by the media-savvy leaders of the BJP. Faith can be more susceptible to social engineering than fact.

While it is necessary to remain critically alert about the perversions of faith through the mediation of the global media, it is essential that the cultural fall-out of globalization should not be reduced to a moralistic lament for the contamination of 'our' traditional culture (*sanskriti*). It would be more expedient to examine how the agencies of globalization are feeding the communalizing tendencies in our culture, not merely in relation to the propaganda of Hindutva but in response to the less recognized failures of secularization in post-independence India.

As outlined earlier in the chapter, a constructive critique of secularism should lapse neither into utopic notions of post-nationality, nor into the assumed tolerance of communities. To seek refuge within the upper-caste patriarchies of traditional and local communities runs the risk of legitimizing the regional hegemonies of culture in which the rights of minorities, women, *dalits*, and tribal communities are presumed to be represented, even if they are denied in practice. For a secular culture to emerge in India on a democratic basis, cultural identities and differences will have to be mobilized through emergent narratives of citizenship across new structures of intracultural exchange and translation. The old mantra of 'unity in diversity' needs to be replaced by an activization of the respect for differences, without which plurality remains a mere chimera, a secular shibboleth.

It becomes obvious, therefore, that there can be no one agenda for the secular struggle in India today, but several intersecting, colliding, overlapping agendas that converge – and clash – around the realities and pressures of communalism, multiculturalism, and globalization. Within the maelstrom of these forces, secularism is at once threatened and resistant. In the process of articulating new dimensions in its philosophy and practice, it is also struggling to survive in a state of profound instability. This chapter resolutely avoids any attempt to resolve this instability, by synthesizing the shifting sites of secularism.

Rather, I would like to end by reiterating this instability. I hope by so doing to counter any complacency about the normativity of secularism or any false reassurance that it belongs intrinsically to the state of India. Secularism is not our birthright; it is a fighting creed for a more democratic form of citizenship. If it is in a state of crisis, it is also in the making. No longer 'Archimedean', as Akeel Bilgrami (1994) has described its non-negotiated origins in the formation of the Indian state, secularism is entering the condition of Heraclitus: unstable, engaged in seemingly ceaseless conflict, yet turbulently alive. I, for one, do not regret this state of restlessness. It is one way of freeing ourselves from the false promises and trysts with destiny that have failed to materialize. New uncertainties are clearing the debris of the past. Utopias can wait.

7

AFTERWORDS

THE BODY IN CRISIS AND THE FUTURE OF THE INTERCULTURAL

It is not just the 'shifting sites of secularism' that need to retain their instability; the 'shifting sites' of this book reject the formality of a conclusion. I would like to interpret this juncture in the narrative not as another beginning, but as an 'interval during politics' (which is the title of a memorable collection of essays by the Indian socialist leader, Rammanohar Lohia). His essays (1965) can be said to have initiated the relatively unacknowledged field of Indian Cultural Studies in their eclectic preoccupations with travel, the colonial heritage of cricket, pilgrimages, the political personae of gods, and the beauty of dark-skinned Indian women (a proto-feminist reflection on the racism that underlies the Indian marriage market). That one of the most alert and oppositional minds in Indian politics should embrace the seemingly small and trivial concerns of everyday culture, is an inspiration for this consciously elliptical end to the book.

I, too, find myself seeking an 'interval during politics'. This book has been charged with so many large agendas – globalization, communalism, secularism – that even my attempts to provide creative alternatives through inter/intra/multi-cultural practices have been subsumed within an undeniably heated, if not occasionally fractious, political discourse. Indeed, I often reached a point in the course of writing this book when I found myself questioning whether it was possible to posit something like the 'non-political'. Was I not consciously rejecting certain areas of subjectivity and play, fantasy and fun that also need to be asserted in and through the 'political'? In Lohia's assertion of lightness in cultural politics, one receives valuable clues as to how one can deal with issues and experiences of worldliness that challenge what is worth being considered 'political' in the first place.

Note that, for Lohia, the 'interval' takes place *during* politics, not *in* politics. I often wondered about the seemingly awkward use of this preposition. But I now realize that for Lohia (as indeed for myself) politics does not stop; it is a continuum of ceaseless activity that is going on all around us, pulsating through the immediacies of conflicting times. Significantly, if politics is suspended, it is also oddly heightened – and transformed – in the 'pregnant moment' of its 'interval'. I had called attention to this paradox in my tract on *The Question of Faith,* in which I had attempted to contextualize Lohia's cultural writings within the larger context of an alternative secular discourse: 'The word "interval" suggests a respite from a certain kind of activity, but it also implies a "break", a conscious "interruption" in which one can anticipate and prepare for the tensions in which one is thrust, and yet, temporarily suspended. Lohia's thought is situated in this rupture between philosophy and action, praxis and theory' (Bharucha 1993: 55). Today I would add that this rupture enables us to imagine the future of the political that has yet to be freed from the immediacies of its ongoing struggles.

What I have to offer here is one such interval that erupted in the course of my intercultural journey, when I was compelled to break my relentless itinerary. Indeed, I had no choice in the matter; this interval was thrust on me, and I had no other option but to embrace its immediacy by reflecting on some disturbing home-truths of my larger intercultural endeavour. Another way of reading this interval is to see it as a moment of crisis that directly affected my body, which became the site of an altogether unprecedented intercultural inquiry. Now I no longer had the luxury of the critic to inspect with seeming detachment the bodies of others (actors, refugees, victims of communal riots). Now I was compelled to confront the breakdown in my own body. Indeed, it is neatly ironic that this narrative, which has been so top-heavy in its preoccupation with the conflicting ideologies of culturalism, should be so decisively ruptured by my relatively unproblematized body. With these introductory remarks, let me now focus on the penultimate site of this book – a hospital in Ljubljana, Slovenia – where I found myself incapacitated with a sudden attack of malignant malaria.

How does one reflect on interculturalism in the state of malaria? Any illness involves an alienation from one's 'normal' self, producing an uncomfortable sense of being entrapped in someone else's body. One has no other choice but to work through this alien body in order to reconnect to one's own. This scarcely reassuring condition becomes all the more unnerving when one falls ill in a foreign country, where, without knowing the language, gestures, or cultural codes, one could be doubly alienated not only from one's own body, but from the environment itself. Such was my experience in Slovenia, a country I had never visited, and where my participation in a theatre conference, which I had eagerly awaited, was cut short in hospital. My interculturalism had finally met its match in malaria.

At the best of times, interculturalism is an enormously taxing practice in the demands that it makes on the body. It is not only a matter of learning other disciplines and techniques – martial arts, Yoga, Kathakali – where one is compelled to 'break' one's existing reflexes and rhythms, balance and co-ordination; the demands on the body in intercultural work are so infinitesimal that they are invisible in their subtle pressures, as one takes in different physical and sensory stimuli from an alien space. These stimuli interact with the memories and sensations that have already been internalized in the body from another space and time – a space and time so intimate that one tends to describe it as 'home'. Contrary to the euphoria that generally accompanies descriptions of intercultural workshops, there is an incredible conflict that takes place within the body, as its psycho-physical assumptions are dislocated. However, the regimen of theatre instils a notion of discipline among actors, which invariably compels them to bear the pain in silence, or even to make a virtue out of it.

What happens to interculturalism in the state of malaria is that the regimen of the body breaks down, so that one is not in a position to conceal the fact that the body is at war with itself. As it collapses, then fitfully recovers as if nothing had happened, only to break down again, the malarial body is subject to periodic fevers, accompanied by intense shivering and hallucinations, which leave one drenched in sweat. In its early stages, malaria can be stopped, but once it rages, the parasites in the bloodstream can work their way insidiously, and with an incremental speed, into the crevices of the brain. Potentially, therefore, malaria is a killer disease, particularly if it remains undetected for too long. This was the source of my terror in Ljubljana. While I knew the symptoms of malaria in my body, the doctor whom I first met was emphatic about his diagnosis: 'Well, you could have malaria, but I think you've got a virus.'

When my body eventually broke down, disproving his seemingly non-negotiable expertise, I found that my greatest source of comfort – my secret therapy – in the Infectious Diseases Ward in Ljubljana, was to drink hot water. Not mineral water but, I insisted, ordinary drinking water: my therapy was just to sip it, after bouts of fever and near-delirium. This water became my 'home' in the hospital.

Gradually, when the fever began to subside for longer stretches of time, I started to explore my environment, at first tentatively, rather like an actor discovering an unknown space in an improvisation. The first moment of self-renewal occurred when I turned around in my bed to confront the eyes of another man lying on an identical bed adjacent to mine. This eye-contact engendered an inexplicable sense of relief, because for the first time in at least three nightmarish days and nights, I was able to cross the barriers of my disoriented self to meet the other. I realized then that the other is not the predatory foreigner demonized in the narratives of communalism that I have narrated in this book. The other is also a source of deep compassion, and someone to whom you are strangely and intimately connected as a fellow-patient, even though it may not be possible to exchange a word with him because he is too seriously ill.

My fellow-patient was an elderly Slovenian dying of Alzheimer's disease. He was a proud man who didn't want any false sympathy. We had no language in common, except a non-verbal set of signs and sounds. We did not even share the same illness. All we could do was to stare at each other at vacant moments, rather like strangers in a subway who meet each other on a regular basis, but who have yet to exchange greetings. I realize now in retrospect that we could never have made such an intimately impersonal contact if we had met each other on the street in Ljubljana. He would have walked past me as if I were a tourist, and I would have pretended not to notice him, another elderly European who has survived the war.

As my health improved with regular doses of quinine, I began to negotiate the corridors outside my room, and, very gradually, the hospital became a comfortably macabre hotel, where my mind was free to wander in strange circuits. As an intercultural worker, you can never quite free yourself from the condition of living in a hotel. Its anonymity almost anywhere/everywhere becomes a 'second home'. From being a patient, therefore, I was becoming an intercultural performer once more, whose initial 'stage fright' was gradually taken care of by the bustle of the 'stage management' surrounding me.

Indeed, once my malaria was diagnosed as 'malignant' and not just as the ordinary 'recurring' kind, I realized that I had become a celebrity of sorts. Now I was compelled to hold forth on this mysterious tropical disease that had not crossed the borders of Slovenia for about a quarter of a century. Clad in my hospital gown, I addressed solemn medical students who asked me obscure questions about 'how I was feeling'. Needless to say, this was my opportunity to dwell on the innermost secrets of my malarial being. But how could I explain to them that the body itself is the deepest repository of secrets, the most deceptive carrier of germs and parasites that can get past even the most nit-picking surveillance of health officials? My body broke down only after I had entered Slovenia, but while I was crossing the border the parasites in my blood were already gestating invisibly, rather like illegal immigrants concealed in the hidden corners of registered vehicles.

It was oddly exciting to realize that my body had facilitated the essentially illegal entry of malaria into Slovenia. But how was I to share this with my captive audience of medical students, whose loyalty as good citizens to the recently constructed state of Slovenia was matched by their ignorance on the subject of a Third World disease? How was I to disturb their professional equanimity by reminding them that malaria itself is the deadliest of performers? As fictionalized so brilliantly by Amitav Ghosh in his surreal novel *The Calcutta Chromosome*, malaria is a 'master of disguises: it can mimic the symptoms of more diseases than you can begin to count – lumbago, the 'flu, cerebral haemorrhage, yellow fever ... What's special about the malaria bug is that, as it goes through its life-cycle, it keeps altering its coat-proteins. So by the time the body's immune system learns to recognize the threat, the bug's already had time to do a little costume-change before the next act' (Ghosh 1996: 47, 207).

Obviously, I was not the only performer in the hospital; my malaria was a hard act to follow. In fact, it never left its seemingly relentless hold on my body. In this agonistic confrontation with my malarial self, I was distracted by yet another, more poignant performance, that I witnessed every afternoon. This monodrama reminded me of Franz Xaver Kroetz's *Request Concert*, the play that had initiated my exploration of interculturalism, in which a solitary working-class woman goes through her household routine silently and then commits suicide. The performance in Ljubljana was different, in so far as another solitary woman expressed her silence through a torrent of words voiced in a hushed breath, rather like a Beckett monologue.

Not disembodied like *Not I*, this voice was very much attached to the composed, dignified body of my fellow-patient's wife, who would enter the hospital room every day, as if she were dropping in on her way to the supermarket. From the moment she entered, she would not stop talking to her silent partner as she comforted and cuddled him, scolded him for messing up, proceeding thereafter in a very matter-of-fact way to shave him with an electric shaver, all the while chatting in a deadly monotone. As she would read aloud the headlines in the newspaper, she would occasionally look in my direction — I was an avid spectator who couldn't stop staring at this incredible display of Bressonian non-acting. With a slight shake of her head and pursing of her lips, she would convey to me, 'He's not going to last, is he?' Finally, with sepulchral calm, she would kiss him on both cheeks; her husband-patient would remain as still as a corpse. Then with a heavily accented 'Good afternoon' — the only English words I heard after almost an hour of Slovene — she would exit with no drama whatsoever. It was only then that this seemingly dour and unprepossessing man would begin to whimper like a child. It was not possible to comfort him; I had to respect his grief in silence.

Intercultural spectatorship prepares one to see what cannot be understood through words. Through the smallest of details, one can 'listen' to how other parts of the body can 'speak'. This peculiarly synaesthetic approach to performances in other cultures is actually a means of compensating for the inadequacies of one's comprehension. Interculturalists are known to focus on fragments in a 'foreign' performance — a movement of the eyes, an involuntary reflex of the fingers — with an almost uncanny concentration. The obvious risk in such atomized seeing is that it can result in an eerie sense of disembodiment, whereby the context to which the fragment is linked can be entirely negated. The intercultural, one can never afford to forget, is also intercontextual. And yet, in any interaction, one context is almost inevitably clearer and stronger than the other. Strangely, in most intercultural processes of learning, it is the known context that gets estranged through displacement, while the unknown context can get transfigured in a state of luminous incomprehensibility.

Such was my discovery of interculturalism in the state of malaria, where I found myself re-reading (and re-thinking) Gandhi's revolutionary tract *Hind Swaraj*, which always accompanies me when I travel. Written in South Africa, and later banned as seditious when it was translated from Gujarati into English in 1908, this tiny book offers one of the most severe, uncompromising critiques of modernity. Gandhi was not known to be euphemistic about his views on the civilizational myths of such modernity. On being asked what he thought about 'western civilization', his audaciously memorable answer was, 'It would be a good idea.' Can I deny that Gandhi was very much on my mind as I recovered from malaria in a very 'western' medical environment, which, at one level, 'cured' me?

And yet, this very environment seemed to deny so many areas and dimensions of the body that are needed not only for our survival, but for our inner vitality.

Technologies of medicine can cure diseases, but can they revive the body? Indeed, are they sufficiently aware of those psychological symptoms that lie outside of a strictly medical diagnosis, but which contribute none the less to the aggravation of a particular illness? Why, for instance, did my malaria have to surface in Ljubljana and not in Calcutta where, in all probability, the parasites had entered my body? Why did it not erupt a few days later in Frankfurt? Surely the timing of any illness is not entirely arbitrary. When the body breaks down, as mine did, there are reasons for it. Reasons that are also enigmas.

The deepest enigma: the moment of freedom, the realization that you are no longer marked by your illness. You are no longer a patient. You are free to be yourself. Both the 'thin smear' and the 'thick smear' blood tests are negative. As always, in medical reports, the negative is positive; metastasis, which sounds like an interesting postmodern construction, is a deadly word, as I learn from my mother's cancer reports. Now in Ljubljana, at the very moment when I am free to leave the hospital, another tragedy strikes. The hospital orderlies rush into the room like extras in a science-fiction film, and wheel out my fellow-patient's bed through the door. He is rushed to the ICU from where he does not return. I am left staring at the empty space in the room – his space, vacated. An empty space becomes empty only when one perceives that it was once filled. It does not pre-exist in some ontological state. As I face this emptiness, I realize that I have lost my other and I have no other choice but to reconstitute myself.

A year or so later, on yet another of my intercultural journeys, I find myself in a theatrical space called DAS ARTS in Amsterdam. The brainchild of Ritsaert ten Cate, the pioneer of Dutch *avant-garde* theatre and host to generations of international artists at the legendary Mickery Theatre, DAS ARTS is not a school or a conservatory or even a laboratory; it is a site for 'advanced theatre research' that pushes the boundaries of the imagination into the unknown of the future. In an unprecedented way, the concrete, yet sceptical, utopianism of this enterprise is one of the very few initiatives in my theatre experience that genuinely breaks new ground in its facilitation of new imaginaries for the theatre in the twenty-first century.

The ways of DAS ARTS are strange. As a traveller passing through town, I have been invited to one of their weekly rituals, which centres around a dinner to which three strangers, who might never have met or even have heard of each other before, are requested to 'speak for their supper'. This is a fairly elaborate meal that the students take it in turn to prepare, but the meal itself is at once the pretext and the background for a ceremony.

In one corner of the meeting place – the central workspace of DAS ARTS which looks like the inner hold of a ship with wooden beams and rafters – there is a massive candelabra with clusters of thick white candles, which cast a warm glow on the entire community, sitting down at three tables, very informally yet elegantly set, with a lectern in the middle for the three speakers. My fellow-guests include a graphics artist and cultural activist (Juul Hondius), who has just returned from Prague where he has been involved in designing anti-racist posters featuring large life-size photographic images of the gypsy community. The other guest is a famous Dutch surgeon (Floris de Graaf), an expert in operating on cleft-palate deformities.

With the gypsies, there are obvious connections with my own research on marginalized and dehumanized communities; with cleft-palate deformities, however, the intercultural connections seem opaque until the surgeon begins to talk about the adaptation of his expertise in Vietnam, where he has operated successfully on numerous patients. With this man, I feel a particular affinity, not least because I have chosen, quite independently of any knowledge of his background, to speak about interculturalism in the state of malaria. Our very different readings of and exposures to the body in pain bring us together in the unwritten narrative of interculturalism.

I recognize in the surgeon's practice a totally different manifestation of commitment from my own search for interculturalism in theatre. Can I deny that I envy its concreteness? Operating on cleft palates seems so specific: the longitudinal fissure in the roof of the mouth has to be marked and measured; it has to be cut and stitched in certain ways; the flesh has to be folded dexterously in particular junctures; redundant passages have to be blocked, so that there is no possibility of, say, the rice coming out of the patient's nostrils while he or she is eating (a common predicament for cleft-palate patients in Vietnam). I am staggered by the surgeon's matter-of-fact way of dealing with pain – he dis-tributes some rather lurid 'before' and 'after' photographs of his patients while we are trying to sip our soup. And he is able to do this precisely because he has *solutions* for the pain in question. In contrast to his precise methodology, my reflections on malaria seem so pointlessly theatrical and self-reflexive.

And yet, the surgeon is a troubled man. His interculturalism is not free of its problems, not least because his expertise has made him into a local hero in Vietnam. While he seeks discretion – he wants to come and go without any fanfare, and, above all, to live in a quiet room in a hotel secluded from the cacophony on the streets – his patients have other plans for him. They would like to honour him in public ceremonies with a display of gratitude. While the surgeon is not making any money on the operations – not because he happens to be altruistic, but because he doesn't need to supplement his income in the Netherlands – his junior Vietnamese colleagues have other, understandably more professional agendas with economic priorities. I realize that this wonder-fully brusque and down-to-earth man, who congratulates me for being alive to narrate my story on malaria, is not free of his own vulnerabilities.

In the warmth that follows our presentations, I encounter yet another intercultural illumination that comes from even farther away than Prague or Vietnam, through the memory of an Indian song that travelled to Surinam. One of the students, a bright and intense Mette van der Sys, finds a quiet moment in the aftermath of the dinner to share something wondrous, the kind of insight that can manifest itself only through the unconscious trajectories of theatre. According to Mette, while she was listening to me speak, she found herself remembering an 'Indian' song from her childhood in Surinam that she had forgotten (or so she had imagined). It appears that one of the Indian expatriate friends of her parents had written this song in Hindi (Devanagiri) script with an English transliteration in her 'poem album' (the equivalent of an autograph book, I would imagine, so coveted by children in their collection of signatures and messages).

After our meeting, Mette went back to her 'poem album' and retrieved the poem, which she xeroxed and later sent me a copy. To my surprise, I found myself encountering a freedom song from India's struggle for independence that was sung by the Indian National Army led by Netaji Subhas Chandra Bose on the borders of north-eastern India:

Kadam kadam barhaye ja
Khushi ke geet gaye ja . . .

At a microcosmic level, the transmission of this essentially untranslatable song from India to Surinam to Amsterdam, catalysed by a description of malaria in Slovenia, counterpointed by real-life stories from Vietnam and Prague, made me wonder about the infinitesimal migrations, travels, accidents, coincidences, and multiple biographies that make such intercultural meetings possible. (Who was this 'Indian' friend known to Mette's parents in Surinam? How did he get there? And what made him remember a militant song from another time? And why would he choose to inscribe that moment of history in a Dutch child's poem album?) None of these insights could have materialized without the narrative structure provided by DAS ARTS, which was sufficiently rigorous, yet open, in bringing strangers together, with no particular agenda beyond sharing the possible insights and pleasure that could be derived from such a meeting.

The pleasure of interculturalism is sometimes forgotten in the rigorous demands of its practice. At one level, such meetings at DAS ARTS can be regarded as risky because there is no guarantee, after all, that anything can be shared in them beyond the voyeuristic curiosities of meeting people from other places. But at another level, it could be said that such meetings are positively indulgent. What is their purpose? How can one measure their insights? What is their lasting significance? They are not workshops, after all, where one learns specific techniques and skills. However, one could counter: Is that all there is in this discipline that we presume to call interculturalism? Is there nothing beyond techniques and skills, the much fetishized secrets of the actor, relating to breathing and pre-expressivity and 'finding one's centre', among other *non-sequiturs* of intercultural performance? Is there no interculturalism worth pursuing beyond performance?

If I respond positively to the DAS ARTS model of not institutionalizing interculturalism as 'theatre anthropology' or 'performance studies', it is because in an altogether original way it opens other, marginalized dimensions of *imagining* interculturalism as another philosophy of living – indeed, the art of living in the new millennium. Crucial to the nurturing and sustenance of this 'art' is the role of the imagination which can no longer be reduced to mere 'fantasy', 'escape', 'elite pastime', or 'contemplation'; rather, as Arjun Appadurai has put it eloquently, though somewhat too confidently, 'the imagination has become an original field of social practices, a form of work (in the sense of both labour and culturally organized practice), and a form of negotiation between sites of agency (individuals) and globally defined fields of possibility' (Appadurai 1997: 31).

While Appadurai would insist that the imaginary ('a constructed landscape of collective aspirations') can be mediated only through 'the complex prism of modern media', notably the new technologies of global communication, I would emphasize that in activizing the imagination we – those of us who are involved in the actual making of cultural practice – should not lose sight of those psychophysical resources rooted in the body that do not necessarily feed 'the new global order' that Appadurai assumes as a norm. It is at this critical juncture that 'the body' can be pitted against 'the world', even as it has been marked, shaped, regimented, and violated by its disciplinary codes. To imagine an absolute autonomy of the body would be as facile as it would be to imagine the innate freedom of the intercultural. What is needed, perhaps, is a more critical imaginary of the body whereby its relatively uninvestigated agency for social transformation can extend beyond the limited horizons of the existing laboratories of intercultural theatre practice.

For all their seeming 'difference', these islands of erstwhile *avant-garde* practice have hermetically sealed themselves from larger interactions with the world. At the start of a new millennium, it would be useful not to repeat their mistakes in 'using' the techniques of other cultures for the articulation of 'different' energies and body-behaviours. We have to get beyond the 'use' of other cultures for the assumed rejuvenation of our inner states of desiccation; instead, we need to develop a more heightened awareness of the ecology of cultures, whereby we do not enrich ourselves at the expense of others.

In this context, another kind of cultural practice becomes necessary whereby a more reflexive ethos of hospitality needs to be activated. It is no longer sufficient to accept that the stranger is a temporary guest whose presence and company should be tolerated. We may need to acknowledge that this guest could also be a resident in our public space, and that he or she could be the most potent interventionist in making us imagine other modalities of meeting that have not yet been envisioned in our dominant world-views. The question is: Are we going to open our doors to this resident-guest? Or are we going to brand him/her as a foreigner who is out to sabotage our most cherished ideals of a 'good society'? Are the intercultural decision-makers – I mean, funding agencies, 'experts', festival directors, impresarios, chairpersons of intercultural research institutes – ready to rethink their hegemonic control over existing frames and circuits of intercultural interaction? Or are they afraid that in doing so their unquestioned rights of representing the other will be usurped?

The intercultural other (which would seem to be a contradiction in terms) is not a usurper: he or she is our potential partner. However, as borders proliferate for large sections of the world's population, even as they seem to have disappeared for more privileged citizens, the bonds of partnership are more threatened than ever before by the increasingly monitored mechanisms of travel determined by the non-availability of visas and the increasing irrationality of border surveillance. While the speed of some intercultural meetings has accelerated with the ubiquity of new communicative facilities like e-mail, the obstacles have increased for larger sections of artists and cultural activists, who continue to be denied the most rudimentary modes of communication and travel, at times within the borders of their own countries. In the process, the ecology of intercultures suffers, as some partnerships proliferate, while others break down even before an opportunity to explore their mutual needs and desires has been tested.

Contrary to reports, therefore, that interculturalism is alive and well, I would say that it could be the least recognized struggle of our times. This struggle extends beyond the making of culture to a confrontation of those global and national forces that actually control – and obstruct – the meeting of different cultures in the first place. Without the creative dynamics of meeting, the intercultural imaginary is stunted. This does not mean, however, that we have no other choice but to fall back on our existing images of the other that could be mere projections of our selves. We need to avoid the predictability of such an impasse by consciously reversing the dominant circuits of intercultural exchange, but also by leaving the routes open to being imagined in unexpected ways. As cartographers of the imagination, we have to accept that the intercultural map has shifting boundaries, shifting sites. If the future is intercultural, the intercultural is also the future that can yet be freed from the fixities of its insufficiently imagined practice.

The book could end here, but in doing so, it would merely succumb to the illusory freedom of cultural choices that could exist for everybody were it not for the inadequacies of existing infrastructures. Perhaps, the act of imagining other cultures is a more difficult enterprise, involving a confrontation of the larger realities of social injustice that are not easily reconciled with the priorities of intercultural practice. While there are no norms as such on how and what one imagines as an interculturalist, this does not mean that the imagination is an entirely subjective resource, or that it need not be accountable for how the world gets interpreted through its trajectories.

Obviously, there are different contexts of life and work that facilitate the construction of specific imaginaries in radically different ways: the post-millennial dreams of the practitioners of DAS ARTS, for instance, function within a framework of privilege that is totally at odds with the deprivation of the social actors in the *mohalla* committees of Mumbai. Without undermining the benefits of privilege by valorizing the assumed integrity of a 'poor' culture, one needs to question how the resources of any kind of privilege can be mobilized and shared. Likewise, there is no reason to deny the capacity of underprivileged communities, as in the Dharavi Mohalla Committee, to imagine a better world for themselves and for others as well. It would be more pertinent to remember that the imagination is not the prerogative of artists alone. Indeed, there is much to learn from ordinary people, who have sustained their creativity through the worst crises – the genocide in Kosovo, or the communal riots in the Indian metropolis.

While accepting that there is more than one way of imagining the world, I would urge a greater openness to those very realities that would seem to annihilate the imagination – poverty, hunger, homelessness, ethnic cleansing. It is out of the harsh, often grotesque provocations of these realities that the moribund narratives of intercultural practice can be most meaningfully challenged and catalysed. Keeping this in mind, I would like to end the book on a particularly painful encounter that has come alive for me through the research of a fellow interculturalist. There are at least two reasons for sharing his story here. At one level, I would emphasize the necessity of inscribing pain in our ongoing narratives of other cultures, which can help us to counter, if not dissolve, the dichotomies of the self and the other. Perhaps, at an even deeper level, the story resonates for me precisely because it links the future of interculturalism to the lives of children, who, hopefully, will inhabit a more peaceful and loving world than ours. This hope, however, cannot be readily assumed.

The story I want to share is drawn from Olu Oguibe's description of an incident in the foyer of a three-star hotel in Guadalajara, Mexico. What he saw shattered the cosmopolitan norms of the international conference in which he was participating:

> [A] child, crudely attired and hastily painted in the colours of an indigenous performer (having perhaps done the make-up himself), gestured towards staff and visitors [in the hotel lobby]. He was at most six, and he was there because he was not in school. He was there because he could not be in school.
>
> The boy gestured, but he did not speak, which is not to say that he could not speak. Evidently, he could only gesticulate to the audience in that hotel lobby because he did not have their language. Our language. Someone offered him money, which he rejected, and at this point he was driven from the lobby by a member of staff. As he fled, the fellow turned to us and explained what the little boy wanted all along: drinking water.
>
> (Oguibe1997: 46)

In the numerous lessons that can be drawn from this story through Oguibe's sensitive guidance – the 'failure of communication' and the 'propensity to misunderstand, and in the process demean' the less articulate and privileged – there is one condition that would seem to be essential for any valid intercultural encounter. Indeed, it is vital for the future of interculturalism as a cross-border phenomenon of human exchange and dialogue: the cognition of the social and economic predicament of underprivileged communities and indigenous peoples in the Third World, without which the recognition of their cultural identity and heritage becomes somewhat redundant, if not fatuous – yet another variation on the neo-orientalist fascination for the Other.

If the future of the intercultural has to be posited in tangible terms, and not just as an empty fantasy, we will have to open ourselves to those realities that resist being imagined easily. The child in Guadalajara, as indeed the Rajasthani child-performer whose dehumanization I had indicated in my essay on the YPO, are there to remind us of the increasingly mechanized indifference to the wretched of the earth in the new world order. We need to take stock of this indifference in order to activate a process of cultural exchange that can be more honestly grounded in a respect for differences, cutting across the inequities of class, race, and citizenship. Only then is the future of the intercultural likely to transcend the conceit of its existing complacencies by igniting new possibilities of being human at the start of the millennium.

NOTES

1 I am reminded in this context of an intercultural art workshop conducted at the cultural complex of Sanskriti Sagar in New Delhi, where one of the foreign participants wanted to incorporate embroidery into his art work. Unskilled in this specific art, he nonetheless drew a sketch of the image he had in mind; this image was taken by an intermediary to a group of local women artisans doing traditional embroidery for a living. Without entering into any dialogue with these women, the artist had no difficulty in accepting their embroidery which he promptly framed, and then claimed as 'his' work of art (for which he obviously got a price when it was sold). Is this illegitimate art practice, or a legitimate rip-off?

2 Emergent debates around 'authorship' have extended both to the avant-garde and popular sectors of contemporary cultural practice in India. For instance, in the 're-mixing' phenomenon of Hindi pop music, old hit songs from early Hindi movies are being electronically transformed into new renditions, with no acknowledgement whatsoever to their original sources (see Jha 1998 for a sharp journalistic account of these commercially legitimized modes of plagiarism). Significantly, while the re-mixing maestro Bally Sagoo is obviously savvy enough to distinguish between a 'lift' and a 'cover version' of the same song, whether he is re-mixing Nusrat Fateh Ali Khan or the veteran Hindi film composer R.D. Burman, the idea of 'quotation' has yet to enter the vocabulary of pop music in India, following the more ironic and reflexive experiments in international pop.

    About the only self conscious mode of quotation in contemporary Indian art practice is to be found in the relatively recent development of 'installations'. Vivan Sundaram's *Memorial* (1993), for instance, draws heavily on an anonymous press photograph (by Hoshi Jal) of a victim in the Mumbai riots – an image that is defaced/framed/concealed/cut/erased in a variety of ways. This installation stimulated a thought-provoking debate on the need to acknowledge all the sources and credits in multi-media work, notably photography as used in the 'art form' of the installation (see Satish Sharma's acerbic 'Still a Fodder for the "Finer" Arts', 1993, for a critical perspective on the issue of acknowledgement). Similar debates have yet to emerge in discussing the 'classical' Indian performing arts, where the routine appropriations of 'folk', 'traditional', and 'tribal' resources are systematically legitimized if not honoured, under the pretence of 'reviving' old traditions or of 'innovating' new ones.

3 The Emergency refers to a two-year authoritarian rule between 1975 and 1977 that was instituted by the ruling Congress Party under Indira Gandhi's leadership. Its non-militarized civic dictatorship was ultimately overthrown by the landslide victory of a coalition of parties that owed their ideological allegiance to the democratic and communitarian ideals of Jayaprakash Narayan. It is one of the lasting misfortunes of Indian democracy that this non-Congress government headed by the Janata Party did not last, resulting in the return of Indira Gandhi to power with an even greater legitimacy of her earlier politics.

4 It is necessary to point out that Brook's 'ultraculturalism' was made possible through the patronage of the Empress Farah and the Shah of Iran, the official benefactors of the

Shiraz Festival in which *Orghast* (1970) had been prominently featured. Such seeming obliviousness to the cultural façade of a political dictatorship reveals the depths at which interculturalists can seek refuge in the platitude that 'art has nothing to do with politics'.

5   'Inroads' refers to an ambitious intercultural project funded by the Ford Foundation, where the basic premise is to open the possibilities of interdisciplinary, cross-cultural collaborative work with artists based in the USA. As the undirectionality of the word suggests, 'Inroads' is restricted by its specific ordering of routes, and the implicit bias in favour of cultures from the South feeding the multicultural agenda of the North (in this case, specifically the USA). There is also an implicit aggression written into the word in so far as you 'make inroads into something'. One would have imagined that the obvious insensitivities of this category, even at a semantic level, would have compelled its sponsors to think of another, more congenial term – 'crossroads', for instance – where the possibilities of cultural exchange are left somewhat more open to being negotiated. It is well known, however, that the traffic (cultural or otherwise) at the 'crossroads' is harder to control – and police – than in the one-way lanes of 'inroads'. It is not surprising, therefore, that foundations should opt for the latter.

6   The Inappropriate Other: 'Not quite the Same, not quite the Other, she stands in that undetermined threshold place where she constantly drifts in and out ... She is this Inappropriate Other/Same who moves about with always at least two/four gestures; that of affirming "I am like you" while persisting in her difference; and that of reminding "I am different" while unsettling every definition of otherness arrived at' (Trinh 1991:74).

7   I was alerted to the intercultural dynamics of the 'respect for imperfection' in a presentation made by Adrian Piper in a conference on 'Frameworks for Art' at the Mohile Parikh Centre for the Visual Arts in Mumbai, February 1998. Piper began her presentation by acknowledging that she was opening herself in an Indian forum to a great deal of risk, if not derision, by speaking on Yoga, one of the disciplines that has inspired her own analytic philosophy and performance practice. Admittedly, Piper's 'imperfections' were real, not least her mispronunciations of basic Sanskrit words (which she herself constantly highlighted), apart from a very literal paraphrase of Patanjali. But this was just the prologue to, if not the preparation for, her own philosophical journey into an exposure of racism and the politics of appearing to be 'white' when one is, in actuality, 'black'.

   This transition from the philosophical context of Yoga into the political realities of racism was a mind-blowing experience for the audience. What impressed and moved me deeply was not Piper's conceptual translation of the rarefied Sanskrit vocabulary within the junctures of her own autobiographical narrative, but the quality of stillness and concentrated energy in her presence. This, for me, was Yoga in action. It was also an illumination of the subversive possibilities of Yoga as a 'political' discipline.

   In retrospect, I would emphasize how much there is to learn from Piper's interculturality, where there is no attempt to demonstrate Yoga as a set of skills, which has become the norm in the fetishization of oriental techniques by intercultural performance 'experts'. Piper demonstrates through her practice how the *principles* of one context can catalyse the formation of narratives in other contexts, without losing their inner resilience and vibrancy. To her colleagues in philosophy as well, Piper offers an altogether unprecedented provocation in her ability to concretize thought through performance.

8   In Bhikhu Parekh's reflections on 'being British' in the multicultural context of Britain today, there is an interesting tension on what constitutes 'the cultural language' of the nation. While this language is posited as an entity, it is also undergoing changes and incorporating a wide spectrum of 'different though mutually intelligible accents and

idioms' (Parekh 1990:75). 'Being British' is not about generalities such as sharing '*values*' or a '*common view of British history*', still less about '*obeying laws*' and '*loving*' British society; it is specifically related to a 'conceptual competence' in being able 'to understand and handle the prevailing variety of accents' (ibid.; emphases in original). Unfortunately, Parekh does not even begin to suggest *how* one goes about developing a cognizance of these 'pluralized' accents. Instead, he falls back on liberal urbanity by invoking 'a new spirit of partnership, a spirit of what the Romans called civic friendship' (ibid.). This prelapsarian mode of utopianizing the multiculturalism of our times is yet another implicit regression, reminiscent of Taylor's endorsement of a 'fusion of horizons'.

9   In economic terms, the privilege of interculturalism can be deconstructed only by those who control the capital that makes its practice possible. This involves much more than a liberalization of existing funding policies, which continue to be based on moribund humanitarian and philanthropic premises that were formulated during the Cold War to promote the privatization of cultural capital. Today, a radical shift in the paradigms of funding is urgently needed, but this is not possible without an infiltration of new ideologies like the 'new abolitionist project' in white studies, which is based on the repudiation of the 'lie of whiteness' and the privileges attached to it (Winant 1997).

This 'new abolitionism' is considered by its proponents as 'the precondition for the establishment of substantive racial equality and social justice' (ibid.: 85). Following the motto 'Treason to whiteness is loyalty to humanity', it exhorts whites to become 'race traitors' (ibid.). While this position is not without its blind spots – not least, as Howard Winant points out, the inscription of 'non-white elements' within existing notions of whiteness – the 'new abolitionist project' is an appropriate challenge, in my view, to the tacit liberal support of prevailing racial and social injustices. Significantly, as the new funding policies around 'cultural diversity' programmes in the USA indicate, there can be no meaningful mobilization of cultural diversity without an acknowledgement of continuing racial discrimination. Finally, one is compelled to add that the implicit privileges of whiteness continue to underlie the very formulation of the funding policies themselves, which refuse to acknowledge their own racial underpinnings.

CHAPTER 3

1   *Gundegowdana charitre* ('The History of Gundegowda') was first performed at the Rangayana Theatre in Mysore, January 1995. The play was adapted and translated by S. Raghunandan, and designed by Pushpamala N., with music composed by B.V. Karanth and Srinivasa Bhat. The title role of Gundegowda was played by three actors – Hulugappa Kattimani, B. Krishnakumar Narakaje, and K.C. Raghunath. The rest of the company, which played multiple roles, included Prameela Bengre, M.S. Geetha, Prashanth S. Hiremath, Mime Ramesh, Basavraja Kodage, Santoshkumar Kusnoor, S. Ramu, Manjunatha Belakere, Mandya Ramesh, Mahadeva, Jagadeesh Manevarthe, Arunkumar, M.C. Krishnaprasad, S. Ramanath, Noor Ahmed Sheik, Vinayaka Bhat Hasanagi, K.R. Nandini, N. Mangala, and B.N. Shashikala.

2   This is one of the platitudinous statements constituting the official multicultural discourse of the Indian state as outlined by the former Culture Secretary B.P. Singh in his book *India's Culture: The State,the Arts, and Beyond* (1998). For a detailed analysis of Singh's pseudo-scholarship, and of his conflation of such categories as 'diversity', 'plurality', and 'composite culture', along with his authoritarian perspective on how 'countervailing forces' need to be 'neutralized' in order to ensure the management of Indian culture by the state, read my review, 'Culture and Power' (1998).

3   Quoted by Saxena and Mahendroo (1993:2447), this statement made by the revolutionary Telugu poet Varavara Rao is worth quoting at length:

   The civil people do not even call poor people's language a language. It is called a dialect of Telugu the way Magadhi and Bhojpuri are called dialects of Hindi. But this is wrong. There is nothing like a standard language of the civil people and the rest are dialects ... Why is a brahmin's language called standard and working people's language dialect? ... Sanskrit words are called natural and the rest are labelled as distortions. This is wrong ... To save the language and cultural identity [of those who have no control over natural and economic resources], the struggle is on.

4   Focusing on the ritual dimensions of anthropology, Victor Turner (1979) has attempted to push the boundaries of ethnography and performance in his experiments on the subject. Unfortunately, his workshops in 'performing ethnography' failed to address with sufficient rigor the contextual differences between ethnography in the field and its simulations in a performance space, as well as the cognitive preparation of actors to adapt their existing acting skills to the 'cultural rules' underlying the anthropological contexts of the Other. Perhaps, in the final analysis, such experiments are more revealing of the anthropologists themselves than their ritualized 'natives'. Indeed, they are testaments to the naivety – and desperation – underlying the ritual anthropologist's desire to ' "get inside the skins" of members of other cultures' (Turner 1979: 81).
   For a critique of the epistemological traps in endorsing a 'native's point of view', read Geertz (1985). An even more incisive reflection on the false models of reflexivity in representing the Other is available in Trinh (1991).

5   Our own postcolonial affinities to English in India enabled us to tune into the contemporary subtleties and 'playability' of Rolf Fjelde's and Michael Meyer's justifiably acclaimed translations of Ibsen's classic, along with a much older, literary, verse translation of the play by R. Farquharson Sharp (from the Everyman Library series) which would be dismissed as archaic and unplayable by any contemporary theatre group in the West today. The point is that 'our' subcontinental English enables us to respond to certain formalities and rhetorical conventions of earlier modes of English literature that were the mainstay of our colonial education. If English became the source-language of the production, therefore, it was 'more than one English' that triggered off the deviations and flights of fantasy in Raghu's adaptation of the text in 'more than one Kannada'.

6   This final direction becomes all the more pertinent today in the context of the recent 'onion scandal' in India when the price of onions increased by almost 100 per cent in the latter half of 1998, making them unaffordable for vast sections of the population. It is also telling that such price-rises over a seemingly negligible food item, onions, had some impact in collectivizing public resistance against the ruling government along with graver issues like communal violence and unemployment.

7   I should add that Peer Gynt's transformation into a Gowda anticipated Deve Gowda's appointment as the Prime Minister of India. While it would have been neatly ironic if the production could have coincided with Deve Gowda's brief and turbulent tenure as Prime Minister, thereby opening vital questions of how a farmer's son can rise to the highest political office in contemporary India, it might also have raised needlessly controversial questions about caste politics that were not specifically addressed in the adaptation of the play. This is not to deny, of course, the manifold problems of casting a play in a multi-caste company like Rangayana, but these conflicts are invariably negotiated within the politics of representation in theatre itself and are not directly linked to the casteism of the *realpolitik*. This is a distinction that needs to be

emphasized, if only to protect the increasingly threatened autonomy of theatre as a cultural practice from the encroachments of caste politics.

8 The Kannada rap song incorporated references to cultural tourism:

Breakfast in Bali
Lunch in London
High tea in Tokyo
Dinner in Delhi.

This is followed by a more menacing celebration of war:

Armoured tank/atom bomb/fighter plane
Hand grenade/machine gun/poison gas
Prathidina kolladakke maarodakke
(Buy and sell them every day).

9 It is important to keep in mind that the original character Huhu is obsessed by his need to return to 'the primal language', 'our real forest-tongue', which was Ibsen's way of satirizing a group of national language reformers in his time, whose aim was to restore the Norwegian language to its former state of purity. Interestingly, this linguistic controversy does not seem to have ended in Norway. From Okwui Enwezor's fascinating 'travel notes', we learn that a group of contemporary Norwegian artists named Struth ('Ostrich') uphold 'the *old* Norwegian language' as 'in fact the *new* language; new Norwegian, a more authentic Norwegian free of the taint of colonial contact with Sweden and Denmark, is truly the old Norwegian' (Enwezor 1997: 10).

From such 'indeterminate histories', I would agree with Enwezor that we continue to discover our 'foreignness' (ibid.), but not without illuminating some of the crises of cultural identity within the unresolved political debates of the past.

10 Though Sheldon Pollock's learned thesis on the 'cosmopolitan vernacular' (1998a, 1998b) lies outside of the historical and conceptual framework of this book, it is worth addressing in some detail in order to highlight some of the difficulties in theorizing the cosmopolitan. Drawing on the widespread vernacularization of local languages in South Asia between AD 1000 and AD 1500, with a particular focus on Kannada, Sheldon Pollock calls attention to how 'the globalizing orders, formations, and practices' of the 'Sanskrit cosmopolis' in the first millennium were 'supplemented and gradually replaced by localized forms' of language, culture, and polity.

One obvious difficulty with Pollock's ambitious thesis has to do with his unproblematized equations of pre-modem 'globalization' with the assertively *cosmopolitan* use of Sanskrit through its dissemination in literature and the public inscriptions of the first millennium. Not only are contemporary categories such as 'global' and 'cosmopolitan' introjected into the past, with no theoretical analysis whatsoever of their political and philosophical legacies in the present, but also Pollock's own scrupulously researched historical evidence of the uses of Sanskrit in the first millennium would seem to refute its 'cosmopolitan' bearings, in so far as it functioned neither as a 'link language' nor as a 'chancery language for bureaucratic or administrative purposes' (Pollock 1998a: 12). Contradicting its seemingly transregional outreach at the level of everyday communication, Sanskrit would seem to have been confined as 'the appropriate vehicle for the expression of royal will', its knowledge being assumed as a vital 'component of kingliness' (ibid.: 14).

Without denying the mutations of the vernacularizing process between AD 1000 and AD 1500, one is nonetheless compelled to question Pollock's unproblematized use of the 'cosmopolitan', which becomes a free-floating signifier in his analysis. It is precisely this elision of the differentiated histories of the 'cosmopolitan' that enables him to conclude that 'indigenous cultures are produced in the course of long-term translocal interactions *by the very same processes* that produce the global itself' (Pollock 1998a: 34; my emphases). The absence of accountability in such large statements is made possible through Pollock's insistence that the 'local/global dualism' needs to be 'historicized out of existence' because 'each becomes the other in constantly new ways'. With such a postmodern predilection for dissolving different periods, times, and concepts of history through the free play of signs in which contexts are interchangeable, it is not surprising that Pollock should acknowledge that his reading of the 'cosmopolitan vernacular' can be read as a 'precolonial complement' to Homi Bhabha's ongoing research on the 'vernacular cosmopolitan'.

My own reading of the 'cosmopolitan vernacular' in relation to *Gundegowda* is more located within a specific historic juncture that is identified with the dual incursions of capitalism and modernity. While there is a jostling of the 'local' and the 'global' within the hybridity of Gundegowda's rhetoric, there is no attempt in the production to neutralize the 'local/global dualism'. Indeed, this would have totally countered the critique of capital in the production by subscribing to a facile, and essentially derivative, postmodernism wherein all conflicts are dissolved.

11   This is not to deny that the practice of rewriting a text, and indeed, of mixing different dialects of Kannada into a 'cosmopolitan vernacular', does not have rich precedents in Kannada poetry and dramatic literature. The theatre critic K.V. Akshara has called my attention in a personal correspondence (December 4, 1999) to the playwright Samsa's 'creation' of a new Kannada drawn from the official archives of the Mysore court, in addition to Kailasam, who 'invented a strange blend of Kannada and English to portray the elite old-Mysoreans of his time.' More recently, in Girish Karnad's play *Taledanda*, the king Bijjala speaks 'a barber community dialect from North Karnataka' that resonates politically in relation to the Kannada spoken by the other characters. Indeed, so distinct are some of these dialects that readers from North Karnataka have apparently demanded a 'translation' of the rural Mysore dialect used in the latest novel of the *dalit* writer Devanoor Mahadeva. I am grateful to Akshara for emphasizing that Raghu's translation of *Peer Gynt* was not only a response to the demands of a specific intracultural project; he was also reacting to already available traditions of translation in Kannada.

CHAPTER 4

1   In this chapter, I will be focusing on dramaturgy rather than on the directorial and acting process of *Kiss of the Spider Woman*, which would require a more extended analysis. For their valuable inputs to the realization of this dramaturgy, I would like to thank Jitu Shastri (Molina) and Arjun Raina (Valentin), Amitabh Srivastav for his Hindi translation of the dramatic text, and, above all, Anuradha Kapur for alerting me to the sexist dimensions from which Puig's narrative is not entirely free. The production was staged at the Siddhartha Art Gallery on the premises of the Max Mueller Bhavan in New Delhi in July–August 1993.

2   Quoted in *Less Than Gay*, 'a citizens' report on the status of homosexuality in India', the first report of its kind in the Indian context, researched and published by AIDS Bhedbhav Virodhi Andolan (ABVA), New Delhi (1991: 31). It is significant to point out that ABVA has initiated a public interest litigation in the High Court of Delhi against the Union of India and other government bodies. The group has appealed for the repeal of Section 377 on the grounds that the authorities of Tihar Jail in New Delhi had refused to distribute condoms to the prisoners, while forcibly testing them for HIV/

AIDS. According to the authorities, this distribution of condoms would have implied an endorsement of homosexuality, if not an acknowledgement of its rampant practice among prisoners (for which they would have had to be formally charged under Section 377). Through their strategic intervention, the members of ABVA have opened a critical debate on the complex relationship between AIDS/homosexuality/sodomy and the necessary de-linking and reconceptualization of their component parts within the legal, sexual, and cultural norms of the Indian state. The contradictions of this debate (which emerged after *Kiss of the Spider Woman* had been staged) inspire a totally different kind of narrative on the politics of homosexuality in India, more grounded in facticity than in the fiction suggested by Puig's text.

3   In one of the many originary myths by which *hijras* trace their ancestry, Serena Nanda (1993) calls attention to yet another transformation of Krishna into a *femme fatale* who manages to seduce – and, thereafter, kill – the demon Araka who had never set eyes on a woman before. After killing Araka, presumably after his virginity has been destroyed, Krishna reveals himself to the other gods testifying that 'there will be more like me, neither man nor woman, and whatever words come from the mouths of these people, whether good [blessings] or bad [curses], will come true' (quoted in Nanda 1993: 548).

Nanda's reference to the 'festival' in Tamilnadu, which she does not name, bears close resemblance to one of the most important ritualistic rites of the *hijras* in the village of Koovagam (around 90 km east of Madras), where thousands of *hijras* congregate towards the end of April on a full-moon night to marry the local deity of the village, Lord Aravan. According to a reportage of this ritual (Banerjee and Mukhopadhyay 1994), Aravan has to be sacrificed by his father Arjuna, one of the central characters in the *Mahabharata*. While it is possible that Koothandavar is yet another local variation of Aravan – both men are sacrificed after a night of love with a female Krishna – there are some interesting differences in the ritual as described in Banerjee and Mukhopadhyay's reportage and Serena Nanda's narrative, which seems to be based on hearsay rather than on actual field-research.

While Nanda specifies that the deity of Koothandavar is carried to a burial ground where the *hijras* begin to enact their ritual of widowhood, Banerjee and Mukhopadhyay mark the moment of widowhood more precisely in the removal of the *hijra*'s sacred wedding-thread by the temple priest. Thereafter, the *hijras* bathe in an adjoining tank, after which they change from their wedding finery into white saris, the traditional dress of Hindu widows. Such details contribute to the poignancy of the *hijras*' 'cursed' life, as they return to reality from their ritualized transformations as divine brides.

Finally, if Aravan is the son of Arjun, whose best friend in turn is Krishna, then the temporary 'union' of Krishna to Aravan opens even more interpretive possibilities linking the act of sacrifice not merely to the heterosexual mediation of marriage but to the less codified intimacies of friendship.

4   While the *hijra* has been a stock character in commercial Hindi cinema for some time, generally appearing in marriage scenes and bawdy dance numbers (which at times inspire the cross-dressed hero to temporarily shed his machismo), there have been some recent attempts in more 'serious' films to represent the *hijra* in a more sympathetic and realistic mode. In Mani Ratnam's *Bombay*, the *hijra* provides shelter to a child who has been separated from his twin brother and parents in the riot-ridden streets of Bombay following the demolition of the Babri Masjid. Likewise Mahesh Bhatt's *Tamanna*, which is based on a 'true story', foregrounds the *hijra* as a single parent who adopts an abandoned girl-child. In a more tragic mode, Kalpana Lajmi's *Daayra* focuses on the almost incestuous bonding (and ultimate suicide) of a hermaphrodite and his film-star mother.

For all these seemingly compassionate breakthroughs in the representation of the *hijras*, what needs to be emphasized is their continued inscription within predominantly patriarchal imaginaries, where they either feed the dominant values of a heterosexual family system or are ultimately apotheosized as victims. In the humanizing of the *hijra*, therefore, the *hijra*'s otherness is also subtly deepened, thereby making him/her a 'safe' choice for an examination of 'our' sexuality. After all, 'we' can never be like 'them'. They may be 'human', but they remain irreconcilably 'different'.

5   It would not be out of place here to insert a blatant piece of homophobia in the Indian context that was legitimized within an allegedly marxist ideological framework. Reacting violently to a report on 'Gay Rights in India' (Balasubrahmanyan 1996) published in the leading Indian social scientist journal *Economic and Political Weekly*, the male respondent (H. Srikanth) attacked the legitimacy of homosexuality on the grounds that 'the natural is not always rational' (Srikanth 1996: 976).

Reducing homosexuality to an aberrant pathology (for which there is always room for a healthy heterosexist cure through marxist 'education, socialization, advocacy, and if necessary, psychiatric treatment'), Srikanth emphasized that the 'social recognition of sexual preferences' cannot be accepted because this would amount to 'asking for a privilege, not a right' (ibid.). Resisting any support for the 'reactionary' and 'backward' nature of homosexuality, which intrinsically works against the 'progressive' and 'social necessity' of a marxist agenda, our comrade ended his diatribe by warning all sexual deviants against making their issues public:

> [I]f some people, much against public conscience, take to the streets on the plea that they have the right to gratify their sexual urges in any way they like, Marxists do not hesitate to use force against such homosexual activists.   (ibid.: 976)

While it would be reductive, if not grossly unfair, to equate such unabashed homophobia with 'marxism' in general, or with 'Indian marxists' in particular, it is chastening to recognize that such positions continue to be affirmed. Needless to say, the *Economic and Political Weekly* published rejoinders to Srikanth's opposition to gay rights, notably by women, but the fact remains that it articulates the kind of masculinist discourse that one would like to identify more readily with right-wing fundamentalists than with secular activists, who are assumed to be more tolerant in their respect for differences. For a reading of the continued non-reflexivity underlying secular (male) critiques of masculinity, read my review of Anand Patwardhan's *Father, Son and Holy War* (Bharucha 1998).

6   Nothing could exemplify the heterosexist biases of the Broadway musical of *Kiss of the Spider Woman* more egregiously than the climactic moment of Hal Prince's production, which ends with a torrid, passionate kiss: not Molina kissing Valentin, but a 'dead' (and heterosexually transformed) Molina locked in the arms of the woman of his dreams, centre-stage, while Valentin stands in the background with a bouquet of red roses in an outstretched hand. The semiotics of this visual is not just ludicrous but obscene, I would say, in its blatant negation of Puig's politics. Perhaps, 'negation' is too strong a word because, arguably, there is no possible frame within the capitalist ideology of the Broadway musical that can accommodate any significant deviation from its celebration of heterosexual/sexist norms.

7   For the reader unfamiliar with the story of the film, it is sufficient to know that *Fire* centres around an urban, middle-class, Hindu family, who run a fast-food restaurant and a video rental business in New Delhi. While the older brother (Ashok) neglects his 'infertile' wife (Radha) in order to devote himself somewhat homoerotically to the service of a *swamiji* (religious man), the recently married younger brother (Jatin) is almost brutally indifferent to his savvy and modern young bride (Sita), favouring the company of a Chinese hairdresser, who is more interested in emigrating to Hong Kong.

The other members of this strange household are Maji, the old invalid mother of the two sons, who can neither walk nor talk, but who has to endure the company of the overworked, sexually frustrated servant (Mundu), who masturbates regularly in front of her while watching blue movies. In this environment, the intimacy of Radha and Sita develops into a lesbian relationship, which is violently exposed when they are discovered in bed by Ashok on Mundu's instigation.

The title of the film refers to the 'test of fire', the *agnipariksha* to which the mythical heroine of the *Ramayana* has to submit in order to prove her chastity to a suspicious husband. In Deepa Mehta's *Fire*, it is Radha who literally survives being burned alive in the kitchen as she escapes the helpless wrath of her disbelieving husband. The final image of the film shows the women together in the serene environment of a Sufi shrine, suggesting a future that remains open. On conflicting interpretations of this final image, read Ghosh (1999) and Naim (1999).

8   This is not the first time that Thackeray has ignited a 'cultural war' by unleashing blatantly vicious anti-minoritarian propaganda through his editorials in *Saamna*. On the power that he wields in editing films, even before they have been released, we need to remember the doctoring of his own screen image in Mani Ratnam's *Bombay*, which deals with the post-Ayodhya riots that were largely engineered by the Shiv Sena on Thackeray's instigation. Despite the highly elaborate investigative report on the riots by the Sri Krishna Commission, Thackeray continues to function as an extra-constitutional political threat by targeting minorities and 'anti-nationalists' (by his own definition). His most recent victims include prominent Muslim artists such as the actor Dilip Kumar and the painter M.F. Husain, whose allegedly pornographic sketch of the goddess Saraswati has been yet another source of manipulation in the communal propaganda of Hindutva.

9   Deepa Mehta would seem to take the question of exclusion beyond gender and sexuality to include problematic issues relating to ethnicity and race as well. In an altogether original intervention in the film, we encounter a rather abrasive encounter between Jatin, the younger brother, who meekly submits to a polemical harangue on 'India' and 'Indians' by the Indian-Chinese brother of his upwardly mobile girlfriend. While this sequence has been yet another source of affront to Hindu chauvinists, it is worth keeping in mind that casual references to the Indian-Chinese community as 'Chinky' (testified by the Chinese character in the film) are not uncommon in India. Indeed, as I will elaborate in Chapter 6 on secularism, there is an unacknowledged racism that extends to the representation of almost all communities in the north-east of India, whose Tibetan-Burmese linguistic roots and mongoloid appearance have isolated them from the rest of the country.

It is worth recording here that this could be the first sequence in Indian cinema where the Chinese minority community has been granted a subject-position. However, a more extended analysis would be needed to show how this subject-position echoes (and distends) the diasporic Canadian cultural politics of Deepa Mehta, which she tends to undermine in her assertion of an 'Indian' identity.

10   The debate around the Uniform Civil Code (UCC) has been intricately inflected through numerous feminist, secularist, and communitarian interventions. No longer viewed unequivocally, the UCC elicits strong reactions in India today. On the one hand, there are those die-hard secularist modernists who would insist on the equal rights of all individuals regardless of considerations determined by gender, religion, and community. This position is staunchly opposed by those who would continue to uphold the validity of separate 'personal laws' for each religious group. A more intermediate position would insist on the internal reform of these laws within the framework of religious communities, with or without state intervention. Resulting from this position is the

increasingly widespread endorsement of what has been described as an 'optional civil code', which enables women to follow the tenets of personal laws, but which also grants them the 'right to exit' their respective communities in those situations where their individual rights may be directly threatened by religious orthodoxy. Yet another variation – 'reverse optionality' – enables citizens to opt for personal laws, even though they may live their everyday lives in compliance with the norms of a common civil code. For a meticulous analysis of the multiple contexts informing the debate around the Uniform Civil Code, read Sangari (1995).

11   I have in mind Gayatri Spivak's valuable formulation of 'the radical interruption of practice by theory, and of theory by practice', and her still more heartening faith in the value of 'crisis', when the 'presuppositions of an enterprise are disproved by the enterprise itself' (Spivak 1990: 44). My only disclaimer would be that the modalities of 'practice' in theatre are dependent on different agencies of 'interruption', which have yet to be adequately accounted for in literary theory.

CHAPTER 6

1   From Gandhi's autobiography we learn that '[t]he principle called Satyagraha came into being before that name was invented' (1982: 291). For a long time the English term 'passive resistance' was used (even in Gandhi's Gujarati discourse), until Gandhi himself became aware of its associations with a 'weapon of the weak', which could also be marked by 'hatred' and 'violence' (ibid.). Realizing that 'a new word' needed to be 'coined by the Indians to designate their [already existing] struggle' (ibid.: 292), Gandhi settled for a down-to-earth activist strategy by offering a prize through the *Indian Opinion* for the best name that could characterize the Indian movement. Maganlal Gandhi was the winner with his contribution of '*Sadagraha*', which Gandhi later altered to *Satyagraha* (*sat* = truth, *agraha* = firmness). The entire process of arriving at this name reveals that there is nothing sacrosanct in the process of naming political principles; it is subject to a combination of thought, change, strategy, and, in Gandhi's case, an element of humour.

2   Significantly, 'racism' is used sparingly in Indian political discourse, subsumed as it is within the dominant usages of 'communalism' in India. At a very literal level, it could be said that the 'communal' more often than not is linked to pejorative associations of other 'religious communities', whereas a 'racist' attitude is generally directed against other 'races' (for example, against black African students in India). However, the distinctions are far from clear, because, as Gyanendra Pandey has elaborated, the Indian meaning of the term 'communalism' can include 'Hindu–Muslim or Hindu–Sikh conflict in northern India, Brahman–non-Brahman conflict in southern and western India, Sinhala–Tamil conflict in Sri Lanka, conflicts between Malays, Chinese and Indians in Malaysia, and between black, brown and white races in the West Indies' (Pandey 1996: 7).
More specifically, within the ideological context of Hindutva, in which the racial foundations of Hindu communalism have been determined, it becomes almost impossible to separate notions of 'religion' from those determining 'race' and 'culture'. The Muslims, for instance, in such an ideological framework, can have no allegiance to India as loyal citizens, because they are unable to identify *pitribhumi* ('fatherland') with *punyabhumi* ('holy land'), quite unlike 'the Hindu', who in 1923 was designated by the primary ideologue of Hindutva, V.D. Savarkar, as 'a person who regards the land of *Bharatvarsha* from Indus to the Seas as his Fatherland, as well as his Holy Land – that is the cradle land of his religion' (Basu *et al.* 1993: 8). Not insignificantly, the recent

conglomeration of communal parties and religious organizations constituting the Hindu Right, is represented as the Sangh *Parivar* (literally, 'family').

While the connotations of 'racism' are elided with or subsumed within the dominant usages of 'communalism' in India, there is no accurate equivalent for 'communal' in western political discourse. The word is still used synonymously with 'communitarian'. In the process, the specific Indian associations with 'religious sectarianism' are negated, so that the conflict in western contexts of religious strife, such as the continuing tensions between Protestants and Catholics in Northern Ireland, is generally described in 'religious' rather than in 'communal' terms.

3 Akeel Bilgrami's caution in categorizing 'religious communities' is well worth emphasizing in this regard: 'The very idea of a religious community is a problematic one since "Muslims" and "Hindus", as categories which we invoke, are meant to describe a collection of people who are in many senses neither religious nor a community. Like all such categories they homogenize diversified social phenomena' (Bilgrami 1997: 2540). None the less, this argument around 'anti-homogenization' can itself be reduced to a banality, as Bilgrami argues, because 'in certain historical and political contexts, religious identities might dominate many of the other identities, in some populations in some parts of the world' (ibid.). There can be situations, for example, as in fundamentalist movements, where the category of 'religious community' becomes unavoidable. On the other hand, in describing (as I do in Site 1 of this chapter) a 'communal' response to a film in the public space of a cinema hall, the category of 'religious community' becomes not merely a false homogenization, but an hermeneutic imposition. In effect, it determines an essentially reductive causality in linking violence to religion, when the process of violence may need to be linked to many other factors that are at once differentiated and elusive.

4 From one of the many erudite digressions in Benedict Anderson's study of the origin and spread of nationalism, we learn how in colonial Indonesia under Dutch rule a 'strange language-of-state' had evolved, based not on the Dutch language (which, contrary to the imposition of English in colonial India, was not instituted by the Dutch as a compulsory language for Indonesian *inlanders*), but on an 'ancient inter-insular lingua franca' derived largely from Malay (Anderson 1983: 132). By the mid-nineteenth century, with the incursions of print-capitalism in Indonesia, this language 'moved out into the market place and the media', and was 'picked up by *inlanders*' at the turn of the century (ibid.: 133). Finally, through the linguistic interventions of urban writers and readers – Anderson fails to emphasize the political advocacy of student leaders like Soekarno in the 1920s for 'one nation, one language' – *bahasa Indonesia* came into existence in 1928. And as Anderson adds, 'it has never looked back'.

5 While I share Chatterjee's opposition to the insufficiently acknowledged anti-democratic components of globalization, I am not in accordance with the way he positions democracy against modernity in the Indian context. Clubbing together civil society and modernity, and political society and democracy, and insisting on a separation of these two dynamics, makes unavoidable the inference that modernity is inimical to democracy. I am also unable to accept the absolutist divide that Chatterjee sets up between civil society and political society. Theoretical discriminations apart, I would argue that the emergent formations of political society in India, while breaking many of the established norms instituted by civil society, are also in the process of transforming, altering, appropriating, and infiltrating these norms in subversive and, at times, blatantly opportunistic ways. Our civil society – the seemingly exclusivist repository of modernist, western values – is becoming increasingly uncivil. Instead of regarding its vulnerabilities as a 'state under siege' (1997: 32), I would see this condition as a positive manifestation of the democratization of society at large.

If Chatterjee had to acknowledge these mutations in postcolonial India, he would not be able to *fix* the sites of community, civil society, political society, and the state so rigidly. This clarity produces a seemingly rigorous theory, but at the expense of taking into account the *shifts* that are actually taking place within the public domain in India today. Nonetheless, Chatterjee's emphasis on the democratization of political society in India compels him, for all his misgivings of the nation-state, to see its site as the most viable meeting ground (or battleground) for the assertion of individual and communitarian rights in India today.

6   The activists of Vimochana, the Forum for Women's Rights, have accurately placed their resistance to the Miss World Beauty Pageant in Bangalore, not within the specious context of defending 'Indian culture and tradition', but in opposition to the 'cosmetic empires' promoted by an international, corporate culture. Protesting against the legitimacy of this 'culture' that recognizes women 'only in so far as they are willing partners in the great global market in which womanhood is iconized', the activists equate the packaging of beauty culture to the fragmentation of women, in terms of their hair, skin, teeth, and toenails. While Vimochana's critique of the standardization of beauty in terms of the 'white, blonde, blue-eyed, svelte' model can be challenged at one level through the increasing adulation of 'Asian' beauty, it continues to be valid when one considers the racism that black women contestants continue to face – a racism, I should add, that was extremely marked in the dismissive, if not derisive, attitude of Indian (male) journalists to the black contestants in the Miss World pageant in Bangalore. For more details, read 'On the Miss World Beauty Pageant and Other Controversies', Vimochana 1996.

7   From the *India Today* report on the Michael Jackson show in Mumbai ('Cashing in on Jackson', 30 November 1996), we learn that 'the glitzy show cost between Rs.12 crore and Rs.15 crore; Jackson brought his own plane-load of equipment and, for reasons known to only a few, waived his performance fee. Wizcraft, the event-management company, claims at least Rs.20 crore from ticket sales and sponsorship deals; 85 per cent of the as yet untabulated profit was promised to the Shiv Udyog Sena (SUS), a Sena offshoot founded by Bal Thackeray's nephew, Raj, supposedly to provide jobs to 2.7 lakh unemployed youth' (p.46). Registered as a society a month after Jackson had agreed to perform in Mumbai, and recognized as a charitable organization a week before the show, and five days after its entertainment tax had been waived by the government of Maharashtra, the SUS has almost flaunted its absence of credibility. In its operation, one recognizes how issues like unemployment and AIDS can serve as 'human' fronts for the propagation of global capitalism.

8   The *rath yatra* ('chariot journey') can be described as a communal pilgrimage undertaken by the BJP leader L.K. Advani through a wide spectrum of locations in India. The purpose of the *yatra* was to incite Hindu communal feelings and religiosity in favour of the construction of the Rama Mandir (temple) in Ayodhya, which still continues to underlie the political agenda of Hindutva despite its strategic suppression in the 1999 elections. It is tellingly ironic that the *rath* used for this pseudo-mythological journey was an air-conditioned Toyota – a very illuminating sign, indeed, of the larger dependency of the Hindu Right on the mechanisms of global corporate culture.

9   A caveat needs to be acknowledged in relation to these well-meaning recommendations, in so far as Dreze and Sen maintain a scrupulously non-confrontationist attitude in relation to global capitalism and the market economy. Emphasizing the essential *incompleteness* of market reforms, the authors none the less acknowledge that '[t]he expansion of markets is *among* the instruments that can help to promote human

capabilities, and, given the imperative need for rapid elimination of endemic deprivation in India, it would be irresponsible to ignore that opportunity' (Dreze and Sen 1996: 203). While the authors promptly go on to prioritize 'government activity' and 'public action', they elide how exactly the 'opportunity' presented by the market can be activated in India.

In this context, it is instructive to note how precisely Dreze and Sen contextualize the market-oriented economic reforms in China. By the late 1970s, the conditions for economic expansion in China had already been prepared through land reform, near-universal literacy in the younger age groups, the foundations of a social security system, and a high participation of women in the labour force, among other achievements (1996: 196). Since India has not realized these conditions, as the authors candidly point out, it does beg the question whether the market can serve as a similar source of social development in India, or whether, in fact, it needs to be negotiated on very different lines, if not opposed through social and political movements like the Narmada Bachao Andolan. With consummate restraint, Dreze and Sen recommend that there is much for India to learn from China on 'a *discriminating* basis' (ibid.: 86). In other words, let us not forget the authoritarianism in China that has made these marketing reforms viable and systematized. Dreze and Sen's qualifications suggest a plethora of contradictions that need to be confronted more sharply within the actual processes of democratization in India at ground level, and in the increasingly inflected critiques of global capitalism as exemplified in C.T. Kurien's *Global Capitalism and the Indian Economy* (1994).

10   This 'battleground' on the Internet has served to incite negative stereotypes of hostility between Indian and Pakistani communities. Fuelled at times by expatriate South Asian children, who have exchanged insidious invectives – 'Pakistanis are all terrorists'; 'Indians would rather starve their cows than eat them as we do here' (Mandli 1997) – the Net has served to unleash communal hostilities through the anonymity of its use. Some of its supporters have attempted to undermine the problems of 'hate-speech' by stressing how the Internet's capacity to create 'a closer community of world states and people' (ibid.) is being hijacked by hate-groups operating *outside* the Net. This sense of an invasion gets even more literalized through the uses of the Net by racist groups like the White Aryan Resistance and the Ku Klux Klan.

At a different level of intervention, there are more nostalgic renderings of violence on the Net through patriotic evocations of past battles, such as the historic 1971 Indo-Pak war, which has now been authenticated on the web-site through a detailed account of the fourteen-day conflict (Anbarasan 1997). Such xenophobic memorabilia invariably serve to enhance the spectre of virtual wars on the Net intensified by the more recent outbreak of violence in Kargil, further accentuated by the nuclear tests in Pokhran.

11   I am referring here to that extraordinary day when the elephant-headed Lord Ganesh was 'miraculously' discovered to be drinking milk – milk of many different brands and qualities, consumed from any number of containers, cups, mugs, and spoons. Nor was he drinking in only one particular location, but in almost every state of India, and in distant parts of the world – in Germany, Hong Kong, Britain, and the United States. Why he stopped drinking milk the following day, however, was not subject to any particular scrutiny by his devotees, who included secularists as well. Ultimately, the law of physics by which this 'miracle' can be explained – the relationship of 'capillary' forces to 'surface tension' – was best demonstrated by a roadside *mochi* (cobbler), who pointed to his iron anvil with some contempt, and said: 'If I pour milk on this, it will drink it up. What miracle are you talking about?'

In retrospect, I would emphasize that the 'miracle' registered primarily in metropolitan and urban centres in India. The rural areas, where one would except such superstitions to circulate, were curiously deprived of Lord Ganesh's milk-drinking propensities. The fact of the matter is that the 'miracle' worked where there were telephones and other communicative devices by which the message spread (and the hysteria built).

REFERENCES

INTRODUCTION

Appadurai, Arjun. *Modernity at Large: Cultural Dimensions of Globalization*. New Delhi: Oxford University Press, 1997.

Bhabha, Homi. *The Location of Culture*. London and New York: Routledge, 1994.

Bharucha, Rustom. 'Eclecticism, Oriental Theatre and Artaud', *Theater*, Vol. 9, No. 3, Summer 1978.

—— *Theatre and the World: Performance and the Politics of Culture*. New Delhi: Manohar Publishers, 1990; London and New York: Routledge, 1993.

—— *The Question of Faith*. New Delhi: Orient Longman, 1993.

—— *In the Name of the Secular: Contemporary Cultural Activism in India*. New Delhi: Oxford University Press, 1998.

—— *Consumed in Singapore: The Intercultural Spectacle of 'Lear'*, Singapore: CAS and Pagesetters, 2000.

Cheah, Pheng. 'The Cosmopolitical – Today', in Cheah and Robbins, 1998 (1998a).

—— 'Given Culture; Rethinking Cosmopolitical Freedom in Transnationalism', in Cheah and Robbins, 1998 (1998b).

Cheah, Pheng and Bruce Robbins. *Cosmopolitics: Thinking and Feeling beyond the Nation*. Minneapolis: University of Minnesota Press, 1998.

Habermas, Jürgen. 'Struggles for Recognition in the Democratic Constitutional State', in *Multiculturalism*, ed. Amy Gutmann. Princeton, NJ: Princeton University Press, 1994.

Kymlicka, Will. *Multicultural Citizenship*. Oxford: Clarendon Press, 1995.

Mufti, Aamir R. 'Auerbach in Istanbul: Edward Said, Secular Criticism, and the Question of Minority Culture', *Critical Inquiry*, 25, Autumn 1998.

Pavis, Patrice (ed.). 'Introduction: Towards a Theory of Interculturalism in Theatre?' in *The Intercultural Performance Reader*. London and New York: Routledge. 1996.

Rawls, John. *Political Liberalism*. New York: Columbia University Press, 1993.

Robbins, Bruce. 'Secularism, Elitism, Progress, and Other Transgressions: On Edward Said's "Voyage In"', *Social Text*, No. 40, 1994.

Rushdie, Salman. *The Satanic Verses*. New York: Viking, 1989.

—— 'In Good Faith', *The Independent on Sunday*, London, 4 February 1990.

Said, Edward. *The World, the Text and the Critic*. Cambridge, MA: Harvard University Press, 1983.

Singh, B.P. *India's Culture: the State, the Arts and Beyond*. New Delhi: Oxford University Press, 1998.

Spivak, Gayatri Chakravorty. 'Cultural Talks in the Hot Peace: Revisiting the "Global Village"', in Cheah and Robbins, 1998.

Shohat, Ella and Robert Stam. *Unthinking Eurocentrism: Multiculturalism and the Media*. London and New York: Routledge, 1994.

Taylor, Charles. 'The Politics of Recognition', in *Multiculturalism*, ed. Amy Gutmann. Princeton, NJ: Princeton University Press, 1994.

Tynan, Kenneth. 'Director as Misanthropist: On the Moral Neutrality of Peter Brook', *Theatre Quarterly*, Vol. 8, No. 25, 1977.

Vanaik, Achin. 'Defence of Multiculturalist Politics', *Economic and Political Weekly*, 21 March 1998.

Walzer, Michael. *Thick and Thin: Moral Arguments at Home and Abroad*. Notre Dame: Notre Dame University Press, 1994.

Wicke, Jennifer and Michael Sprinker. 'Interview with Edward Said', in *Edward Said: A Critical Reader*, ed. Michael Sprinker. Cambridge: Blackwell Publishers, 1992.

Williams, Raymond and Edward Said. 'Appendix: Media, Margins and Modernity, in *The Politics of Modernism: Against the New Conformists*, ed. Tom Pinkney. London and New York: Verso, 1989.

Žižek, Slavoj. 'Multiculturalism, or, the Cultural Logic of Multinational Capitalism', *New Left Review*, No. 225, September/October 1997.

CHAPTER 1

Appadurai, Arjun. *Modernity at Large: Cultural Dimensions of Globalization*. New Delhi: Oxford University Press, 1997.

Bharucha, Rustom. *Theatre and the World: Performance and the Politics of Culture*. New Delhi: Manohar Publishers, 1990; London and New York: Routledge, 1993.

Boyle, James. *Shamans, Software. and Spleens: Law and the Construction of the Information Society*. Cambridge, MA: Harvard University Press, 1996.

Chatterjee, Partha. 'Beyond the Nation? Or Within?', *Economic and Political Weekly*, 4–11 January 1997.

Fanon, Frantz. *The Wretched of the Earth*, trans Constance Farrington. Harmondsworth, Mx: Penguin Books, 1967.

Frow, John. 'Information as Gift and Commodity', *New Left Review*, No. 219, 1996.

Hall, Stuart. 'Dialogue', in *The Fact of Blackness: Frantz Fanon and Visual Representation*, ed. Alan Read. London: ICA 1996; Seattle, WA: Bay Press, 1996.

Jha, Subhash K. 'Just "Beat" It', *The Telegraph*, 10 April 1998.

Kapur, Geeta. 'Globalisation and Culture', *Third Text*, 39, Summer 1997.

Kloppenburg, Jack. *First the Seed: The Political Economy of Plant Biotechnology, 1492–2000*. Cambridge: Cambridge University Press, 1988.

Lazarus, Neil. 'Disavowing Decolonization: Fanon, Nationalism, and the Problematic of Representation in Current Theories of Colonial Discourse', *Research in African Literatures*, Vol. 24, No. 4, Winter 1993.

Mercer, Kobena. 'Interculturality Is Ordinary' in *Intercultural Arts Education and Municipal Policy*, ed. Ria Lavrijsen. Amsterdam: Royal Tropical Institute, 1997.

Mohanty, Satya P. *Literary Theory and the Claims of History: Postmodernism, Objectivity, Multicultural Politics*. New Delhi: Oxford University Press, 1998.

Omi, Michael and Howard Winant. *Racial Formation in the United States*. London: Routledge, 1986.

Parekh, Bhikhu. 'Britain and the Social Logic of Pluralism', in *Britain: A Plural Society*. London: Commission for Racial Equality and the Runnymede Trust, 1990.

Pavis, Patrice. *Theatre at the Crossroads of Culture*. London and New York: Routledge, 1992.

——(ed.) 'Introduction: Towards a Theory of Interculturalism in Theatre?', in *The Intercultural Performance Reader*. London and New York: Routledge, 1996.

Rushdie, Salman and Elizabeth West. *Mirrorwork: 50 Years of Indian Writing 1947–1997*. New York: H & Holt, 1997.

Schechner, Richard. 'Intercultural Performance', *The Drama Review*, Vol. 26, No. 2 (T94), 1982 (1982a).

—— *The End of Humanism: Writings on Performance*. New York: PAJ Publications, 1982 (1982b).

—— 'Interculturalism and the Culture of Choice', in *The Intercultural Performance Reader*, ed. Patrice Pavis, London and New York: Routledge, 1996.

Sharma, Satish. 'Still a Fodder for the "Finer" Arts', *The Economic Times*, New Delhi, 11 December 1993.

Shiva, Vandana and Radha Holla-Bhar. 'Piracy by Patent: The Case of the Neem Tree', in *The Case Against the Global Economy and For a Turn Towards the Local*, ed. Jerry Mander and Edward Goldsmith. Sierra Club Books, 1996.

Shohat, Ella and Robert Stam. *Unthinking Eurocentrism: Multiculturalism and the Media*. London and New York: Routledge, 1994.

Sivanandan, A. 'RAT and the Degradation of Black Struggle', *Race and Class*, No. 26, Spring 1985.

Smiers, Joost. 'Threats and Resistance', typewritten proposal on 'the consequences of economic globalisation' and 'strategies to promote conditions by which artistic cultures can flourish on both local and regional levels', 1997. [Personal correspondence]

Taylor, Charles. 'The Politics of Recognition', in *Multiculturalism*, ed. Amy Gutmann. Princeton, NJ: Princeton University Press, 1994.

Trinh, T. Minh-ha. *When the Moon Waxes Red: Representation, Gender and Cultural Politics*. London and New York: Routledge, 1991.

Weiss, Linda. 'Globalisation and the Myth of the Powerless State', *New Left Review*, No. 225, September/October 1997.

Winant, Howard. 'Behind Blue Eyes: Whiteness and Contemporary US Racial Politics', *New Left Review*, No. 225, September/October 1997.

Wolf, Susan. 'Two Levels of Pluralism', *Ethics*, No. 102, July 1992.

—— 'Comment', in *Multiculturalism*, ed. Amy Gutmann. Princeton, NJ: Princeton University Press, 1994.

Žižek, Slavoj. 'Multiculturalism, or, the Cultural Logic of Multinational Capitalism', *New Left Review*, No. 225, September/October 1997.

CHAPTER 2

Bharucha, Rustom. *Theatre and the World: Performance and the Politics of Culture*. New Delhi: Manohar Publishers, 1990; London and New York: Routledge, 1993.

—— *Chandralekha: Woman/Dance/Resistance*. New Delhi: HarperCollins, 1995.

Carlson, Marvin. 'Brook and Mnouchkine: Passages to India?', in *The Intercultural Performance Reader*, ed. Patrice Pavis. London and New York: Routledge, 1996.

Cixous, Hélène. 'The Language that Speaks in Many Tongues,' included in publicity material of Sarthi, no date indicated.

Cobb, C. and J. Cobb (eds.). *The Green National Product: A Proposed Index of Sustainable Economic Welfare*. New York:. University Press of America, 1994. Cited in Sachs 1996.

Kaviraj, Sudipta. 'The Imaginary Institution of India', in *Subaltern Studies*, Vol. VII, ed. Partha Chaterjee and Gyanendra Pandey. New Delhi: Oxford University Press, 1987.

MacCannell, Dean. *Empty Meeting Grounds: Tourist Papers*. London and New York: Routledge, 1992.

Miyoshi, Masao. 'The Postcolonial Aura: Third World Criticism in the Age of Global Capitalism', *Critical Inquiry*, No. 20, Winter 1993.

Moi, Toril. *Sexual/Textual Politics: Feminist Literary Theory*. London and New York: Routledge, 1985.

Sachs, Wolfgang. 'Sustainable Development. On the Political Anatomy of an Oxymoron', typed manuscript, 1996, contribution to *Living with Nature: Environmental Discourse as Cultural Politics*, ed. F. Fischer and M. Hajer. London: Oxford University Press, 1999.

Sarthi. Brochure of *The Hidden River*. Sponsored by the Young Presidents Organisation, Mukesh Mills, Mumbai, 25 February 1996.

Schmid-Bleek, Friedrich. *Wieviel Umvelt braucht der Mensch?* Berlin and Basel: Birkhauser, 1994. Cited in Sachs 1996.

CHAPTER 3

Al-Azmeh, Aziz. *Islams and Modernities*. London: Verso, 1993.

Asad, Talal. 'The Concept of Cultural Translation in British Social Anthropology', in *Writing Culture: The Poetics and Politics of Ethnography*, ed. James Clifford and George Marcus. Berkeley: University of California Press, 1986.

Bassnett, Susan. *Translation Studies.* London and New York: Routledge, 1991.

Benjamin, Walter. 'The Task of the Translator', in his *Illuminations.* London: Collins Fontana, 1969.

Bhabha, Homi. *The Location of Culture.* London and New York: Routledge, 1994.

Bharucha, Rustom. 'Culture and Power', *Sangeet Natak*, Nos. 127–128, 1998.

—— *Theatre and the World: Performance and the Politics of Culture.* New Delhi: Manohar Publishers, 1990; London and New York: Routledge, 1993.

Enwezor, Okwai. 'Travel Notes: Living, Working, and Travelling in a Restless World', in *Trade Routes: History and Geography.* 2nd Johannesburg Biennale, 1997. Johannesburg: Greater Johannesburg Metropolitan Council and the Prince Claus Fund for Culture and Development.

Geertz, Clifford. ' "From the Native's Point of View": On the Nature of Anthropological Understanding', in his *Local Knowledge: Further Essays in Interpretive Anthropology.* New York: Basic Books, 1985.

Leach, Edmund. 'Ourselves and Others', *Times Literary Supplement*, 6 July, 1973.

Mohan, Peggy. 'Market Forces and Language in Global India', *Economic and Political Weekly*, 22 April 1995.

Pattanayak, D.P. *Multilingualism and Mother-Tongue Education.* New Delhi: Oxford University Press, 1981.

Patterson, Michael. *Peter Stein: Germany's Leading Theatre Director.* Cambridge: Cambridge University Press, 1981.

Pavis, Patrice. *Theatre at the Crossroads of Culture.* London and New York: Routledge, 1992.

Pollock, Sheldon. 'The Cosmopolitan Vernacular', *Journal of Asian Studies*, Vol. 57, No. 1, 1998a.

—— 'India in the Vernacular Millennium: Literary Culture and Polity, 1000–1500', typewritten manuscript, 1998b.

Sangari, Kumkum. 'Politics of Diversity: Religious Communities and Multiple Patriarchies,' *Economic and Political Weekly*, 23 and 30 December 1995.

Saxena, Sahnna and Kamal Mahendroo. 'Politics of Language', *Economic and Political Weekly*, 1993.

Singh, B.P. *India's Culture: The State, the Arts, and Beyond.* New Delhi: Oxford University Press, 1998.

Trinh, T. Min-Ha. 'Outside In Inside Out', in *When the Moon Waxes Red: Representation, Gender and Cultural Politics.* London and New York: Routledge, 1991.

Turner, Victor. 'Dramatic Ritual/Ritual Drama: Performative and Reflexive Anthropology', *The Kenyon Review*, Vol. 1, No. 3, 1979.

CHAPTER 4

ABVA (AIDS Bhedbhav Virodhi Andolan). *Less Than Gay.* New Delhi: ABVA, 1991.

Almagauer, Tomas. 'Chicano Men: A Cartography of Homosexual Identity and Behaviour', in *The Lesbian and Gay Studies Reader*, ed. Henry Abelove, Michele Aina Barale and David M. Halperin. London and New York: Routledge, 1993.

Alonso, Ana Maria and Maria Teresa Koreck. 'Silences; "Hispanics", AIDS, and Sexual Practices', in *The Lesbian and Gay Studies Reader.* London and New York: Routledge, 1993.

Balasubrahmanyan, Vimal. 'Gay Rights in India', *Economic and Political Weekly*, 3 February 1996.

Banerjee, Partha and Bhaskar Mukhopadhyay. 'India's Hijras: Ostracised yet Accommodated', *The Saturday Statesman*, 3 September 1994.

Bharucha, Rustom. 'Dismantling Men: Crisis of Male Identity in *Father, Son, and Holy War*', in his *In the Name of the Secular: Contemporary Cultural Activism in India.* New Delhi: Oxford University Press, 1998.

Butler, Judith. *Bodies that Matter: On the Discursive Limits of 'Sex'.* London and New York: Routledge, 1993.

Cohen, Lawrence. 'Holi in Banaras and the *Mahaland* of Modernity', *GLQ: A Journal of Lesbian and Gay Studies*, Vol. 2, 1995a.

—— 'The Pleasures of Castration: The Postoperative Status of Hijras, Jankhas, and Academics', in *Sexual Nature, Sexual Culture*, ed. Paul R. Abramson and Steven D. Pinkerton. Chicago and London: University of Chicago Press, 1995b.

Ghosh, Shohini. 'From the Frying Pan to the Fire', *Communalism Combat*, January 1999.

John, Mary E. and Tejaswini Niranjana. 'Mirror Politics: "Fire", Hindutva and Indian Culture', *Economic and Political Weekly*, 6–13 March 1999.

Kapur, Ratna. 'Is *Fire* about Free Speech? Sex? or Culture?', *Communalism Combat*, January 1999 (1999a).

—— 'Cultural Politics of *Fire*', *Economic and Political Weekly*, 22 May 1999 (1999b).

Naim, C.M. 'A Dissent on "Fire" ', *Economic and Political Weekly*, 17–24 April 1999.

Nanda, Serena. 'Neither Man nor Woman: The Hijras of India', in *The Lesbian and Gay Studies Reader*. London and New York: Routledge, 1993.

O'Flaherty, Wendy Doniger. *Women, Androgynes and Other Mythical Beasts*. Chicago: University of Chicago Press, 1980.

Puig, Manuel. *Kiss of the Spider Woman*, trans. Thomas Colchie. New York: Vintage Books, 1980.

Sangari, Kumkum. 'Politics of Diversity: Religious Communities and Multiple Patriarchies', *Economic and Political Weekly*, 23 and 30 December 1995.

Spivak, Gayatri Chakravorty 'Questions of Multi-culturalism', in *The Post-Colonial Critic: Interviews, Sttrategies, Dialogues*, ed. Sarah Harasym. London and New York: Routledge, 1990.

Srikanth, H. 'Natural Is Not Always Rational', *Economic and Political Weekly*, 13 April 1996.

CHAPTER 5

Bhargava, Rajeev. 'Introduction', in *Multiculturalism, Liberalism and Democracy*, ed. Rajeev Bhargava, Amiya Kumar Bagchi and R. Sudarshan. New Delhi: Oxford University Press, 1999.

Bilgrami, Akeel. '*Mukti* from the "Majority", "Minority" Mantras', *Communalism Combat*, October 1997.

Butalia, Urvashi. *The Other Side of Silence: Voices from the Partition of India*. New Delhi: Penguin Books, 1998.

Das, Veena. 'The Spatialization of Violence: Case Study of a "Communal Riot" ', in *Unravelling the Nation: Sectarian Conflict and India's Secular Identity*, ed. Kaushik Basu and Sanjay Subrahmanyam. New Delhi: Penguin Books, 1996.

Gupta, Dipankar. 'Secularisation and Minoritisation: Limits of Heroic Thought', *Economic and Political Weekly*, 2 September 1995.

Ilaiah, Kancha. *Why I am Not a Hindu: A Sudra Critique of Hindutva Philosophy, Culture and Political Economy*. Calcutta: Samya, 1996.

Pandey, Gyanendra. 'In Defence of the Fragment: Writing about Hindu-Muslim Riots in India Today', *Economic and Political Weekly*, annual number, March 1991.

Pinto S J, Ambrose. 'Atrocities on Dalits in Gulbarga: Upper Caste Hold on Police', *Economic and Political Weekly*, 16–23 April 1994.

Said, Edward. *Orientalism*. New York: Vintage Books, 1979.

Sitaraman, Sudha. 'Burdens of Interpretation: The Case of Kannappa', *Economic and Political Weekly*, 11 June 1994.

Tendulkar, Vijay. 'Muslims and I', *Communalism Combat*, No. 32, April 1997.

CHAPTER 6

Alam, Javeed. 'Tradition in India under Interpretive Stress', *Thesis Eleven*, No. 39, 1994.

Anbarasan, Ethiraj. 'Pakistanis Angry over Internet Site on '71 Conflict', *The Asian Age*, 27 June 1997.

Anderson, Benedict. *Imagined Communities: Reflections on the Origin and Spread of Nationalism*. London and New York: Verso, 1983.

Appadurai, Arjun. *Modernity at Large: Cultural Dimensions of Globalization*. New Delhi: Oxford University Press, 1997.

Barve, Sushoba. 'A Tale of Ganapati Bappa and Four "Minor" Priests', *Communalism Combat*, October 1996.

Basu, Tapan, Pradip Datta, Sumit Sarkar, Tanika Sarkar, and Sabuddha Sen. *Khaki Shorts, Saffron Flags*. New Delhi: Orient Longman, 1993.

Bharucha, Rustom. *Theatre and the World: Performance and the Politics of Culture*. New Delhi: Manohar Publishers, 1990; London and New York: Routledge, 1993.

—— *The Question of Faith*. New Delhi: Orient Longman, 1993.

—— *In the Name of the Secular: Contemporary Cultural Activism in India*. New Delhi: Oxford University Press, 1998.

Bilgrami, Akeel. 'Two Concepts of Secularism: Reason, Modernity, and the Archimedean Ideal', *Economic and Political Weekly*, 9 July 1994.

—— 'Secular Liberalism and Moral Psychology of Identity', *Economic and Political Weekly*, 4 October 1997.

Chatterjee, Partha. *The Nation and its Fragments*. New Delhi: Oxford University Press, 1994 (1994a).

—— 'Secularism and Toleration', *Economic and Political Weekly*, 9 July 1994 (1994b).

—— 'Beyond the Nation? Or Within?', *Economic and Political Weekly*, 4–11 January, 1997.

Datta, Pradip. Intervention in discussion on 'The Secular-Communal Question', a study week conducted at the Institute of Advanced Study, Shimla, May 1997.

Dreze, Jean and Amartya Sen. *India: Economic Development and Social Opportunity*, New Delhi: Oxford India Paperbacks, 1996.

Gandhi, Mahatma. *An Autobiography or, The Story of My Experiments with Truth*. Harmondsworth, Mx: Penguin Books, 1982.

Hall, Stuart. 'The Whites of Their Eyes: Racist Ideologies and the Media', in *Silver Linings: Some Strategies for the Eighties* ed. George Bridges and Rosalind Brundt. London: Lawrence & Wishart, 1981.

—— 'On Postmodernism and Articulation: an Interview with Stuart Hall', ed. Lawrence Grossberg, *Journal of Communication Inquiry*, Vol. 10, No. 2, 1986.

—— *The Hard Road to Renewal: Thatcherism and the Crisis of the Left*. London: Verso, 1988.

Kothari, Rajni. 'Rise of the Dalits, and the Renewed Debate on Caste', *Economic and Political Weekly*, 25 June 1994.

Kurien, C.T. *Global Capitalism and the Indian Economy*. New Delhi: Orient Longman, 1994.

Lash, S. and J. Urry. *The End of Organised Capitalism*. Madison: University of Wisconsin Press, 1987.

Mandli, Murtaza. 'Indo-Pak Hate War on the Net', *The Asian Age*, 12 June 1997.

Nandy, Ashis. 'The Politics of Secularism and the Recovery of Religious Tolerance', *Alternatives*, Vol. XIII, 1988.

Oguibe, Olu. 'Forsaken Geographies: Cyberspace and the New World Order', in *Trade Routes: History and Geography*. 2nd Johannesburg Biennale, 1997. Johannesburg: Greater Johannesburg Metopolitan Council and the Prince Claus Fund for Culture and Development.

Pandey, Gyanendra. *The Construction of Communalism in Northern India*. New Delhi: Oxford University Press, 1996.

Patnaik, Arun Kumar. 'Burden of Marx and Morals', *Economic and Political Weekly*, 20 May 1995.

Rajadhyaksha, Ashish. 'Beaming Messages to the Nation', *Journal of Arts and Ideas*, No. 19, May 1990.

Sangari, Kumkum. 'Politics of Diversity: Religious Communities and Multiple Patriarchies', *Economic and Political Weekly*, 23 and 30 December 1995.

Shohat, Ella and Robert Stam. *Unthinking Eurocentrism: Multiculturalism and the Media*. London and New York: Routledge, 1994.

Spivak, Gayatri Chakravorty. 'Subaltern Studies: Deconstructing Historiography', in *Subaltern Studies*, Vol. IV, ed. Ranajit Guha. New Delhi: Oxford University Press, 1985.

Vachon, Robert. 'Presentation' and 'Editor's Note' to Hassan Zaoual's monograph 'The Economy and the Symbolic Sites of Africa', *Interculture*, No. 122, Winter 1994 (Intercultural Institute of Montreal).

Vimochana, 'Is Beauty Only Skin Deep?', *Deccan Herald*, 27 October 1996.

Zaoual, Hassan. 'The Economy and the Symbolic Sites of Africa', *Interculture*, No. 122, Winter 1994 (Intercultural Institute of Montreal).

CHAPTER 7

Appadurai, Arjun. *Modernity at Large: Cultural Dimensions of Globalization*. New Delhi: Oxford University Press, 1997.

Bharucha, Rustom. *The Question of Faith*. New Delhi: Orient Longman, 1993.

Ghosh, Amitav. *The Calcutta Chromosome*. New Delhi: Ravi Dayal, 1996.

Lohia, Rammanohar. *Interval during Politics*. Hyderabad: Rammanohar Lohia Samata Vidyalaya Trust, 1965.

Oguibe, Olu. 'Forsaken Geographies: Cyberspace and the New Order', *Trade Routes: History and Geography*. 2nd Johannesburg Biennale, 1997. Johannesburg: Greater Johannesburg Metropolitan Council and the Prince Claus Fund for Culture and Development.

INDEX

actors: and caste, 121; decontextualizing of, 69; dehumanization of, 18, 55–6; and the folk, 74; poverty of, 56; of Rangayana Theatre, 74; and singing, 74, 107; violence in biographies of, 120
Advani, L.K., 143
Africa, 141
ahamkara, 75
Alam, Javeed, 134
All India Radio, 74
altruism, 8
Amarcord, 84
Ambedkar, Dr Babasaheb, 15, 50, 108–10
Amin, Samir, 4
Anderson, Benedict, 8, 173(n4)
androgyny, 52, 53
Appadurai, Arjun, 1, 4–5, 7, 19, 136, 137, 138, 139, 147, 148, 149, 159
Arabian Nights, 84
Asad, Talad, 701
atman, 75
Attenborough, Richard, 50
Auerbach, Eric, 15
authors, and intellectual property rights, 23–4
Azmi, Shabana, 95, 96

Babenco, Hector, 93
Babri Masjid, demolition of, 71, 95, 104, 112, 127, 143, 149
Bajrang Dal, 95
balladeers, 47
Bandit Queen, 99
Banu, Saira, 96
Barba, Eugenio, 27, 56
Barthes, Roland, 116
Bauls, 47
Baywatch, 134
Beckett, Samuel, 155
Beggary Act, 56
Bellow, Saul, 38
Benjamin, Walter, 70
Bergman, Ingmar, 82
betrayal, of culture of origins, 42

Bhabha, Homi, 6–7, 28, 64–6, 72
Bharat Ratna, 81–2
Bharathipura, 71, 121
Bharatiya Janata Party, 79, 143, 150
Bhatt, Mahesh, 169(n4)
bhavageetha, 77
Bhiwandi, 143
Bilgrami, Akeel, 108, 109, 110, 173(n3)
BJP *see* Bharatiya Janata Party
blacks, 2, 33; as artists, 40
body: and communal violence, 119; in crisis, 152–7; as evidence, 118; fictional bodies, 56; imaginary of, 159; as source of pollution, 117–18
body-culture, 139
Bombay, 169(n4), 171(n8)
Bose, Netaji Subhas Chandra, 50, 158
Boyle, James, 23
Braga, Sonia, 93
brahmins, 77, 114–15 *see also* caste
Brecht, Bertolt, 19, 130
Brook, Peter, 1, 2, 27, 51, 72
Buchner, George, 105
Buddhists, 108
burakumin, 18
Butalia, Urvashi, 114, 115, 116
Butler, Judith, 94, 98–9

Calcutta Chromosome, The, 154
capitalism: global (*see* global capitalism); print, 7–8, 132–3, 159
caste, 8, 9, 29 *see also* brahmins; dalits; *harijans*; untouchables; and actors, 121; and cultural authenticity, 98; dominance of, 17; upper, and Hindu culture, 111, 112
Cat People, 88
catachresis, 14
censorship, 52–3, 95, 101, 136, 137
Chakyar, Ammannur Madhava, 47
Chatterjee, Partha, 14, 15, 44, 110, 137, 142
chauvinism, 29, 69
Cheah, Pheng, 6–8, 16